Praise for *Mistrial*

"*Mistrial* is the story of extraordinary careers as the go-to lawyers for the celebrated (or notorious, or both) defendant. Don't miss it!"

—Jeffrey Toobin, *New York Times* bestselling author of
The Nine: Inside the Secret World of the Supreme Court, legal affairs
writer for *The New Yorker*, and senior legal analyst for CNN

"A win: engaging, enlightening, and entertaining . . . provides a salutary reminder that criminal-defense lawyers, far from being criminals themselves, play a vital role in our adversarial system of justice."

—*The Wall Street Journal*

"Two high-profile defense lawyers pull back the curtain on the U.S. criminal justice system and find much to criticize. . . . A no-holds-barred indictment of the system, filled with memorable anecdotes and accessibly written."

—*Kirkus Reviews*

Mark Geragos is the head of Geragos & Geragos, a Los Angeles–based law firm that focuses on both criminal- and civil-trial work. In his thirty-plus-year career, he has tried more than three hundred cases and has served as a regular legal analyst on CNN, Fox, and ABC shows.

Pat Harris was recently named as one of the top 100 trial lawyers in America and is a partner at Geragos & Geragos. He is a regular contributor on legal issues for shows on Fox and CNN, is the coauthor of Susan McDougal's *New York Times* bestselling memoir *The Woman Who Wouldn't Talk*, and speaks regularly at law schools across the country.

MISTRIAL

AN INSIDE LOOK AT HOW

THE CRIMINAL JUSTICE SYSTEM WORKS . . .

AND SOMETIMES DOESN'T

Mark Geragos *and* Pat Harris

I Love u.
maxine!

GOTHAM
BOOKS

GOTHAM BOOKS
Published by the Penguin Group
Penguin Group (USA) Inc., 375 Hudson Street,
New York, New York 10014, USA

USA | Canada | UK | Ireland | Australia | New Zealand | India | South Africa | China

Penguin Books Ltd, Registered Offices: 80 Strand, London WC2R 0RL, England
For more information about the Penguin Group visit penguin.com.

Published by Gotham Books, a member of Penguin Group (USA) Inc.

Previously published as a Gotham Books hardcover

First trade paperback printing, October 2013

10 9 8 7 6 5 4 3 2 1

Gotham Books and the skyscraper logo are trademarks of Penguin Group (USA) Inc.

The Library of Congress Cataloging-in-Publication Data has been applied for.

ISBN: 978-1-59240-844-3

Printed in the United States of America
Set in Bembo STD   •   Designed by Elke Sigal

While the author has made every effort to provide accurate telephone numbers and Internet
addresses at the time of publication, neither the publisher nor the author assumes any responsibility
for errors, or for changes that occur after publication. Further, the publisher does not have any
control over and does not assume any responsibility for author or third-party Web sites or
their content.

Some names and identifying characteristics have been changed to protect the privacy of the
individuals involved.

This book is dedicated to my father, Eugene Harris, a man who has lived life with integrity, a strong sense of devotion to others, and an unwavering dedication to his family. He is as good and decent a man as I have ever known and has set a standard for character that I will never live up to but which I strive for every day.

—Pat

I would like to dedicate the book to my father, Paul (Pops) Geragos. Pops taught me long ago that the single most honorable thing a man can do is to fight for those who have no one to fight for them. He has spent every day as an attorney living up to that belief. He has also made sure that I never forget the genocide of our ancestors, the Armenian people, at the hands of the Turks, and that I should continue his life work to make sure that the Armenian people always have someone to fight for them.

—Mark

CONTENTS

MISTRIAL

Introduction: Mark

From the time I was five, it was as if I was programmed to be a lawyer. For the first thirteen years of my life my father was a prosecutor for the Los Angeles County District Attorney's Office. I have fond memories of going to court and watching him and thinking to myself what a great job he had. You get to go talk with people, tell stories, go out to eat, and occasionally argue with people in court. And people pay you to do this. It seemed like a pretty sweet deal.

By the time I got to college, though, all that had changed. When I was a senior at Haverford College, I actually had thoughts about going in a wholly different direction. During college I majored in Sociology and Anthropology with a concentration of classes in the Philosophy of Religion. One of the professors whom I idolized was named to head the Divinity School at Harvard, and I gave serious thought to following him there after graduation. I even considered becoming a priest, which I suppose was a throwback to my days as an altar boy at St. Gregory Armenian Church of Pasadena. When I tell people that today, I usually have to pause for them to stop laughing, but at the time it was no joke. My sainted mother assumed I would follow in my father's footsteps and become an attorney, but I seriously considered going to divinity school. I spent the better part of my senior year in college agonizing over the decision.

Finally I went to Archbishop Vatche, who at the time was the head of the Western Diocese of the Armenian Apostolic Church, and told him my dilemma. I had known him since I was twelve years old and attended Armenian summer camp, and I respected him immensely. I fully expected him to encourage me to pursue divinity school and the priesthood, but as I explained my passion for my religious studies, he just kept shaking his head. After patiently listening to me pour my heart out, he finally responded in the tell-it-like-it-is fashion he was known for:

"Mark, I have seen you at church camp since you were twelve years old. We have spent the last five years disciplining you for drinking, smoking pot, and chasing the girls that have come to camp. I can't afford to spend the next forty years trying to slow you down. Go be a lawyer and help represent the Church when we need you one day."

So with what I guess was God's blessing, I started law school. Sure enough, in law school I found a second calling—it just wasn't to be a lawyer. In an effort to make a little extra money, I began moonlighting by booking bands at a local venue in Pasadena. It was the era of the B-52s, X, Oingo Boingo, Missing Persons, the Ramones, and the Plasmatics, bands that drew huge crowds partly due to their music and partly due to their penchant for blowing up things on stage. A young rock promoter could do very well for himself as long as he could afford the insurance. My last year in law school I was spending much more time promoting concerts than worrying about the arcane details of writing a will or setting up a trust.

Graduation from law school was not a foregone conclusion, but I managed to convince the registrar that my real-life experiences writing contracts and dealing with police raids were every bit as valuable as time spent in the classroom. In reality, the law degree was gravy. I was busy setting up a business empire in the music industry.

It didn't take long for me to find the perfect opportunity. Having developed a relationship with one of the local radio stations, I was approached by a group that was attempting to buy a small but potentially powerful rock station in Los Angeles. The station was new, but I believed it had incredible potential. Even more incredible was that I could own a large share of the station for approximately $200,000. A quick check of my bank account showed that all I needed to come up with was $198,500. Thankfully, the bank was inclined to give me a credit line for the purchase if my father would cosign for the loan.

My father, Paul Geragos, or Pops as he is more widely known, had been a legend in the L.A. County District Attorney's Office for more than a decade before leaving to set up a practice as a criminal defense attorney. He had been an immediate success in private practice largely due to his reputation as a take-no-prisoners courtroom attorney, and he was now reaping the financial rewards. I went to Pops and pleaded with him to loan me the money or at least cosign a loan with me. He turned me down flat. And of course, being a lawyer, he didn't simply say no. Pops used the opportunity to lecture me on the instability of the music industry and how I needed to get a job at the D.A.'s office, work for a few years, and then join his law practice.

Unable to raise the money, I passed on the opportunity, and the investors turned to someone else to supply the $200,000. Five years later the radio station was number one in the entire L.A. market and the $200,000 share I was to have purchased eventually sold for $84 million. Pops loves retelling that story, always laughing uproariously at the end. My kids used to think it was hilarious too, until I explained the concept of inheritance.

The decision to become a criminal defense attorney rather than a prosecutor or corporate lawyer was an easy one for me because I am Armenian. If ever there has been a country in the world that has achieved permanent underdog status, it would be Armenia. Yet Armenians are a race of people who, despite repeated obstacles, have never stopped fighting no matter the odds. To me that is the essence of the job of the defense attorney and is branded into my DNA.

Armenia is a small country strategically located between Europe and Asia. It is bordered on the west by Turkey, or what I like to call "Occupied Armenia," and on the southeast by Iran. It was not always small. Around 600 B.C. and again in the Middle Ages, Armenia was a major geographical and political force in the region, taking up parts of what are now Turkey, Iran, and Georgia. Unfortunately, the Armenians were not very good at warfare and kept losing land.

The total population of the country is approximately 3 million people. The diaspora of Armenians is a much heftier number, estimated at 8 million around the globe. California alone has an estimated 1 million ethnic Armenians. For most of the twentieth century, Armenia was a part of the Soviet Republic, having been taken over by the Soviet army after World War I. Since declaring its independence in 1990, Armenia has struggled to scrape away its Soviet barnacles, to become a democratic society, and in time to become a member of the European Union.

During my life, I have on countless occasions had to explain to people that Armenians are not Iranians, are not Albanians, are not from a country in South America, don't speak Persian, aren't fire worshipers, and, most especially, that their capital city isn't Glendale, California.

All four of my grandparents were Armenian and survivors of the Armenian Genocide. Largely forgotten and ignored, it was the first genocide of the twentieth century. Ottoman Turkey under the tutelage of the Germans engineered the slaughter of more than 1.5 million Armenians between 1915 and 1923. It is rare to find an Armenian who does not have a relative who was killed by the Turks. The murdering and driving into the desert of millions of Armenians is why the diaspora of Armenians in other countries is nearly three times the number of Armenians in Armenia.

Like all children of Armenian ancestry, upon learning the stories of the genocide, I felt a heavy burden to someday grow up and do whatever I could for Armenia and to honor my grandparents and great-grandparents. The law has allowed me to do that. There will always be cases of mine that receive more publicity, but to me, my legal career will always be defined by what I am able to do to honor the victims of the Genocide. That is the spirit of the Armenian people. It was best expressed by the well-known Armenian writer William Saroyan:

> I should like to see any power of the world destroy this race, this small tribe of unimportant people, whose wars have all been fought and lost, whose structures have crumbled, literature is unread, music is unheard, and prayers are no more answered. Go ahead, destroy Armenia. See if you can do it. Send them into the desert without bread or water. Burn their homes and churches. Then see if they will not laugh, sing and pray again. For when two of them meet anywhere in the world, see if they will not create a new Armenia.

With that heritage, there was no way I was going to be anything but a defense attorney.

The idea behind *Mistrial* is to go behind the scenes as never before and let the reader get a glimpse of the good, the bad, and the ugly. At times, *Mistrial* may come across as a diatribe about how the system is becoming unfairly weighted to the prosecution, and there is definitely some of that in the book. But although I have my cynical and even bitter moments, I hope that *Mistrial* also makes the reader understand that I love what I do—absolutely love it. It is not only my job; it is my only real hobby. Do I get frustrated? Absolutely. Would I want to do anything else? Absolutely not!

Furthermore, whining about it isn't going to do any good anyway. It is important to recognize what is going on in the system and adjust accordingly. We talk a lot about how the system used to work twenty to thirty years ago, not because we expect it to go back to that, but because it is important to recognize the changes and adapt. For example, if a defense attorney fails to realize the effect that media coverage has had on jurors in the past two decades, he or she is headed for trouble.

Over the course of thirty years of practicing law, I have tried more than three hundred cases and represented thousands of clients. I may not have seen it all, but I have seen more than my fair share. I think Pat and I are uniquely situated to write about the criminal justice system and how the perceptions have changed over the years. We have worked on cases that have involved celebrities such as Michael Jackson, Chris Brown, Winona Ryder, and Mike Tyson. We have worked on cases that have made ordinary people into celebrities, like Susan McDougal, Scott Peterson, and Gary Condit. And every single day we work on cases, from murder to shoplifting, where nobody knows the defendant but the case is just as important to that defendant as any high-profile case. We have traveled across the country and worked on cases in twenty-three states, including Arizona, Texas, New York, Pennsylvania, Washington, and Florida. In short, I doubt there are two lawyers anywhere who have seen both ends of the spectrum and everything in between from as many different places as we have.

We have talked about writing this book for a number of years. A couple of months ago we were sitting in a cigar bar in New York when some semiloaded lawyer wandered over to our table and asked to sit down. He then proceeded to tell us how despicable we were for representing people like Scott Peterson and Michael Jackson, and how we were what was wrong with the system. Given his condition, I didn't want to engage with him, but when he walked away I looked at Pat and said, "It's really gotten bad when we are at the point that even lawyers don't understand what the hell is going on in the system. We really need to write the book!"

Introduction: Pat

The first time I met Mark Geragos was when I went to his office to fire him. At the time, I was engaged to Susan McDougal, the woman who was sitting in a jail cell in Los Angeles because she refused to talk to Kenneth Starr's Whitewater jury. She also had a pending case in Los Angeles involving false accusations of embezzling from a former employer. Before she was transferred to Los Angeles, I had been working as a public defender for two years in Nashville, Tennessee, but after she was moved to L.A. I quit my job to move there and work on the case. Since I had no California bar license, my first order of business was to find a California lawyer who was willing to take the case. That was not an easy task, because we had no money and we were essentially asking a lawyer to do the case pro bono.

When I arrived in L.A., I made contact with the name lawyers— Vincent Bugliosi, Leslie Abramson, Johnnie Cochran—but I could not drum up any interest. Over the next few weeks, I met with at least ten lawyers, pleading with them to take the case and telling them that the media coverage would help their careers. Nobody was buying it.

Then one Sunday, Susan made her nightly call from jail. She sounded a little sheepish, which was very un-Susan-like, and I could tell that something had happened that she was nervous talking about. Finally, she blurted it out.

"I think I hired a lawyer!"

"You what? What do you mean you think you hired a lawyer?"

"Well, I signed a retainer with this guy."

"Oh my Lord! Susan, why would you sign a retainer with some guy that I haven't even spoken to or done any research on?"

"I liked his shoes."

"That's why? You hired a lawyer because you liked his shoes?"

"I also like his briefcase. He just gives off the appearance of being very successful."

"What is this guy's name?

"Mark Geragos."

"I've never heard of him. You can't sign a retainer because you liked his shoes and briefcase. You realize that I am going to have to go see this guy and fire him."

The next day my brother, Ron Harris, who was in town visiting, and I drove to downtown Los Angeles and walked into Mark's office unannounced. I didn't want him preparing for what was coming. When we were ushered into his office, he was very gracious and polite and seemed somewhat amused that we were there. More than that, he had a plan and he knew exactly how he was not only going to help Susan on the L.A. case, but he was going to help her fight Starr and the Office of Independent Counsel. His father, who was also his law partner, was an old-time Roosevelt Democrat, and he had approached Mark about representing Susan, even though he knew that it could cost the firm a lot of money. His father had told him that "if that little girl can stand up to Starr, then the least we can do is stand up for her."

When we left the office, I was a little too dazed to speak. Not only was his demeanor impressive, but this was a lawyer who was extremely enthusiastic about representing Susan. I looked at Ron and asked him if it was possible that we had really gotten lucky enough to stumble into a lawyer this good.

The answer turned out to be yes. Not only did I not fire him, within a month he hired me to work at the firm, where I have now been for fifteen years. He won Susan's case in Los Angeles, and then we went to Arkansas, where we whipped Starr and the Office of Independent Counsel in a trial there. Oddly enough, Susan and I split up, but Mark and I stayed together.

Unlike Mark, I always planned on being a lawyer. My grandfather George Patterson was a lawyer and later a judge in the small town of Clarksville, Arkansas. He died when I was only three, but I grew up having people stop me on the street to tell me stories about how he had represented them for free or for a bushel of corn because they had no money. My mother would tell us how widely respected he was and about the large number of people he had helped. He was a real-life Atticus Finch, at least in the mind of an impressionable young boy. My brother, Ron, and my sister, Cheryl, also had the same experience, and they became lawyers too.

My route to law school was a little more circuitous than most students' as I worked in politics, entertainment, real estate, restaurants, baseball, and taxi driving before I made it to law school at the age of thirty-one. I always knew I was going to be a lawyer; I just wasn't in any hurry.

Unlike a lot of my law school classmates, I didn't love the law. I wasn't interested in analyzing an appellate court decision on some obscure antitrust statute from 1931 as an academic exercise. What I was interested in doing was getting into a courtroom, and law school was the necessary evil to get me there. Other than a brief fling with First Amendment law, my only real law school relationship was with criminal law and the classes that pertained to evidence and criminal procedure.

My confidence in my future courtroom abilities bordered on cockiness. I had always done a lot of public speaking, beginning at the age of sixteen when I preached a sermon at my church. My confidence took a hit, however, at an oral argument competition during my second year of law school at the University of Michigan. Each participant gave a ten-minute argument in front of a panel of three actual judges, who then critiqued the person and offered suggestions. After I finished my argument, I was relatively sure I had done well so I waited for the praise to flow. It came from the first two judges, who were very complimentary of most of what I had done and who also offered good insights into how I could improve. The third judge had a different take. The first words out of her mouth were "I don't know whether or not you think that is the best way to be charming, but I can tell you right now that the Matlock crap is not going to work in front of a judge."

I then made the mistake of trying to interrupt her and explain that this was not an act, this was how I talked, accent and all. That just made her angrier as she seemed to assume that now I was trying to make a fool out of her by denying it was an act. At the time, I was very upset, convinced that maybe she was right—my accent would hold back my career. It didn't turn out that way. After almost every jury trial I have done, some juror or jurors have come up to me and told me how much they loved the accent. In fact, far from playing down my accent, I find that when I get into trial it magically gets a little more pronounced. Women lawyers tease all the time about how they can wear shorter skirts or low-cut blouses in front of a jury. The accent is all I've got.

At the beginning of my legal career, I took my Matlock-crap accent back down south to Nashville, where I was hired by Davidson County public defender Karl Dean to be a public defender in his office. A couple of years later I left the office to go to California and work on Susan's case, which is how I eventually ended up in Mark's office. We ended up hitting it off because we both have the same sick sense of humor and a love of the courtroom. He has taught me to be absolutely fearless, and I have taught him to be less of a smart-ass in court. Actually, that last part is still a work in progress. Regardless, the relationship has worked for fifteen years.

We had discussed writing a book as early as 2000. The original impetus was to give the public a behind-the-scenes look at the justice system and how it really works. It was obvious from the number of questions people ask that there is a lot of curiosity about what really goes on and a lot of misunderstanding about the system. We thought it would be fun to give people an unvarnished version of lawyers, judges, jurors, prosecutors, etc. When I was approximately ten years old, a landmark book about baseball was written called *Ball Four.* The author, Jim Bouton, was a player who wrote about things like drinking, sex groupies, and drug use in the big leagues, but with a writing style that showed how much he loved the game he played. Major-league baseball management went crazy claiming that the book would ruin the game and traumatize young fans. It had the opposite effect on me. Knowing the dirt, the craziness, and the reality of major-league baseball made me love it even more. I use to tell Mark that we should try to do the same type of thing for the judicial system. People are curious about what really goes on, yet they have very little sense of how the system operates. What they think they know is largely distorted by television. I have always felt that a behind-the-scenes look at the real judicial system would make the system more interesting to people and maybe even make them more interested in participating.

Unfortunately, trials and life in general interfered with any real efforts by us to sit down and write. But as time wore on, a second reason to write the book began to crystallize. The system itself was undergoing dramatic changes as the pendulum was beginning to swing heavily in favor of the prosecution, and the balance that is so necessary for the system to work was being upended. It began with what we refer to in this book as the politicization of the criminal justice system. The ugly, negative side of political campaigning began to bleed over into the justice system, with politicians at all levels, from president to tax assessor, now realizing that by screaming that the system was "soft on crime" and more concerned with defendants' rights than victims' rights, they could scare the public into voting for them.

Stories of murderers being released on technicalities and criminals being given short sentences became standard fodder in many campaigns.

The idea that the system had gone soft on crime was totally absurd and untrue, but remarkably effective. The truth was that from 1968 until 1992, a span of twenty-four years, with the exception of the four-year Carter presidency, the Supreme Court and federal courts had been filled with Nixon, Ford, Reagan, and Bush appointees who were conservative, pro-police, and victims' rights oriented. By 1992, when the soft-on-crime campaigns were in full swing, the courts were actually tougher on crime than at any time in the past century.

The pendulum has swung so far at this point that Mark and I agreed we needed to make the time to write this book. Thus, it ended up being written with a twofold purpose. One reason was still to give the reader a look at how the system operates, complete with stories of oversexed jurors, lying witnesses, and clients who want to bribe the judges. The other purpose was to provide a sense of how the system has lost its balance, resulting in overcrowded jails, frightened judges, and prosecutors with a Batman complex. This book is not a legal treatise, nor does it require a legal degree or some legal experience to understand it. The first thing we realized was that a serious critique of the legal system, complete with tables, charts, and statistics, would be enjoyed by only the twelve people who would read it. This book is meant to be more of a fun look at a system that rarely lets you see behind the scenes. At the same time, it is our fervent hope that some of the stories will generate debate over such issues as confessions, eyewitness identifications, and media coverage of high-profile trials.

It is also our hope that when the readers of this book walk into a courthouse as potential jurors, they will remember that the system has to have balance or it fails. A major part of that balance is jurors who will follow their oath to be fair and to listen to both sides before making a decision. If this book helps in having potential jurors think about that while they are serving on a jury, then I will consider it a success. Of course, if the book also sells a million copies and I can finally afford a house on the beach, then I will also consider it a success. I never claimed to be Atticus Finch.

CHAPTER ONE

Politics, O. J. Simpson, and the Rise of the Angry Blond White Women

In July 1997, a recently married eighteen-year-old woman, Michelle Moore-Bosko, was raped and murdered in her Norfolk, Virginia, apartment while her navy seaman husband was not at home. A short time later, the police arrested Danial Williams, another navy seaman who lived in the apartment complex, and brought him in for questioning about the incident. Norfolk police detective Robert Glenn Ford took Williams into an interrogation room, where at first he adamantly denied any involvement. Twelve hours later, Williams signed a written confession to the rape/murder. He was subsequently charged with the crime.

When the DNA samples from the crime scene came back from the laboratory, none of the semen or blood samples matched Williams's. He was then brought back for further questioning by Detective Ford, and within a few hours he had fingered Joseph Dick Jr., another navy seaman, as his accomplice in the rape/murder. Joseph Dick Jr. was then interrogated by the same detective, Robert Ford. At the outset he denied he was involved in the crime, but several hours later he too signed a written confession and was charged with the crime. Unfortunately for the police, his DNA sample did not match the DNA from the crime scene either. Furthermore, the details of neither of the men's confessions matched the actual details of the crime. Nor did any other physical evidence match them to the crime scene. In fact, evidence was produced that showed Dick had been on his ship, the USS *Saipan*, at the time of the murder.

Ford brought Dick back in for questioning, and after a few hours of interrogation Dick named two more navy seamen, Eric Wilson and Derek Tice, as taking part in what was rapidly turning into a mass orgy of sex and violence. Both of the newly named seamen, as had the other two, initially proclaimed their innocence, denying any knowledge of the crime. Both were interrogated by Detective Ford, and in the end both confessed. In fact, Tice not only confessed but named three other seamen involved. Fortunately for those three men, they all had alibis that put them either out of town or on a ship at sea during the crime. Still the Norfolk police believed these men took part in the murder, although only the four original seamen were eventually charged. All four were sent to jail to await trial. They all recanted their confessions, and their lawyers pointed out that the DNA evidence and other evidence from the crime scene were totally supportive of their innocence. The D.A.'s office never flinched or even investigated. They were sure they had the culprits.

A few months later, a career criminal with a lengthy record was arrested near the apartment complex for committing a rape. While in jail, he wrote a letter to a friend admitting to murdering Moore-Bosko. The letter was turned over to the police. His DNA not only matched the crime he was charged with, but also the rape and murder of Moore-Bosko. The man had no previous connections to any of the four navy seamen charged. Rather than reevaluate their view of who committed the crime, the police and the D.A. instead speculated that perhaps he had met the four men in the parking lot that day and the men needed help breaking into the apartment, so they let him in on their plan to rape and murder Ms. Moore-Bosko. Despite not knowing any of these men, the police opined that he jumped at the chance to kill her.

In the end, all four seamen asked for and were granted separate trials. Two of the seamen chose to go to trial. Both were found guilty largely based on their confessions to the crime. The other two seamen, watching what had happened to their codefendants, decided to plead to lesser time rather than face a jury. The career criminal, who not only admitted to committing the crime but denied anyone else was with him, simply pled guilty and was sentenced to life in prison.

No one on the jury could believe that these four strapping young navy seamen could be intimidated by a police officer into confessing to a murder they did not commit. The fact that all four of them had confessed meant that there had to be something to it.

Yet all four were stone-cold innocent. Twelve years after the convictions, the governor of Virginia granted three of the four men partial pardons and they were released from jail (although they were still stuck with their felony convictions). The fourth man, Derek Tice, had his conviction overturned by a federal appeals court. Eleven of the jurors who convicted the four men wrote sworn affidavits stating they now felt the men were innocent.

In 2010, it was discovered that Detective Ford, the architect of the four confessions, had been illegally selling confidential police information to outsiders. He was charged, convicted, and is currently serving a twelve-year prison sentence. As for the seamen, they spent a total of forty-five combined years in custody for a crime they did not commit. Their lives were ruined by accusations borne out of confessions.

Was this simply a perfect storm of bad cops, bad prosecutors, a bad jury, and bad luck? You can read the story that way, but if you do then you have simply not been paying attention. Consider this: over the past decade, the Innocence Project group and its progeny have managed, on very limited funds, to conclusively prove the innocence, through DNA testing, of more than 297 people who have been convicted of crimes. In 30 percent of those cases, the wrongly convicted person had confessed to the crime. They are currently working on hundreds of other cases that appear to have evidence problems. All over the country the wrongfully convicted are being released from custody on a weekly and sometimes daily basis.

One would think, with advancements in DNA techniques and the new research that has proven that confessions and eyewitness identifications are extremely faulty, as well as the success of organizations like the Innocence Project, that this is a golden age for defense attorneys. Potential jurors must be entering courthouses filled with doubts about the strength of the prosecution's case. After all, it has been shown repeatedly, by irrefutable scientific evidence, that innocent men and women are frequently brought into court as defendants.

The reality is that the exact opposite is occurring. When we were doing trials in the eighties and early nineties, an average jury pool had one or two jurors who admitted that they could not give the defendant a fair trial because they felt that anyone charged with a crime was likely guilty. Ten years later, the number of jurors who say that has grown exponentially. When we ask the question "How many of you think the defendant is guilty simply because he is charged?" anywhere from 10 to 30 percent of a jury panel (a panel can range from 50 to 150 people), will now raise their hands. And those are just the ones willing to admit it. Nor is this a phenomenon that only we have noticed. It is such a hotly debated topic at defense attorney conferences across the country that panel discussion topics frequently include new approaches to take with jury selection to combat these attitudes.

Why the huge change? In an era of conclusive scientific proof that the system often gets it wrong, how is it possible that so many people can walk into a courtroom and emphatically tell you that they believe there is no way the system can get it wrong? They refuse to entertain the idea that an officer or the prosecutor can even make a mistake!

We believe that three separate events that began in the eighties and nineties led to an increase in this attitude.

THE POLITICIZATION OF THE JUSTICE SYSTEM

The first event had its origin in the late sixties but reached its zenith in the late eighties and nineties. This is what we refer to as the politicization of the judicial system and the subsequent misconception that the courts were soft on crime. It would be easy to blame Richard Nixon for politicizing the judicial system, because it's easy to blame Nixon for pretty much everything that went wrong in the late sixties and the seventies. But of all his political tactics, we're just concerned with one: his campaign against all the liberal judges who were supposedly letting criminals loose. At the time, the nation's major cities were in decline, whites were fleeing to the suburbs, and Nixon hit on a winning strategy by blaming it all on liberals who weren't tough enough on crime. But Nixon was an amateur. By the time Lee Atwater and other political consultants in the eighties and nineties picked up on the concept, it had been perfected. The commercial pretty much wrote itself and usually went something like this:

> The candidate poses with his wife and three very well-scrubbed children and tells us that he wants a future that is safe and wholesome for his family. He plays with the kids in the yard, and a big golden retriever comes and jumps up on them, and they all roll around on a big green lawn with a large barbecue grill in the background, the grill being the ultimate symbol for the American way of life. Then the music turns menacing and the candidate begins to talk about how worried he is that his children are going to be growing

up in a very different America, an America where those who are soft on crime, especially liberal judges, have allowed murderers and rapists to roam the streets. The screen fills with images of nasty-looking individuals being released from jail or perhaps passing through a revolving door into and out of prison. Cut to the candidate standing in front of a jail cell door and promising that if he is elected, criminals won't go free on his watch. The door to the jail cell loudly slams shut. Cut to the candidate back in front of his fireplace, family intact and dog sedated. He repeats that he is going to make our neighborhoods safe again, and they all smile as the screen fades into a waving American flag.

Perhaps someday a candidate will shoot a commercial standing in front of a prison and complaining that we don't provide adequate medical care for our prisoners and that prisons are so dangerously overcrowded that inmates sleep on the concrete floors in some facilities. He will then open the jail door and help a prisoner in a wheelchair who has been in jail for thirty years and has terminal cancer to leave the facility, all the while saying that this country is not judged by how we treat our best, but how we treat our worst. Perhaps someday we will give up being attorneys and form a rock band that rivals the Beatles in popularity. The latter is actually more likely than the former.

But the commercials were not enough. Soon every stump speech included some anecdote about a murderer or rapist who was set free only to kill or rape again. (What the stump speech didn't say was that in the vast majority of these cases the murderer or rapist was set free because of conduct by the police officer or prosecutor so egregious that a judge deemed it necessary to overturn a conviction. No judge ever woke up one day and said, "I think I will let a killer loose today just for fun.") In the 1988 presidential race, Michael Dukakis saw his campaign implode when he didn't respond with enough "toughness" to a misleading ad about a career criminal named Willie Horton, who had gotten out on a prison furlough and subsequently raped a woman after assaulting her fiancé. Instead of responding with a tough thirty-second sound bite, Dukakis tried to explain what had actually happened—and this sealed his fate.

Before long, no candidate, Democrat or Republican, could afford to be branded with the label that he or she was soft on crime. It was the death knell for any campaign. In some contests each candidate would desperately try to outdo the other in being tough on criminals. Small towns and communities across the country that hadn't seen a murder in thirty years were now locking their doors at night because of all those murderers being released by liberal judges. This type of political advertising has had a dramatic effect. Polling data shows that 74 percent of the American public believes that crime has gotten worse every year over the past decade, despite statistics showing the exact opposite.

The kicker to the story, of course, comes when a person arrested for drunk driving or getting in a bar fight or possessing a small amount of marijuana stands by in total disbelief at the tough sentencing from a judge who shows no sense of leniency. Where are the liberal judges they were told were running the system? And why are they being treated like . . . well, criminals? Criminals were the ones on TV, like Charles Manson and Jerry Sandusky. When the politicians were ranting about criminals and making the community safe, they weren't talking about *them*!

THE O. J. SIMPSON TRIAL

And then, sure enough, it turned out those griping about a nation that had gone soft on crime were right. Murderers *were* going free and they had the proof in the person of one Orenthal James Simpson. The O. J. Simpson trial would turn out to be the ultimate "I told you so." A liberal judge, a bunch of slimy defense lawyers, and a racially biased jury were exactly what the public had been told the system was full of, and now they had exhibit A to prove it.

The Simpson trial was the first time the majority of the American public had seen the criminal justice system at work for anything longer than a sixty-minute courtroom drama series. The public got to see from start to finish how a lengthy murder trial unfolds, complete with motions, sidebars, jury instructions, and a number of other processes that are not always TV-friendly. The ratings surprised everyone, including the networks that were covering the trial almost nonstop. And what everyone saw was the justice system at its worst.

The trial was so popular because it had a little bit of everything. It starred a wealthy black celebrity accused of murdering his gorgeous white ex-wife in a violent outburst of jealous anger. It hit on hot-button topics of the day, like race, violence, sex, drugs, fame, fashion, sports, and crime. If O.J. had been an illegal alien, it would have been the entire package. People all over the country used the trial as a focal point to debate issues like interracial marriages, police conduct, the use of racial epithets, and the advantages of celebrity. For almost a year it was inarguably the single most captivating event in the country. If you don't believe that, ask yourself where you were when Bill Clinton signed the Welfare Reform Act. Now ask yourself where you where when O.J. was riding in his Bronco down the 405 Freeway, or when the verdict came in.

The problem was that the O. J. Simpson trial was not real. Of course it happened—it just wasn't real. This was not the criminal justice system or any reasonable facsimile of it. To most courtroom attorneys, it was unrecognizable. To compare the O. J. Simpson trial to the everyday workings of the criminal justice system would be like comparing Angelina Jolie to Queen Elizabeth just because they belong to the same species.

But for most Americans, the Simpson trial was not only the best example of the criminal justice system at work they'd seen, it was their only reference. Even before the verdict, the public opinion of the judicial system was not positive. Much of what went on during the trial was hard to understand, and at times it felt like the entire thing was spinning out of control.

The verdict simply confirmed much of the public's suspicions about the entire justice system. O.J. was clearly guilty, but he had gotten off. The soft-on-crime advocates were right. You could kill people in this country and get away with it if you had a good lawyer. And worst of all, to white Americans, the African-American community seemed to be happy about it. The country was angry and divided.

Of course, the O. J. Simpson verdict had to do with race. And that started with the jury selection. The prosecution in the case made an incredibly bizarre decision that didn't take into account the feelings of the black community and didn't seem to reflect any understanding of what their experience was like living in L.A.—and the prosecution paid for it. The murder of Nicole Simpson and Ron Goldman occurred in Brentwood, which is in the western part of Los Angeles. Based on that location, the case should have been heard in the Santa Monica courthouse, an old nondescript building about two blocks from the ocean. Jurors would have come from high-income communities like Palos Verdes, Manhattan Beach, Brentwood, and Malibu. This was not going to be a jury panel with many minorities, especially African-Americans. We did the Susan McDougal trial in Santa Monica just four years later, and we had a total of three African-Americans in a jury pool of about 120 people. The people in that area are also used to celebrity and wealth and would not likely have been swayed by O. J. Simpson's star power. Santa Monica was ideally suited for the prosecution.

But in a move that shocked the local bar, the L.A. district attorney willingly agreed to move the trial to the downtown Criminal Courts Building, commonly referred to as CCB. The makeup of the jury pool at CCB was the exact opposite of Santa Monica. It was drawn from South Central Los Angeles, Inglewood, and East Los Angeles, none of which is affluent. The jury pool during the nineties was often 30 to 40 percent African-American and more than 50 percent minority. Every defense attorney in L.A. wanted trials in CCB because the juries were notoriously defense-friendly. People in those communities had often had bad experiences with law enforcement and thus were suspicious of the prosecution's case. And every trial attorney in L.A. knew that Johnnie Cochran owned CCB. Going up against Cochran in CCB was like going up against the lions in the Roman Colosseum. You were not going to win.

But the head D.A.'s office was located in CCB downtown, and that allowed the head D.A. to manage the trial from an office a few floors above. That, however, was not the only reason the prosecution agreed to move it downtown. In a show of either remarkable arrogance or remarkable stupidity, they believed that the African-Americans from South Central L.A., especially women, would not relate to the rich football star with the white wife. They may have been correct about that, but apparently no one bothered to tell them that these jurors sure as hell were not going to identify with the L.A. Police Department. Had anyone in the D.A.'s office ever heard the name Rodney King? Although the LAPD was one of the best trained, best funded, and most celebrated police departments in the entire world, it also had a fraught history of race relations that would have made Bull Connor proud. The images on television of L.A. burning following the King verdict had stunned the entire nation, but apparently the D.A. believed the riots were just an aberration perpetrated by a few thugs.

They weren't. The African-American community in Los Angeles had lived with years of LAPD harassment, and it understood how the system worked. The LAPD did not invent racial profiling, but they were expert practitioners. Many people stereotyped South Central L.A. as filled with nothing other than gangs, drug dealers, and thugs. In reality South Central had problems, but it also had a large community of hardworking, deeply religious families who were close-knit and wanted to see that their children had better opportunities than they'd had.

Despite the fact that they were law-abiding and responsible citizens, the residents had had bad experiences with the police. For example: during a seminar we were teaching, we met a twenty-two-year-old African-American college graduate who had just been accepted to Georgetown University Law Center, one of the most prestigious law schools in the country. His father was a minister in South Central L.A., and the student also had a part-time job—he was a park police officer for Santa Monica. When we talked about his experiences with the police, he told us that because he drove a nice car, he had been pulled over more than a dozen times, usually on suspicion of having stolen his car. On four of those occasions, the police had ordered him to the ground and put a gun at his head. Most of us cannot imagine the fear of having a police officer standing over us with a gun pointed at our head, wondering if the cop will make a mistake and shoot. Yet it happened to this student four times, a kid who had no criminal record and who was actually a part-time police officer himself. Being harassed by the police had been a regular part of his life. He had heard way too many stories of people who had mouthed off to the police or run from them and ended up dead.

Virtually every African-American in the area had similar stories. To some, it was not even an issue that aroused anger as much as a deep sense of mistrust. Many times when they would write a complaint about being harassed, the police officer would write a report denying their assertions, and the entire thing would be swept under the rug. Without proof, it was their word against the word of a cop.

It was in this atmosphere that the prosecution chose to leave eight African-Americans on the jury. These people were intelligent individuals with strong character—but they had grown up with a different American experience from most of the people watching the trial on TV. It was not going to take much to convince them that the police would lie or even frame a black man. They saw it on a regular basis. When the defense produced tapes of Detective Mark Fuhrman using the n-word and bragging about beating up suspects, the jury had heard all they needed.

The verdict shocked most of the country, but it did not surprise defense attorneys in L.A. Almost the entire defense bar, including us, believed that O.J. was guilty, but we also felt that there was very little chance this jury was going to convict. All they needed was a couple of mistakes by the police and the prosecution: Fuhrman's getting caught lying under oath, the glove not fitting in court, and the officer carrying O.J.'s blood around for several days before taking it to the lab. Combine those with Cochran's charm and skills, and our predictions proved right.

But people wanted to blame someone other than the police or the prosecutors, so misguided criticism fell on Judge Lance Ito. If you took a poll at the time of the trial—or even today—of defense attorneys and prosecutors and asked them to name the three best judges in L.A., Judge Ito would be on both lists. He is widely respected both for his intelligence and for his sense of fairness. He was not some crazed liberal judge; in fact, he had been a tough-as-nails prosecutor before he took the bench. Pops worked with him in the L.A. County District Attorney's Office and often said that he was one of the best prosecutors he had ever met. He was given an impossible task with the Simpson trial and managed to get the jury to a verdict. Given the numerous opportunities for mistrials along the way, that was no small feat.

The public response to the Simpson trial verdict bordered on hysteria. People took to the latest fad, the Internet, and began campaigns to do away with the jury system and decried the fact that all a murderer had to do was be wealthy enough to hire a great defense attorney who would lie, cheat, and steal to make sure murderers roamed the streets. Although no one could point to an actual lie that Johnnie Cochran told in court, it became an assumed fact that defense attorneys lie regularly in court—that it was part of the job.

Pat: Whenever I win a trial, some of my acquaintances will smile knowingly, as if to say, "We know what you do to win." When I was hired to be the legal consultant for the TV show Shark, *I was told the premise of the show was that a defense attorney suddenly becomes a prosecutor and "uses all those*

*dirty tricks he learned as a defense attorney on behalf of the government." I
explained to them that I wouldn't be much help in the "dirty tricks" department, but that most of the lawyers who could help them would have plenty of
free time, since they had likely been disbarred.*

Let us make this very clear. We don't lie in court, and neither do
the vast majority of defense attorneys we know and have seen practice
in court. Beyond the ethical ramifications, there are simply the practical ones, such as getting caught and having your bar license taken.
We love our clients, but we have yet to meet the client for whom we
are willing to lose our bar license. We are both way too old and un-
skilled to go looking for another job.

In addition, we've had far more experience with incredibly ethical defense attorneys—for example, John Climaco, a well-known
Ohio lawyer who has become a great friend to our firm, is one of the
most prominent and skilled attorneys in the country. He had a case in
Cleveland involving a suspected domestic terrorist that was both potentially financially lucrative and was garnering a great deal of national media attention, including an hour-long show on *Dateline*. It
was a defense attorney's dream. John, however, knew the judge that
the case was assigned to—their families did things together socially—
so he knew that the case would be transferred to another judge if he
stayed on it. Recognizing that the best thing for his client was to keep
this judge, he chose to step off the case and referred it to us. He gave
up a lot of money and a huge amount of publicity to make sure the
client was best served. That took a lot of character, but John did not
even hesitate. Actions like John's, however, never draw media attention, and the more outrageous or unusual cases end up informing the
public's opinion of defense attorney ethics.

THE RISE OF THE ANGRY BLOND WHITE WOMEN

Perhaps the most interesting thing about the Simpson case was the
Nielsen ratings. Crime did in fact pay, especially if you could televise

it and sell commercials. The Simpson trial proved that people would not only watch the trial, but they would watch people who talked about the trial, and they would even watch the people who talked about the people who talked about the trial. CNN, Fox, Court TV, and even the three major networks all saw their ratings spike with anything Simpson-related. Cable news was looking for programming to fill up a twenty-four-hour cycle. What could be better than a real-life celebrity murder trial? It wasn't giving a bone to a starving dog; it was giving the dog a forty-eight-ounce porterhouse steak.

The problem was that there were just not enough celebrities accused of murdering people. Sure, you did get the occasional Phil Spector or Robert Blake, but by the time they were arrested they couldn't even have gotten on *Dancing with the Stars*. For a while, Court TV, which had been perhaps the biggest benefactor of the Simpson trial, tried to fill the void by showing trials from around the country that usually involved a doctor or lawyer killing his wife. But they soon learned that the people who had tuned in for the Simpson trial were not going to invest their time and energy in watching tedious trials in which they had no emotional investment. So what were the networks to do?

The answer soon came in the rise of the angry blond white women. The phrase "angry blond white women" is one we coined based on the poster child of faux hysteria, Nancy Grace, and the legion of imitators that followed her. To be classified as one of the angry blond white women, you don't have to be blond, white, or even a woman. You only have to be angry, not very bright, and willing to say outrageous things without the slightest hint of self-awareness. Pandering to the angry O.J. crowd and to a growing number of Americans, in a post-O.J. world, now convinced that the courts were soft on crime, these people began ranting and raving about how the court system was stacked against the victim and for the defense. Under the guise of "advocate for victims," they would argue that if you are arrested then you must be guilty of the crime, or even if you are not guilty of that crime you must at the very least be guilty of some crime and a general sleazebag who deserves what happens to you. Meanwhile, as they were busy whining that defense attorneys were running wild destroying the system, the National District Attorneys Association was releasing statistics that showed that D.A.s acquired convictions in more than 90 percent of all cases. From those statistics, put out by the D.A.s themselves, it does appear that the deck is stacked—but not against the prosecution. However, the angry blond white women were only interested in one statistic—ratings points.

Part of the problem that we have with all of these professed victims' advocates is that they have a very narrow definition of what constitutes a victim. The woman who is sexually assaulted is clearly a victim and deserves justice. But is the man who is falsely accused of sexual assault and spends twenty years in jail during his twenties and thirties before he is freed not a victim too? How about his family who lost his companionship and love, not to mention his earning power; are they not victims as well?

In the beginning, cable television programs were leery about how far the envelope could be pushed. The answer soon came back that there were no limits—the more outrageous the better. Large numbers of viewers were not really interested in facts or the actual evidence in a case as much as they were interested in hearing the latest rumor or the latest speculation by the commentators on what the next rumor might be. And coincidentally enough, the rumors and speculation they heard were always something negative about the defendant. Possessing the right combination of anger and sarcasm, the commentator could not only get ratings but could sell a book, create merchandise, and hit the public speaking circuit. Victim advocacy turned out to be mostly advocating for a much larger bank account.

As the competition between the angry blond white women increased, so did the level of rhetoric. At times it appeared it was not enough just to repeat rumors; they actually needed to create them. If it sounds like we believe they are lying, we do. It's almost as if they took a page from Nazi propagandist Joseph Goebbels: "When one lies, one should lie big and stick to it."

ANN COULTER

The evolution of the angry blond white women began back during the Clinton administration, when for the first time you could turn on the television and see a tall, lanky bleached blonde with eyes so wide that they appeared to be propped open by toothpicks. The moniker under her face identified her as Ann Coulter, and it listed her profession as "Constitutional Lawyer." In the beginning we were struck more by this job title than by what she was saying (which just sounded like rehashed Ayn Rand). Having been lawyers for quite some time, we had come across corporate lawyers, immigration lawyers, patent lawyers, family law lawyers, etc., etc., but neither of us had ever heard anyone who listed his or her profession as constitutional lawyer. It raised a number of interesting questions: Did the Constitution pay her a flat fee or was she on a retainer? When she sued on behalf of the Constitution, who was the plaintiff (I believe Jefferson, Adams, and Monroe are all unavailable)? Most important, which Constitution was she representing, since, judging by her comments, it was obvious she had never read ours?

Eventually we decided that "constitutional lawyer" was a synonym for "unemployed lawyer incapable of holding down a real legal job." This turned out to be a description that seemed to be quite common among the angry blond white women.

Pat: The constitutional lawyer bit might have been enough for me to dismiss Coulter as a total lightweight, but as luck would have it, I had the opportunity to meet her shortly after seeing her on television. I had just flown to Washington, D.C., for a political function, and while in town I picked up a copy of the Washingtonian *magazine. Oddly enough, Coulter had written an article for the magazine complaining that Washington men were wimpy, and whining about how she could not get a date. My first reaction was that this woman was a two-time loser—unemployable and undatable. But later that night, when I attended the political function, who should show up but Ms. Coulter, wearing a remarkably short black miniskirt that accentuated a nice pair of legs and a rather fetching figure. This produced a total revamp of my thinking. Given the fact that men are dogs (a scientific fact—look it up) and will basically sleep with anything, how was it that this semi-attractive, semi-famous single woman was unable to get a date? Just exactly how repulsive did her personality have to be?*

Later I began to realize that the reason she was not dating was that she already had her eyes set on one man, and she was clearly obsessed with him. Night after night she would pop up on numerous TV shows ranting about the rule of law and how Bill Clinton should be charged with perjury. The hatred she had for him was unbelievable. Then it hit me: she didn't hate Clinton— she was in love with him. I thought back to my own grade school experience when the only way I could get DeAnn Dickerson's attention was to push her down. The ranting night after night was Coulter's way of pushing Clinton down—she was desperately trying to get his attention. Anyone could see she was obsessed with the man. As they say, the opposite of love is not hate—it is apathy, and she was clearly not apathetic about Bill Clinton. In fact, in February 2012, Ann Coulter gave a speech to a conservative convention in which she made a series of Clinton penis jokes. Fifteen years later! Fifteen years later and she still has Clinton's penis on her brain. In California, we get restraining orders for less than this.

NANCY GRACE

The O. J. Simpson trial, the Scott Peterson trial, the Michael Jackson trial, and the Casey Anthony trial each produced its own huge media circus. Every circus has to have a clown, which brings us to Nancy Grace. The undisputed breakout star of the angry blond white women, Grace was once a Georgia prosecutor known for being tough and for committing multiple acts of prosecutorial misconduct. "Prosecutorial misconduct" is legalese for saying she lied and cheated. In fact, appellate courts in Georgia found that she had committed prosecutorial misconduct three separate times in a nine-year career. To put that in perspective, in our experience, most prosecutors, in a twenty- or thirty-year career, will not be admonished even once for prosecutorial misconduct. It is a very harsh—and rare—finding by a court. But Grace wouldn't make her name in the courts—she'd make it on Court TV. She began her broadcast career there in the late nineties, before getting her own show on HLN in 2005. From this perch she offers running commentary on the cases of the day—usually ones that involve an innocent young woman as the victim.

Grace's professed enemies are not just the accused—she also despises the liberal courts. One of the most scathing opinions of Grace's career as a prosecutor was written by federal judge William Pryor. Judge Pryor became somewhat well-known during the George W. Bush presidency because his nomination to the federal bench was vetoed repeatedly by a Democratic Senate due to his extreme conservative views. He was later put on the bench by Bush via a recess appointment. He was as law-and-order as it gets, somewhere to the right of Supreme Court Justice Antonin Scalia. His exact quote about Grace was that he agreed with the lower court opinion that she "played fast and loose" with her ethical duties and that it was difficult to conclude that Grace did not knowingly use apparently false testimony from a detective. Of course Pryor, to Grace, is just another liberal judge.

But her prosecutorial misconduct is in the past. The problem today is that she is an entertainer pretending to be a lawyer—she is an actress playing a role. She has cleverly marketed herself as the voice of those angry at an America allegedly soft on crime. She has created a character who whines about perceived injustices and then sneers at anyone who has opposing viewpoints. In short, she has become the Morton Downey Jr. of our time.

It would be easy to dismiss Grace as a joke, someone with zero credibility who is just looking to make a buck. However, that would be a huge mistake. She has an audience of millions, most of whom are allowed to serve on juries. When we do jury questionnaires before a high-profile case, a number of potential jurors always put down her show as one they regularly watch.

She also broadcasts lies. She is not a spinner, someone who takes a fact and spins it in one direction or the other. She propagates untruths. If this were limited to her show and her viewers, that would be a problem in itself. But in the fishbowl world of the media, her lies get picked up by other commentators who don't want to appear out of the loop. Before long, her story becomes a truism that is repeated by the media throughout a trial. For example, before the Scott Peterson trial started, Grace announced, based apparently on some nonsense in the ether, that the police had arrived at Scott's house the day of his wife Laci's disappearance and were immediately suspicious of foul play because of the smell of bleach, as if someone had tried to clean up a crime scene. This was a totally fictitious story that was even denied by the police. That did not stop Grace from repeating the story, and soon much of the press was following suit. It became an accepted fact, and in our defense of Scott Peterson we had to confront reporters who constantly brought up this lie, and we had to face a jury pool tainted by it.

Grace's success is having a demonstrable effect on young prosecutors who see that she is famous for her snit fits. Professor Jonathan Turley described it perfectly in an article for his blog when he said, "The Grace effect is not lost on aspiring young prosecutors who struggle to outdo one another as camera-ready, take-no-prisoners avengers of justice." As we discuss in Chapter 4, the system has always functioned best when each side has a respect for the other's job. A lot of the young prosecutors we now see every day in court, however, believe that their role is to treat the defense with the same disdain and sarcasm they see coming from Grace and to refuse to even look at any other side to the story.

Refusing to admit she is wrong is also part of Grace's shtick. Even in the face of irrefutable evidence she will not admit that she is wrong. At various times she has preached the guilt of, among others, Gary Condit, JonBenét Ramsey's parents, Richard Ricci (in the Elizabeth Smart case), and the Duke University lacrosse team, all of whom were later shown to be innocent. When confronted with her prior statements assuring her audience these people were guilty, she usually hides behind the notion that the police are the ones investigating these people; she is simply reporting on their investigation, so if you are criticizing her, you are really criticizing our brave men and women in uniform. Or when she is not hiding behind the police, she just doesn't show up for work. The night the D.A. dismissed the charges against the Duke lacrosse team, whom she had viciously attacked on a nightly basis, she was a no-show for her own broadcast. The irony is that she repeatedly skewers criminal defendants for not taking "personal responsibility" if they offer an excuse for their behavior. Yet she offers up more excuses than anyone and refuses to make any attempt at taking personal responsibility when she is dead wrong.

Ultimately, though, she is an entertainer, not a prosecutor. (Many of the prosecutors we speak to despise her and hate that she puts herself out there as the voice of the prosecution.) In the end, we give her kudos for creating a character with an appeal to a large segment of the population. But that is what she is—a character. She is playing a role, even if some believe she is a real person.

The people really responsible are the networks and the shows that continue to give her a forum. They are not deaf and blind—and they certainly are aware that she has repeatedly accused innocent people of committing crimes. In many countries, you are stoned for falsely accusing someone of a crime. At the very least you are charged with a crime yourself and thrown in jail. Here, you get your own TV show. Only in America.

WENDY MURPHY

Anytime someone finds a formula for success, there are going to be copycats, and the success of Ann Coulter and Nancy Grace is no exception. Most of the women who auditioned for the copycat roles were cut from the same cloth: i.e., former prosecutors with varying degrees of telegenic aura and a willingness to make outrageous comments. They learned the game very quickly—court cases on TV were not about evidence; they were about what you could say to get the highest ratings.

Our favorite of the copycats is sex crime specialist Wendy Murphy. While the rest of the Grace acolytes learned that there are boundaries even on cable TV, Murphy revels in acting crazy. In most advanced European countries, she might have been committed to an institution for her own good (and certainly the public's). But in the United States she has not only been allowed to freely roam the streets, she has been given a regular forum, on several different cable shows, to present her views on the criminal justice system. We appreciate more than most the protections of the First Amendment and the whole concept of the marketplace of ideas. However, the First Amendment does not guarantee you the right to appear regularly on Fox News.

Yet somehow Murphy has managed to slip through the cracks. Representing herself as the ultimate heroine for all victims of sexual abuse, she stands out for her insane statements, such as:

1. She has never heard a false claim of rape. She made this statement despite overwhelming evidence from DNA and blood samples that proves that many, many rape claims are false. This does not even include the large number of people who have actually admitted to falsifying rape charges, oftentimes to gain an advantage in a divorce or child custody issue.

2. She stated that the ACLU wrote a brief that argued it should be a constitutional right for children as young as thirteen to have sex with adults. And she took it further, saying the ACLU did not want any laws on the books that made it a crime for a child to be abused by an adult. The ACLU actually argued that an eighteen-year-old boy convicted of sexually abusing a fourteen-year-old boy should receive the same sentence as any person accused of abusing a female child. In other words, the sex of the victim, male or female, should not be a determining factor in sentencing.

3. She stated in an interview that "I'm really tired of people suggesting you're somehow un-American if you don't respect the presumption of innocence because you know what that sounds like to a victim? Presumption you're a liar." By the way, she claims to be an adjunct professor at New England Law. Presumably the school is okay with her lectures entitled "The Ridiculous Presumption of Innocence—Who Made That Stupid Idea Up Anyway?"

4. She believes that the Duke lacrosse team is still guilty. Years after it has been conclusively proven that the entire rape report was phony, Murphy still insists the Duke lacrosse players are guilty. As recently as a few months ago, she went on a tirade that the defense was hiding and should produce documents that would prove their guilt. (One of the common themes among wackos is that there are secret papers or tapes that are being kept from the public that will prove them right.) It turned out that the papers that were being held back were actually the psychological records of the alleged victim, which the defense was kind enough to not release.

DR. KEITH ABLOW

Although the women dominate this category of the tabloid media, there is at least one male who could qualify under the heading of "angry blond white women." His name is Dr. Keith Ablow, a psychiatrist who used to appear regularly on Fox News and a few other assorted shows but who, we believe, has thankfully begun fading into oblivion. We became acquainted with Dr. Ablow during the Scott Peterson trial when he wrote a book called *Inside the Mind of Scott Peterson*. The book was a deep psychoanalysis of Scott and his sociopathic tendencies as well as an in-depth discussion of the troubled family he came from. It was a truly amazing piece of work especially because Ablow had never (a) talked to Scott Peterson, (b) met Scott Peterson, or (c) been in the same area code as Scott Peterson. Nor had he ever spoken to the troubled family. Ablow is the Kreskin of psychiatrists—who needs to actually ask questions of a patient when you can read minds? Or, better yet, get the necessary information from the *National Enquirer* to do your analysis.

The capper (we hope) was when he announced in 2011 that parents should not let their children watch Chaz Bono on *Dancing with the Stars* because they might turn gay. Parents should probably be more worried that their children might watch Dr. Ablow on Fox News and turn stupid.

|||||

The politicization of the criminal justice system, the O. J. Simpson trial, and the rise of the victims' advocates have yielded predictable results: emboldened prosecutors, nervous judges, cowed defense attorneys, and juries primed to convict.

Much of the public views this as a good thing—being tough on crime is very popular. Until, of course, it happens to them. Every single day people come into our office who have led upstanding lives until they suddenly find themselves or a close relative facing what they feel is an unfair criminal charge. They are often the same ones who the week before were cheering on Nancy Grace and smugly feeling sure that any person charged with a crime must be guilty. After all, people who haven't done anything wrong don't have anything to worry about. Just try telling that to the four navy seamen.

CHAPTER TWO

Defense Attorneys— We Sleep Very Well at Night, Thank You Very Much

Let us clarify one thing to begin with about being a criminal defense attorney. If you picked up this book expecting us to apologize for what we do for a living or, even worse, to offer some mealymouthed rationalization of a criminal defense attorney's job, then you need to put this book down immediately. Go buy Nancy Grace's autobiography: *An Idiot's Guide to Criminal Law.*

We don't apologize for being criminal defense attorneys. We don't apologize for fighting for people who have no one else to fight for them and, in most cases, who have been deserted by everyone around them—people they used to call friends. We will not apologize for taking unpopular cases. And we will never apologize for the pride we take in standing up in court and announcing that we represent the defendant.

Given the current environment, people often expect us to act a little embarrassed about what we do for a living. Whenever we attend a party, some stranger eventually will get enough alcohol in them to sidle up and in a tone filled with disgust ask, "How the hell can you represent someone when you know he is guilty?" We now have come up with a standard answer that we deliver with the same level of disgust: "How can you just stand by and do nothing when thousands of innocent people are sitting in jail cells all across the country?" Not coincidentally, we get invited to fewer and fewer parties each year.

It used to be that people had to actually see us at a party and work up the nerve before asking that question. But with the Internet, now anyone can fire off thoughts to us, often in e-mails that pray for our deaths, usually in a manner that involves some kind of inventive prolonged torture. It's best to just ignore these e-mails, but sometimes we can't help but respond to some of the more interesting ones. When we were representing Michael Jackson, we responded to one particular e-mailer who was adamant about Michael's guilt and unwilling to listen to any argument to the contrary. After a couple of back-and-forth exchanges in which we tried to explain why his reasoning was faulty, he sent us one final e-mail that was both eloquent and succinct. It simply said, "DIE SCUMBAG LAWYERS! DIE!" Hard to argue with that.

It is incredible to believe that twenty to thirty years ago, when we were starting our legal careers, it was the criminal defense attorneys who were considered the heroes of the justice system. Atticus Finch was an icon—the ultimate example of strong character and morality. For years, TV had been filled with shows like *Judd for the Defense*, *Owen Marshall: Counselor at Law*, *The Defenders*, *The Bold Ones*, and, of course, the show featuring the greatest defense attorney of all, *Perry Mason*. In 1972, noted defense attorney F. Lee Bailey published a book called *The Defense Never Rests*, which became an instant best seller.

But that has all changed. The defense lawyers in dramas today are all sleazebags, win-at-all-costs whores who live for the opportunity to get some guilty guy off and put him back on the street.

THE DEFENSE ATTORNEY'S JOB

Perhaps it's best to start off by confronting the notion that it is our job to get guilty people "off." Not only is that a silly description of our job, but anyone who has spent one week in a courtroom knows it is not true. Let's walk through some hypotheticals that show why this is nonsense.

A man walks into our office charged with a crime. Now, let's say there is a mountain of evidence against him—perhaps a videotape of him committing the crime or maybe a confession that is ironclad. With that scenario, we would likely assume the man is guilty and also assume that the prosecution would be able to prove it easily at trial. Why would we be foolish enough to take that case to trial in order to "get him off" when we know it is almost certain he would lose and receive an even harsher sentence? The answer is we wouldn't. A client like that hires you to work hard for him, negotiate like hell, explore sentencing options, and try to make the landing as soft as possible. He is paying you for your expertise in negotiating and for your relationships with the people (i.e., prosecutors and judges) who can help him achieve that soft landing.

Now let's take a second scenario. This time the man walks into our office charged with a crime and there is some evidence pointing toward his guilt and some evidence that suggests he may be innocent. In our experience someone in this situation will always proclaim his innocence. Our job is not to try to figure out if he is indeed guilty or innocent. Our job is to determine how a jury will look at the evidence. As for personal feelings, if he says he is innocent and we see evidence to back that up, then we are going to believe him and treat him as the innocent man the law tells us he is. If during the course of proceedings evidence is produced that shows he is lying and that he is indeed guilty, we are not going to foolishly press on to trial to try to "get him off." Instead, we would revert to scenario one and explain to him that the jury will almost certainly find him guilty, and if we go to trial, he would end up with a harsher sentence. When cases like this do go to trial, it is generally because the prosecution believes the man is guilty based on how they view the evidence and we believe he is innocent based on how we view the evidence. This is why we have trials. Because both sides have a good-faith belief they are right.

And then there is the third scenario. The client walks into our office and this time it is clear that the prosecution has very little evidence and it is a stupid case. Sound far-fetched? It happens on almost a daily basis. As we will explore later in the book, sometimes cops don't want to deal with a confusing situation, with conflicting claims and inconclusive evidence, so they just arrest somebody or everybody and let the courts sort it out. Other times it is clear the police made a mistake. The *Los Angeles Times* reported in 2011 that 1,480 people in Los Angeles had been falsely arrested in the past five years based on simple misidentification by the police. That may sound simple to sort out, but as the article makes clear, it can often take weeks and even months before they get it right.

Sometimes the prosecutor overcharges a case—adding a number of superfluous counts or charging a defendant with the most severe crime possible when a lesser crime would be more appropriate. In most of these situations, either the prosecutor comes to his or her senses or the judge steps in and dismisses the case. Either way, the case is not likely to go to trial.

|||||

As you will note, none of these scenarios involves a defense attorney trying to get a client he or she knows is guilty "off." The system just does not work like that. If a case goes to trial, the defense attorney usually has a good-faith belief that the client is indeed innocent—that is why the attorney is taking the case to trial and risking a loss plus a likely harsher sentence for the client. The defense attorney is not eagerly rubbing his or her hands together and gleefully thinking of sending a murderer or rapist back out into the community.

There are some exceptions. Sometimes you just can't work out a deal that is acceptable to both parties, and the defendant is looking at so much time anyway that you might as well roll the dice and see what happens at trial. This is the one time when you may know your client is likely guilty, but you go to trial because even if you lose, the judge's sentence will likely be better than the prosecutor's offer. For example, say that on a series of residential burglary cases the prosecution makes your client an offer of five years in state prison, which you believe is too high. If the case goes to trial and your client is found guilty, you suspect that the judge will not give your client more than three years. You might as well go to trial and lose—your client will actually end up with a better deal.

The other exception is when the client is clearly delusional and, even though the evidence is overwhelming, thinks he or she will get off. Against your strong advice, the client insists on going to trial. This scenario rarely ends well.

The true role of the defense attorney is to fight for the client by any legal means possible. Fighting means crossing swords with people and sometimes making enemies. It's a part of the job that, frankly, some defense attorneys can't stomach. Despite the common perception that defense attorneys will do anything to get the defendant off, we see a number of defense attorneys who are simply afraid to piss off people. A couple of years ago we were hired to take over an attempted murder case in a small California community. The defense attorney was trying to convince his client to plead to twenty-five years for a crime the client was adamant he did not commit. He failed to file even a simple discovery motion that would have backed up his client's claims, perhaps because it was a small town and he did not want to be perceived as a troublemaker. It was more important for that attorney to not rock the boat in his community than to fight for his client. We always wonder why these lawyers do criminal defense work if they are so afraid of being adversarial.

Even worse is the story of Cameron Todd Willingham, who was

found guilty of arson and murdering his three children in Texas in 1991 and was put to death in 2004. Before he was killed, scientific evidence was produced to show that the arson testimony used in his trial was not only faulty, it was dead wrong. Despite this, he was put to death, and since that time the evidence has grown stronger that he was in fact not guilty of the crime. Virtually every expert who has looked at the case now agrees that the fire was not set intentionally. But one person who refuses to admit it was a mistake is Willingham's own defense attorney. In an interview, he actually argued for his own client's guilt. Apparently he would rather suck up to the prosecutors, who clearly made a huge mistake, than take up for his poor dead innocent client.

Mark: I believe this attitude is ridiculous—it is the defense attorney's job to zealously defend his or her client at all peril to the attorney. Good judges and good prosecutors understand that and respect you if you do it well, even if they don't like it very much at the time. As a general rule I have good relationships with the prosecutors I face because I don't take it personally when they call me an egotistical media whore or a smartass slimeball, and they don't take it personally when I call them wimpy cop wannabes who got beat up in high school and are now looking for revenge. So far I have only had one D.A. take a swing at me and that was because I questioned his manhood at a time when he was apparently having some sexual identity issues.

THE UNDEFEATED LAWYER

There is another myth that has arisen in the media age: the great defense lawyer who has never lost a case. Let us explain why you should never, ever, ever even consider hiring a lawyer who has told you he or she has never lost a case. Either one of two things is true: (1) the lawyer is lying or (2) the lawyer has tried very few cases. Whenever we hear an opposing lawyer with some experience brag that he or she has never lost a case, we immediately know the lawyer is lying.

You can be smart, charismatic, and well versed in the law, but you cannot be a great trial attorney until you have tried dozens if not hundreds of cases. There is a saying among attorneys: "Some gotta burn so you can learn." It's not a lovely thought, but it's true. There are a lot of attributes that go into being a great trial attorney, but the most important thing is to try cases and then try some more, even cases you know you will likely lose. If you want to be a great trial attorney, you must have no fear. You can't cherry-pick only cases you think you can easily win. You have to try the tough ones too, and you can't be afraid to lose.

You learn something new from every single trial, and often more from the ones you lose. Combined we have tried well over four hundred cases, and we are still learning. No matter how many trials you watch or how many books on trials you read, every trial produces situations that you have never been through or even thought about. A few years back we did a trial where the judge was fine in the morning session and then after lunch would come back clearly intoxicated. They don't teach you how to handle that in law school.

The greatest skill a defense attorney can have is to be able to think fast on his or her feet. A lawyer may have some natural ability to do that, but what you really need is a wealth of experience to draw from.

Mark: I like to think that I was born with the ability to think fast in tough situations, but when I was first thrown into a courtroom, I lost the first seven cases I tried. Ten years later I had a winning streak of twenty-five trials in a row, spanning three years. What was the difference? Over those ten years in between losing seven in a row and winning twenty-five in a row, I had tried more than one hundred cases: three-day trials, three-week trials, three-month trials. Won some, lost some. But by the time I finished, I sure as hell knew how to try a case.

That is why the "I have never lost a case" quote is such a joke among real trial attorneys. You aren't trying cases if you haven't lost cases. When we flew to Little Rock, Arkansas, to defend Whitewater figure Susan McDougal on criminal contempt charges, the United States attorney prosecuting that case introduced himself to us and quickly made us aware that he had never lost a case and was not planning on losing this one. Our research showed that he had indeed never lost a case, but he had also tried a grand total of eleven cases with the U.S. Attorneys' Office. At the trial, we discovered he was indeed a very talented lawyer, and we came to have enormous respect for him—but that turned out to be the last time he could say he had never lost a case.

Along the same lines as the mythical undefeated trial attorney is the attorney who can help you get away with murder if you can afford to pay the attorney enough. As you can guess, O.J. did little to put this theory to rest, so let us try. O. J. Simpson can get away with murder because he can afford to hire a great lawyer—you can't. Hiring Johnnie Cochran did not mean you got a get-out-of-jail-free card. Johnnie was a great, great lawyer. One of the best ever. But even Johnnie lost cases—a lot of them. Which is exactly why he was such a great lawyer—he was not afraid to try tough cases.

THE UNDERDOG PROSECUTOR

Speaking of Johnnie Cochran, the concept of the dream team of defense attorneys has promulgated another misconception—that poor, hardworking, understaffed, underfunded prosecutors face off against huge defense juggernauts with unlimited resources and battalions of lawyers. You'll often hear commentators in high-profile cases push the image of the prosecution as these scrappy underdogs fighting against a system that heavily favors the defendant. The truth is the exact opposite. In the vast majority of cases, especially the high-profile ones, the prosecution has at their beck and call the full force of law enforcement, experts, law clerks, technology, interns, etc. We recently tried a case where the D.A. and the lead detective spent lavish sums on trips to interview witnesses in Colorado, New England, Montana, San Francisco, and Hawaii. Amazingly, every single one of the witnesses had telephones.

In contrast, the defense is usually lucky if the client can afford a part-time investigator. And these investigators, beyond their limited budgets, face an uphill battle in attempting to gather evidence. If the police come to your door to interview you as a witness, most people are more than willing to talk. When a private investigator comes to your door and identifies himself as working for the defendant, the majority of the time the investigator is asked to leave.

In the Scott Peterson case, the prosecution brought in more than 150 law enforcement officers from seven different agencies and used helicopters, expensive underwater sonar equipment, tracking devices, and wiretapping equipment. They spent more than $6 million to prosecute Scott, and their investigation involved tens of thousands of manpower hours. Contrast that with a defense team that had to beg the court for enough money to pay a part-time investigator and a couple of experts. Yet virtually every media outlet sold the story of how a David prosecution team was going up against a Goliath defense.

One could counterargue that because prosecution must prove their case beyond a reasonable doubt, it makes sense that they need to employ more resources than the defense. After all, judges regularly lecture jurors that the accused is presumed innocent until the prosecution *proves* that he or she is guilty.

But as we mentioned earlier, over the past decade jurors have started coming into court with the exact opposite state of mind: they believe that anyone accused of a crime is likely guilty. The job of the defense attorney now includes getting those jurors who don't understand the presumption of innocence to disqualify themselves.

During jury selection (known as voir dire), we almost always ask this question:

"Is there anyone here who thinks that just because the defendant is sitting here in court he must be guilty?"

Over the years we would get a smattering of hands raised, sometimes none. Today that question always garners numerous raised hands and the same standard answers:

"Where there is smoke there is fire."

"He wouldn't be here if he had not done something!"

"Why would the police arrest him if he hadn't done anything wrong?"

And of course the always relevant "I think O.J. was guilty as sin."

Further questioning of the jury panel invariably produces even more people who feel this way but did not want to raise their hands. In the past most judges would remove these people for "cause," which means that the judge finds they are not suitable to serve on a jury. It is now so commonplace to hear potential jurors say these things that judges are no longer removing for cause in these circumstances unless the person says something really egregious or outrageous.

So we have to get them to say something totally outlandish during the jury selection process. We will often agree with people like this, making them feel comfortable and letting them know that their opinions are not unusual. We tell them that we want to know more about why they feel that way, and then we let them explain. The more puzzled you act, the more they will volunteer. They are almost desperate to make you understand why they feel the way they do. And sooner or later they are likely to say something that will get them disqualified.

PROSECUTORS V. DEFENSE ATTORNEYS

The majority of the television shows today portray the prosecutor's role in the courtroom as similar to the defense attorney's—mostly cross-examining witnesses. In truth, the jobs are dramatically different. A good prosecutor will slowly and methodically build a case. Prosecutors are trained to follow a certain script to make sure that they get what they need for the conviction. For example, they make sure that all the elements of the crime are presented, that proper exhibits get introduced, that the crime scene is laid out, etc. Often a witness is called simply to establish the credibility of a later witness. A good prosecutor is there to not wow the jury, but rather to educate them.

The defense attorney has a very different job. In most cases the prosecution puts on a lot more witnesses than the defense, meaning the prosecution handles mostly direct examinations and the defense counters with cross-examinations. Defense attorneys have police reports and some witness interviews, but for the most part we don't have access to the prosecution witnesses and have no idea what their demeanor or truthfulness will be. Thus we can't follow a script. And if you script a cross-examination prior to seeing the witness, you are asking for trouble.

It's like the difference between a stand-up comic and an improv comic. Prosecutors are like stand-up comics. Night after night they go on stage and deliver mostly the same material, with a few tweaks here and there. When he or she does the job well, a stand-up comic can control an audience. Defense attorneys are more like improv comics. They have to react quickly and figure out what is working and what is not while they're in the middle of thinking up new ideas. Done well, improv is a work of art. Done poorly, it is painful to watch.

Most of the time prosecutors do their direct examinations in some sort of chronological order. Some will literally read from notes as they walk their witnesses through a series of questions. It's the best way for them to get the jury to see their case as a story. When we really want to get under the skin of prosecutors, we tell them that we could train a dog to be a prosecutor. All we'd have to do is teach him how to say, "And then what happened?" (That is obviously an oversimplification. The dog would also have to be trained to ask, "And what happened next?")

Although the defense can put on its own witnesses and experts, the defense usually makes its case during cross-examination of the state's witnesses. Cross-examination is where the defense builds reasonable doubt, and thus it is the lifeblood of the defense attorney. It is far and away the most difficult trial skill to master, yet it is without a doubt the most important for the defense. Cross-examination is where an attorney's reputation is gained or lost. Any number of things in a trial can make the difference between winning and losing. But it is the defense attorney's cross-examination of the prosecution's witnesses that sets the tone for the trial, and it is that cross-examination that jurors remember most.

THE ART OF CROSS-EXAMINATION

Cross-examination is not for weak at heart, but if you don't love cross-examination, you have no business being a defense attorney. It needs to be aggressive, and because of the latest television shows it can be. As the years have gone by, cross-examinations on television shows have become more and more hostile and exaggerated. A few months ago one of the legal shows portrayed a defense attorney barking questions at the dead victim's grieving mother, something no intelligent defense attorney would ever do. But it demonstrates how jurors are now primed to not object if the same aggressiveness is used in a real-life courtroom.

Nowadays jurors not only don't object to it, they expect it. It seems like they are actually disappointed these days if they don't see some fireworks. They think that a good defense attorney should berate all witnesses. They might even think your client must be guilty if you're not attacking prosecution witnesses.

Mark: I learned cross-examination from one of the all-time greats: my father, Paul Geragos. Pops was a D.A. for twelve years and a defense attorney for more than thirty years. He is a legend in L.A., and the stories of his cross-exams are still discussed in courthouses across the county. I rarely go into a courthouse in Los Angeles where I am not stopped by a D.A., judge, or defense attorney who asks about him and wants to tell me a Pops story. One of the classic Pops stories involved a rather arrogant L.A. society woman who strolled into court letting everyone know exactly who she was and that she was not afraid of anybody. She was a witness to a robbery, and her attitude was that the court was lucky she had bothered to show up. Pops was known for going for the jugular, and he was not about to let this Beverly Hills blue blood off easily. Minutes into the cross-examination, she was being made out to be a fool. Pops got her to admit that she didn't really see anything and that she was not even at the location she'd told the police she was. At the twenty-minute mark she had become completely unraveled. Rather than continue, the woman abruptly snatched up her purse, got off the witness stand, and silently walked out of the courtroom, leaving behind a dumbfounded judge and jury. When she reached the back door, she slammed it loudly, never to return.

But Pops saved his best cross-examinations for his three young sons. At home he was as relentless as he was in the courtroom. People often think I am kidding when I say I learned how to cross-examine at home, but trust me, it was no joke. By the time he finished questioning me about what I had been doing out so late on a Saturday night, I was confessing to things I hadn't even thought of doing. If Pops had been alive during the Spanish Inquisition, there would have been no need for the rack. He had his own form of torture—you either learned how to match it or you didn't survive in our house.

Cross-examination is an art form that, like any art form, requires practice. It also requires learning to listen to what the witness is saying. As we said, it's like improv. That is why we cringe when we see a lawyer stand up for cross-examination with a huge binder filled with dividers and a perfect categorizing system. Cross-examination is not smooth; you have no idea where it is going to go or what opportunities may open up when you listen carefully and adjust your questions to what you just heard.

You also want to create great rhythm—to get into a zone while at the same time making sure the witness doesn't get into one. A smart witness can see what direction the examination is going in and begin to anticipate the questions or, at the very least, figure out what points the defense is trying to make. A good defense attorney will focus on an area and then after a few questions abruptly jump to another area, to keep the witness off-kilter.

A smart prosecutor knows when and, most important, how often to object to trip up the defense attorney. If he objects too little, he allows you as the defense attorney to get into a rhythm. If he objects too frequently, then he runs the risk of antagonizing the jury. But just because a prosecutor objects and the judge sustains the objection does not mean you should necessarily move on. Way too many attorneys take a sustained objection as a personal affront or an embarrassment in front of the jury. A judge's ruling is not the same as God speaking from the burning bush (although some judges would dispute this). Just because the objection has been upheld does not mean that you should not pursue the question. A good lawyer knows that asking the same question multiple times but in slightly different forms may ultimately make it admissible. Eventually the judge may allow the question, but even if the judge does not, the jury will start wondering why the prosecutor is so scared of that particular line of questioning.

Another huge mistake to avoid as a defense attorney is not quitting when you are ahead. When you do a cross-examination and it is going extremely well, the witness is putty in your hands and you are congratulating yourself for being the greatest attorney since Clarence Darrow. The temptation is to just keep going—keep beating up the witness. After all, you have exposed the witness as a liar, the jury dislikes the witness, and you are having a lot of fun. But if you keep pushing you're going to look like a bully.

Mark: During an arson trial I was doing several years ago, a dubious eyewitness to the fire repeatedly contradicted himself for the better part of an hour as I cross-examined him. It became clear that the witness was lying about what he saw. While the frustration mounted in the courtroom, the witness appeared to be blissfully oblivious to the carnage going on around him. Finally I realized that this prosecution witness was simply incapable of telling the truth. I calmed down, backed off a little, and then asked the witness, in the interest of saving time, to please just raise his hand before he answered the next question if he was planning on lying. The prosecutor objected, basically on the grounds of me being a smart-ass, and the judge admonished me to stick to the cross-examination. So I asked the witness the next question. To everyone's amazement, the witness raised his hand before he answered. The judge nearly fell out of her seat laughing. Even the prosecutor was trying to stifle a giggle. For one of the few times in my life, I was speechless. The judge explained to the witness that he really did not have to raise his hand if he was going to lie—instead just try to tell the truth. The witness looked genuinely befuddled. I had more questions, but it wasn't going to get any better than this for the defense, so I thanked the witness, walked back to the counsel table, and sat down.

Even a great meal starts going downhill when you are getting bloated, and that is what can happen on cross-exam. At some point, human nature takes over and jurors start feeling sorry for even the worst witness if they feel it is going too far. Just because the defense can beat up the witness for another three hours does not mean they should. This is especially true in a trial where the prosecution is not going well. We have heard hundreds of jurors complain about dead-end trials dragging on too long; we have yet to hear from one who complained the trial was too short.

The reverse is also true. One of the most frustrating things in cross is when we are not getting what we expect out of a witness. Whether the witness does not have the information we want, or is very good at deflecting questions, or is just so sympathetic that we are wasting our time, the frustration can build. While the instinct can be to keep going after the witness until we either break down the witness or get something good, the likelihood is that neither will happen. At this point we have to cut the examination short and live to fight another day.

The defense cannot approach every witness the same way, with the same style. In the Scott Peterson case the most anticipated witness was Scott's girlfriend Amber Frey. The pundits were debating how Geragos v. Frey would go down, with most assuming that the defense would brutally grill her. Gloria Allred, who represented Frey, was busy holding press conferences in the parking lot (where she does her best work), building up the confrontation as if she were Don King at a pre-fight weigh-in. The entire thing was ridiculous. Why would we attack Amber Frey? She didn't do anything wrong. Based on our background investigation, she was not exactly a candidate for Our Lady of the Chastity Nunnery, but so what? The worst thing you could say about her was that she appeared to enjoy sex, and we have rarely held that against a woman. Attacking her was only going to make her sympathetic. The best thing to do was just make a few minor points and get her off the stand as quickly as possible.

The courtroom was packed in anticipation for a battle that never came. It was very anticlimactic. Most of the questions asked were simply to reinforce that Scott Peterson had never told her anything during any of their conversations that would lead her to believe he killed his wife, Laci. He certainly never confessed anything to her. The press left disappointed, but Gloria Allred, still in full Don King mode, had a press conference in the parking lot holding a trash bag making some reference to the questions being trash.

Some clients want to see every witness embarrassed, destroyed, and beaten. We have had cases where the client was more interested in destroying a witness than in winning the case. Clients love screaming—they want a show, and it is hard to explain to them that the most effective way is not always the loudest way.

But what they want even more than screaming is the Perry Mason moment when the witness breaks down or so screws up on the witness stand that the case is quickly dismissed. It doesn't happen often, but we love it just as much as clients do when it does.

Mark: A couple of years ago I was representing a man accused of running an escort service. He denied it and said that the two women making the accusations were prostitutes who were caught running their own escort service and were trying to shift the blame.

The first woman took the stand at the preliminary hearing and began crying in record time. She wailed that our client had forced her into prostitution and she was being sent out on calls against her will. She insisted that since her initial arrest she had been freed from forced prostitution.

The cross-examination took less than a minute.

First I asked her, "Are you sure you are no longer engaging in prostitution on your own?"

"Absolutely not!" she answered. "I escaped from that life the day your client was arrested."

I asked the judge if I could approach. In my hands was a picture taken from a Web site that morning that showed her very prominently displayed in a state of virtual undress and holding on to what appeared to be a man's penis. The page had her name and a phone number featured at the top and a suggestion that she would be happy to hold on to anyone's penis for the right amount of money. As I approached the witness stand, the woman took one quick look at the picture, looked at me, and then loudly proclaimed, "Oh, shit!"

| | | | |

The importance of cross-examination is not always in the facts you get out; sometimes it is in repeating facts so that they sink in. The truth is that all attorneys tend to forget that they are familiar with the material and have read over it numerous times at their leisure, but jurors are having information thrown at them in a rapid-fire manner on a subject they knew nothing about before they walked in the door. On top of that, attorneys expect them to concentrate on details for six or seven hours a day without letting their minds wander. Even if we are doing a gripping cross-examination, the jurors may not catch everything or even most of what is going on.

For example, in the Scott Peterson case, the prosecution put a computer expert on the stand to testify that Scott had been looking at tidal charts in the San Francisco Bay. The expert's testimony was lengthy, detailed, and put 90 percent of the room to sleep. During cross-examination, we asked him about some notations in his records that seemed strange. The prosecution was arguing that Scott had killed his wife at night and then taken her body to the bay the next morning. But the computer expert's records seemed to show that someone had been on the Peterson's home computer at around 8 A.M. on the morning of Laci's disappearance. That person had gone on the Internet and looked up women's sweaters and umbrella stands that had sunflower designs. Laci loved sunflowers and even had a sunflower tattoo.

This certainly showed that Laci may have been alive when the prosecution was claiming she was dead, and it should have created reasonable doubt about the prosecution's entire case. We brought it up twice more and emphasized it in the closing argument. After Scott was found guilty, the jurors were interviewed on *Larry King Live*, and King asked them what they thought about that particular computer evidence. As we watched the blank looks on their faces and their inability to articulate a response, the real answer was clear—they had no idea what he was talking about. In a six-month trial with more than one hundred witnesses and thousands of pages of documents, perhaps the single most important piece of evidence had gone right past them.

What jurors do retain, however, is the tone of the cross. If cross-examinations are consistently causing the prosecution witnesses to stutter or misstate things, jurors will remember that. After a trial, we will sometimes talk with the jurors, and, invariably, they will remember whether a witness was good or bad; but when you ask them for specifics about the testimony or why they feel that way, they frequently have a hard time coming up with anything.

It's possible to undermine witnesses without yelling at them. In fact, sometimes the most effective method is to quietly expose the absurdity of the witness's testimony. In a trial a few years back, the prosecution put on an expert witness whose background was impeccable: he taught at Stanford, Harvard Medical School, etc. He was also a seasoned expert—well-spoken, made eye contact with the jury, was a grandfatherly type with a Stephen Hawking résumé. The issue in the case was whether our client had picked up his four-year-old daughter and thrown her over a cliff to her death in the ocean. The prosecution hired the expert to opine that based on the young girl's injuries and an experiment he ran on the cliff, she had to have been thrown off. His direct testimony was well prepared, well presented, and utter and complete bullshit.

As with a lot of experts, his Achilles' heel was his hubris. A smart expert readily admits to potential errors or possible flaws in his opinion, a trait that endears him to the jury and actually makes his testimony more credible. But this expert, with his prestige in question, was not about to have some Los Angeles attorneys question his opinions. The first question on cross-examination was that if someone threw a body off a cliff, wouldn't the thrower fall forward as well, especially on a surface that was slanted downward toward the edge? The expert smugly quoted Newton's third law of motion: for every action there is an equal and opposite reaction, implying that if someone stepped forward and threw something, that person would actually recoil backward. We then showed the videos he had provided of his own assistant in his backyard conducting a throwing experiment with a large watermelon, and in all nine of his throwing attempts, the assistant fell forward, often nine or ten feet. The expert, flustered, tried to explain that his assistant was just moving forward to pick up the object. We reran the videos over and over, showing that, far from going to pick up the watermelon—which, by the way, had splattered—the assistant had hurled his whole body forward in order to launch the object. Nevertheless, despite repeated viewings of the video, the expert stubbornly refused to admit the possibility. At no time during the cross-examination was there a voice raised, nor did the questioning ever get too sarcastic—we just smiled at him a lot and laughed along with the jury—he was doing all the damage himself. That case eventually ended in a hung jury (i.e., they were unable to reach a unanimous verdict) not just once but twice.

We are taught in law school to never ask a question that we don't know the answer to. Like many things attorneys are taught in law school, it sounds good in theory but is questionable in a courtroom. Attorneys should be daring, take risks, and ask questions they do not know the answers to, as long as the answers aren't likely to hurt the case. A certain amount of questioning into unchartered areas can yield amazing results.

A case in point occurred in the Arkansas trial of Whitewater partner Susan McDougal. After the prosecution rested, we announced that the first witness for the defense would be Hickman Ewing Jr. Ewing was a former U.S. attorney in Tennessee who was working for the Office of Independent Counsel led by Kenneth Starr. Ewing was one of Starr's closest advisors and was by all accounts dead set on bringing down President Clinton. As soon as it was announced that we were calling him as a witness, the television commentators began criticizing us, saying that Ewing was a seasoned attorney who knew his way around a courtroom and would certainly be able to handle a simple cross-examination.

But from our viewpoint, there was little to lose. The prosecution had already fired all their ammunition during their case, and Ewing could add nothing that could help that case further. And we'd also found over the years that lawyers make lousy witnesses. It is one thing to ask questions, but a whole different one to be under oath in front of twelve people and have to answer them. As witnesses, lawyers are always trying so hard to measure their words and to sidestep questions that they come across as disreputable.

As it turned out, Ewing was not just bad—he made Mark Fuhrman look like a model witness. He couldn't sit still on the witness stand and was sweating profusely. At one point, Ewing admitted under oath that he had drawn up an indictment of Hillary Clinton. When asked what he based the indictment on, he stated that he thought she lied in front of the grand jury. Asked for specifics, he replied that he was deeply concerned that she had answered so many questions with "I can't remember" or "I can't recall." He was then asked if this inability to answer questions indicated a person was lying. He replied that in his mind it did. But apparently in Ewing's mind he was exempt from his own rule. In his brief one-hour testimony, Ewing answered numerous questions with "I don't remember" or "I don't recall," a fact pointed out to the jury during closing arguments.

If a lawyer does ask a blind question and gets burned by the answer, the best thing to do is to not belabor it. Trials are not perfect specimens, with every question perfect and every objection correctly made. Law school tends to scare the hell out of young lawyers by training them about all the things that could go wrong and all the potential mistakes they could make. Imagine an airline pilot training school that spent three years teaching you all the ways you could crash—by the time training was finished, you wouldn't be able to find a pilot graduate willing to go up in a plane.

What they don't tell you in law school is that you can walk into any trial in any part of the country on any given day and see those mistakes being made over and over again by some of the best attorneys in the country. Trials move fast; lots of mistakes are made. Very few are costly; most are not even noticeable. However, new attorneys are not told this, and they are almost universally scared to go to trial.

In fact, very few young men and women who graduate from law school will ever try a case. Some of them end up in areas of law where trials are virtually nonexistent, such as intellectual property or antitrust. Others go into large law firms where they are never the ones allowed to actually try a case. But many are frankly just too scared to do it. There are a large number of lawyers, many calling themselves trial lawyers, who are petrified of going to trial. You can identify the really nervous ones because they are always the biggest blowhards, screaming and threatening that if they don't get what they want they will just go to trial. Invariably if you look at them and say, "Okay, let's pick a jury," they fold like a cheap suit.

PUTTING ON A DEFENSE

The hardest decision we have to make in a trial is whether to put the defendant on the stand to testify in his or her own defense. If we put the defendant on the stand and lose the case, we'll always second-guess the decision. If we don't put the defendant on and lose, we'll still second-guess it.

The judge will tell the jury both at the beginning and the end of a trial that the defendant has an absolute right to not take the stand. During jury questioning we frequently remind the jury that our client may not take the stand and that they cannot hold that against the client. None of that matters, because jurors want to hear from the defendant. They can sit there all day and say they won't consider the defendant's decision in reaching a verdict, but they will—it's human nature. Just for fun we asked a crowd at a conference we were speaking at whether, if they were serving as a juror, it would make a difference to them if the defendant testified. Every hand in the room shot up. The consensus among the group was "Why would the defendant not want to get up and tell his or her story if the defendant was truly innocent?"

In spite of the way the jury will view it, there are a myriad of reasons why it might be best for the defendant to not testify. The most common reason is that the defense team is very happy with the way things went during the prosecution's case and feel that the prosecution did not come close to establishing the defendant's guilt. Essentially, in such a situation, we are confident that we have won the case. Why put on the defendant and risk losing the case? It's like having a two-touchdown lead in a football game with time running out. You take a knee. But you had better be damn sure that you are reading the case right. There is nothing worse than thinking that the case is in the bag, putting on no defense, and then getting a guilty verdict.

Another reason has to do with clients who have been in custody for a while, especially given the current conditions in jail. The client may start to become a little paranoid and begin creating all kinds of conspiracy theories. One client of ours became convinced that the prosecutor had been following him for years and had even disguised himself as a waiter at a pizza place in Nevada where he was eating. The client was stone-cold innocent, but there was no way we could put him on the stand at that point.

A third reason is that it is not uncommon for clients to have a past conviction or even a very bad act in their background that would not be admissible at trial unless the defendant takes the stand. Nothing gets a jury to convict faster than to find out the defendant has been found guilty of another crime in the past.

One of the most frequent questions we are asked is why we did not put Scott Peterson on the stand. After all he is nice-looking, articulate, and smart. But we had to weigh the good testimony we would get out of Scott on direct against the pounding he would take on cross. And we knew he was going to take a pounding. Earlier in the trial the prosecution had played tapes of Scott's conversations with his girlfriend Amber Frey. He repeatedly lied to Frey, telling her stories about being in Europe while fireworks were going off at the Eiffel Tower or being in various other parts of the world while he was actually home in Modesto. The tapes were devastating not only for their content but for his carefree demeanor during the conversations. We could visibly see changes in a number of the jurors' faces when the tapes were played. If we put Scott on the stand, the prosecution could replay the tapes going line by line through every lie for three days. And the last thing in the world you want your defendant having to say on the stand over and over is "Yeah, I lied about that." Given the fact that we had already rebutted most of the rumors and false accusations against Scott, we just felt that what we would get from his testimony was not going to be worth having the jury listen to the tapes again.

If we do choose to put the defendant on the stand, we take an unconventional approach to prepping him or her for testimony. Obviously we talk to the defendant about his or her version of events and play devil's advocate on some points to give the defendant a feel for cross-examination. But we don't want the defendant rehearsed, because the best testimony comes from defendants who are natural in their retelling of events, even if that means flubbing up a detail or two. Jurors will forgive that and even embrace it as a sign that a person is telling the truth. Furthermore, if you start telling a client too much about what to say and how to say it, on the stand the client will often be so busy concentrating on getting your instructions right that he or she will mess up the basic story. Thus, we will talk to the client about the testimony before the client takes the stand, but we shy away from coaching him or her about what to say or even how to say it. If the witness is telling the truth, prepping him or her for hours just makes the testimony worse.

CONCLUSION

We are often asked by young lawyers what they need to do to become defense attorneys. We tell them that they must become fearless—they cannot be afraid of walking into a courtroom and fighting like hell for their clients even if it is unpopular or against long odds. The best way to get there, to that state of fearlessness—in fact the only way to do it—is to try cases. You try enough cases, you will be fearless.

It sounds simple, but it is not. A judge in San Jose once told us a story about a lawyer who was a partner at one of the most prestigious firms in San Francisco. Although he had been a lawyer for twelve years, he had never tried a case. He finally got his chance to be co-counsel on a trial where his firm was representing the defendant. At the beginning of the trial he went to the podium to give the opening statement. He looked at the podium then announced, "My name is _____, and I represent the defendant in this case." At this point he stopped, paused for a long time, and then walked back over to the counsel table and began looking through his notes. After one minute had passed, he walked back to the podium and again announced, "My name is _____, and I represent the defendant in this case." Again there was a long pause, and then he walked back over to the counsel table and started going through his notes. Finally, after another minute or two had passed, he abruptly sat down and stared straight ahead. The judge had to call a recess and the lawyer was replaced the next day.

There is no shortcut to getting over that fear. You get thrown into the pool, and if you're going to swim, you learn to swim very quickly.

CHAPTER THREE

Clients—Thirty-Nine Floors Is a Long Way to Fall

Pat: I sat quietly facing Mark's desk, where he sat going on and on about an upcoming trial. Our offices were located on the thirty-ninth floor of one of the tallest buildings in Los Angeles. Even on the smoggiest of days, we could see for miles—from my vantage point in Mark's office I could see the incredible views of downtown Los Angeles and beyond into the Santa Monica mountains.

Sitting with us in the office was a large, hulking man dressed entirely in black, with a hair-dye job to match his clothes. The word "menacing" came to mind, but since he barely spoke it was difficult to determine his mood. He just stared ahead as he listened to Mark explain his brother's case and what we were doing to defend it. His brother was about to go on trial for having arranged the murder of a rival businessman.

For the next twenty minutes, the man just continued to stare while Mark explained what was needed to prepare for the trial. Finally, Mark ended the unilateral conversation by saying that he fully believed that we were ready for trial and that if we could get all our evidence admitted, there was a good chance we could win this case.

The man rose from the chair, shook Mark's hand, and without even a hint of a smile on his face said, "I hope so. Thirty-nine floors is a long way to fall."

We began to laugh, but we stopped quickly when we realized that the man was not laughing with us. He turned and exited the room without saying another word.

Six months later, perhaps coincidentally, perhaps not, we moved into a new office building that used to be an old fire engine company. The building only has four floors.

| | | | |

A few months ago we were sitting in a courtroom watching a very good defense attorney, Tony Brooklier, do a masterful job of cross-examination, completely destroying a government witness. After he was finished, he walked back to the table and sat down next to his client, who proceeded to give him an earful about what he should have asked and how he should have done this instead of that.

During a recess, Tony walked over to us, shook his head, and laughed. "This would be such a great job if we didn't have clients."

Several times a week, every defense attorney feels the same way. In truth, most clients are pretty easy—they hire you and trust that you know what you are doing. However, a minority can drive you absolutely crazy. Most of them fail to realize that it is this very same crazy behavior that got them into trouble in the first place. Recently we had a client who was accused of stalking because she was obsessively calling her ex-boyfriend thirty to forty times a day. She denied it, but the day after she hired us the phone calls to our office started. The first day there were more than thirty calls—the next day more than fifty. By the third day we had to get one of our secretaries to help the receptionist deal with this client's phone calls. We finally got her to slow down the calls by explaining that if she continued this behavior, we were going to be called as the first witness against her at trial.

To be fair, the reason some clients act out is because they've lost absolutely all control over their own lives. Their fate is now in the hands of an attorney they've likely just met, and they don't really understand what he is doing. That is why the attorney has to understand why clients constantly ask questions and why they get angry if you don't immediately return phone calls. Imagine for a minute what your life would be like if suddenly you could not make any plans for the next two or three years and you didn't even know if at the end of that you'd be free or imprisoned. That is why people often plead guilty to crimes they didn't commit or take a deal that might not be the best they could get. As crazy as it sounds, the certainty of a fixed sentence becomes tempting—anything to relieve the uncertainty and to gain back some control.

There is an old defense saying that every case gets better with time—memories fade, witnesses move or even die. Prosecutors and judges are constantly accusing defense attorneys of aging cases to gain an advantage. But many times the client can't take the wait. The uncertainty is just too much. A lot of clients would rather take jail time now and get it over with than wait it out and possibly walk free. They would rather know what they are going to be doing for the next year than live in limbo wondering what their future holds.

Our experience is that there is one method that is often effective in getting the client past this—yelling in court. Clients love it when you yell, assuming it is not them you are yelling at. Seeing you in court yelling at the D.A. or at a witness against them gives them a type of personal catharsis. It doesn't actually matter if you are accomplishing anything—yelling usually doesn't. But clients need to know that you are fighting for them, and yelling seems to convey that. It does make a lot of sense. These are people who are frustrated because they can't talk. They have been accused of something and they can't even say a word; they have to depend on someone else. Imagine your spouse coming home and accusing you of having an affair with a close friend, and you have to just shut up and take it without ever responding, even if you know the accusation is false. You would want to yell too. Fortunately, we get paid to yell for you.

GETTING CLIENTS

Before we can defend a client we first have to get a client. No matter how many times its name is in the paper, a law firm can't survive without a constant influx of clients. The common assumption is that many of our clients come from our media appearances. While it is true that our e-mail and phone traffic increase dramatically after an appearance on television or in an article in the newspaper, many of those people requesting representation want us to help sue the government for placing transistors in their brains affected by low-flying aircraft, or to go after President Obama because he has been stalking them. We politely decline these cases and refer them to Gloria Allred. She reciprocates by referring some of the same ones to us.

Most of our cases actually come to us from word of mouth, people who know someone we represented in the past. We are fortunate in that we get a lot of referrals, so we can somewhat pick and choose whom we represent. There is no set formula for how we choose; sometimes we just like the person and want to help. Oftentimes we choose a client because we find the facts of the case fascinating and want to litigate the legal issues. And of course sometimes it depends on whether "Mr. Green" is generous enough. The old lawyer story goes like this: A lawyer would ask to be relieved from a case and the judge would ask the reason. If the lawyer had not been paid, he did not want to appear crass enough to say this in front of his client. So instead he would tell the judge that it did not appear that "Mr. Green" was going to show for trial. This was the signal to the judge that the client had not or would not pay and almost always resulted in the lawyer being relieved from the case.

Even though we can be selective in whom we choose to represent, there are three types of clients that we universally reject. The first one is the client who expects us to bribe the judge. This is much more common that most people realize. Because of the Armenian connection, a part of our client base comes from Armenia or from other countries that were under the control of the former Soviet bloc. The old Soviet system may have been communist, but the criminal justice system was very much based on capitalism. A few years ago, a case we were working on sent us to the former Soviet country of Moldova, where we met an outstanding young lawyer who had been educated in Europe and the United States. When we asked him about a witness in our case who was in jail in Moldova, he explained that the witness was waiting to see if his family could come up with the money to have him freed. We assumed he was talking about bail money, but he quickly disabused us of that notion. He explained that for approximately 5,000 U.S. dollars, the judge would dismiss the case and set our witness free. If his family failed to raise the money before he was sentenced, they could still pay to get him free later on appeal, but it would cost more, around $10,000, because the appeals court had more judges.

A couple of times every month a prospective client will ask how much we charge for a case and then ask if that fee includes the judge. When we explain that the fee does not include the judge, the client asks how much extra for the judge. The reason that we end up rejecting these clients is because they almost always end up unhappy that we have not found somebody they can pay to get out of the mess. If we don't know who to bribe, we must not be very good lawyers.

The second type of client we reject is the client who wants the mythical third option. More often than not, this is a client who has already hired another attorney, gotten an offer from the prosecution

that he or she is not happy with, and is now shopping for a new lawyer who will tell the client what the client wants to hear. When we
meet with these types, they are upset that they did not get what they
think is a fair offer, and they are refusing to take it. We explain to them
that we will be happy to take the case and go to trial. The problem
is that they don't want to go to trial either. They want the third option. You can spend hours, days, even weeks explaining to them that
there is no third option—they have to either take a deal or go to trial.
Yet no matter how many times you explain this to them, when you
ask them which way they want to go, they invariably say neither.
They want the third option.

The third type of client we reject is the client who wants a guar-
anteed win. Our firm has a very strong policy—never, never, never,
never ever guarantee a result. Even if a result seems obvious in a case,
we have been practicing long enough to know that nothing works
out the way you expect. If you guarantee a result, you are guaranteeing trouble. Even if you don't guarantee a result, a lot of clients will
come back at the end and say, "But you promised me that I would get
_____." By having a policy of never guaranteeing a result, you
can always tell the client that this is simply not true. The only promise we make is that we will work extremely hard to give the client the
softest landing possible.

A close cousin to the guarantee-seeker is the client who constantly asks you what the chances are for success and wants you to put
a percentage on it. These clients are scared to death, and they want
some reassurance that they have a reasonable chance. We try to explain to them that the criminal justice system is just not an exact science. There are a number of factors that go into the equation, such as
who the prosecutor is, who the judge is, how angry the victims are,
how crowded the jails are at the time, etc. That answer never satisfies
them. At that point we explain that we have multiplied the algorithm
of the court case number, divided that into multiples of the courtroom section, multiplied it times pi, and added the square root of

the penal code section they are charged with to determine their probability of success. Based on our calculations, they have a 36.1 percent chance of acquittal, a 43.9 percent chance of conviction, and a 19 percent chance of a mistrial. There is a 1 percent chance the D.A. will drop all charges and issue an apology. What we've learned from giving this answer is that defendants do not hire lawyers for their sense of humor.

So what really does happen when a potential client walks in the door? When we meet a client, we are interested in the very sketchy details, such as when and where the alleged crime was committed, what courthouse the case will be in, what the exact charge is, and if the client said anything to the police. Most people are surprised that we do not ask for an in-depth explanation of the facts. We don't do this for a couple of reasons. First and foremost, we do not want to be tied down to a defense. We have a one-word motto at our firm—fluidity. A defense evolves depending on what we learn—it is better to not be wed to any defense early on. Second, until we go to court and see what the prosecution has for evidence, it is pretty stupid to set up a defense. You don't want to build a defense around something a witness is believed to have done, only to get to court and find out that the witness isn't even being accused of that. Finally, clients sometimes forget certain details—like the truth. One of the worst things an attorney can do is stand up in court and argue, based on a client's representations to the attorney, that the client has lived a crime-free life—only to find out that the client failed to mention spending twenty-five years in prison for chopping up the mailman with an ax.

Do clients lie to us about the crimes they are accused of? Yes, they do, but not as often as you would think. We tell clients early on that the second stupidest thing they can do is lie to their lawyer (we assume that the stupidest thing they did is probably what put them in our office). We can handle virtually any issue that comes up because we have seen just about every scenario. The one thing we can't deal with is if a client lies to us and we find out during a court hearing or, even worse, during trial. A few years ago we did a commercial burglary trial involving several thefts from a retail store. There was a videotape of the burglar skirting the checkout line, but it was blurry and the person in the video was not recognizable. Our client was absolutely insistent that the man in the video was not him. Two days into trial, the D.A. handed us an enhanced version of the tape that was much clearer. Sure enough, there was our client's smiling face, looking as if he were posing for a professional photographer. The jury was out for about twenty minutes before returning the guilty verdict. All we could think of was what took them so long.

Stories like that are common among defense attorneys. This is one reason that we get a reputation for being cynical, especially about a client's story. But sometimes if you become too cynical it can affect the way you represent a client.

Pat: I learned a very valuable lesson early on when I almost let a client take a plea bargain for something he insisted he didn't do and I didn't believe him. The defendant was a nineteen-year-old kid who one night was driving around with some friends. It was around midnight and they got hungry, so one of them suggested that they go by the local Safeway grocery store and get some chips and doughnuts. Shortly after leaving the store, they were all four arrested for confronting a man in the parking lot with a gun and taking his wallet.

From the very beginning my client denied he was involved in the robbery. He told me that his friends wanted some cold food, but he wanted hot food, so he dropped them off at the Safeway and went to a nearby Wendy's and got a cheeseburger and fries. When he came back to pick them up, they jumped in the car and told him to take off. He didn't even make it out of the parking lot before the police pulled them over. The story was suspicious to start with, and then the D.A. told me that she had a tape where my client was in the police station with his three other buddies talking about committing the crime. She also said that the police had surreptitiously taped him with one of his buddies in the backseat of the police car, and he had admitted to the crime there as well.

Armed with that information, I went to the jail and explained to the client that he could probably get three to five years if he pled early. The client got tears in his eyes and kept saying that he didn't do it. I was not going to force him to plea, but I wanted to confirm that the client had indeed admitted to the robberies on the tapes the D.A. had mentioned. When I finally got the copies of the tapes, they revealed the client not admitting to the robbery, but rather chewing out the other guys for being so stupid and getting them all in trouble. On the videotape, he refused to sit by them at the police headquarters and was heard periodically screaming at the others for being idiots. I was coming around to the idea of his innocence, but I could not figure out a way to prove it.

A few days later, I went through a drive-thru window at my favorite barbecue restaurant, paid at the window, and got the change along with a receipt. Later that night I was getting something out of my wallet when I noticed the receipt. That's when it hit me. What if the client had done the exact same thing with his receipt from Wendy's? It would still be in his wallet. The next day I went to the police property room and asked to see the wallet. Sure enough, right in the folds was a receipt from Wendy's dated that night. The receipt also had on it the exact same time as the robbery. That proved to be enough for the D.A. to lower the charges, and the client was subsequently freed. I walked away from that case vowing to back off the cynicism.

CELEBRITY CLIENTS

Our firm is well-known for handling a lot of celebrity clients. Some of those relationships are public knowledge and some are not and will never be. What would surprise people is that we reject more celebrity clients than we take on. The reason we reject them is almost always the same—they want us to represent them for free. These are people with an extremely strong sense of entitlement who are used to getting freebies from restaurants, sporting venues, travel agencies, etc., and just assume that legal fees should fall into this same category. One young actress who was constantly getting into trouble came to our office and became absolutely furious when we quoted her a price. She kept saying that we should consider representing her an honor. We didn't.

We also largely reject what we refer to as celebrity abuse cases (that is, cases where a celebrity is being accused of abusing someone else), which is too bad because that is a real growth industry. Los Angeles is filled with celebrities, semi-celebrities, and people convinced they are celebrities. Not surprisingly, some of these people are narcissistic, out of control, and mentally and sometimes even physically abusive toward the people around them. We have been approached by potential clients who have had hot coffee thrown on them by these people, ex-lovers who have contracted sexual diseases from them, relatives who have loaned these people money and never gotten paid back, and, of course, the cottage industry of women who have slept with Tiger Woods. With very few exceptions, we do not take these cases for two reasons. One is that it is a bad business model. These cases often require a great deal of time, and they usually provide very little financial benefit in the end. The real damage that most of these potential clients have suffered is hurt feelings, and most jurors are just not that sympathetic to a person's feelings being hurt. The second reason is that a large number of these potential clients turn out to be crazier than the celebrity they want to sue. They think that because a person is famous they can extort huge sums from them. A celebrity throwing a notebook at them becomes a million-dollar emotional trauma. Those cases never go well.

Because we have been a little more discerning than usual about which cases to take, our celebrity clients have tended to be among the very best clients we have had. No one was kinder and more down to earth than Winona Ryder, despite the fact that she was being destroyed in the media on a daily basis during her shoplifting trial. She knew that the charges were going to harm her career, yet she never complained or second-guessed anything. She must have been very sad during the whole process, but she never let it show—she was the one always asking how everyone else was doing, and even in the middle of her own trial, she was begging us to represent the famous West Memphis Three. She was probably the least self-absorbed of any movie star we have ever met.

Likewise, Chris Brown came to us after a violent episode with his girlfriend Rihanna, and we were all a little hesitant to deal with him. From the first time he came to the office he was extremely humble, almost to the point of being shy. First and foremost, though, he realized he had messed up and he was up-front about accepting responsibility and whatever punishment came with it. Part of his plea bargain included community service, and he has never hesitated to pick up trash and wash buses and do whatever he was asked to do. He never made any excuses or tried to justify his actions, which is probably why most of his fans have stuck by him.

NATE DOGG

Another of our favorite clients was Nathaniel Hale, aka Nate Dogg. Nate was a legend in the rap music industry. He was a cousin to the more famous Snoop Dogg and did vocals on tons of top-selling West Coast rap albums. He was one of the most beloved figures in the entire industry. We of course had no idea who he was when he walked into the office, since the last collection of music that either one of us purchased was in the form of an 8-track tape.

His trouble started when his tour bus was driving through Kingman, Arizona, late one night when they were pulled over by a police officer who smelled marijuana. A quick search of the bus revealed a small amount of pot and a gun that was not registered. Nate stepped up and said both the pot and the gun were his, so he was arrested and given a court date one month later.

Pat: On the day he was to be in court in Arizona, Mark was in the middle of a trial, so I went with Nate. When Nate and I met at the airport in L.A., we shook hands, said hello, and then did not speak for the next four hours. We flew to Vegas and drove to Kingman in total silence. Nate had a scowl on his face and didn't seem to want to talk, and I knew so little about rap that I thought Puff Daddy was a Saturday morning cartoon character, so I didn't really care if we talked.

As it turned out, Kingman is a hotbed of libertarianism, and having a bag of pot was not something they cared a lot about. As for the gun, they seemed even less interested. Most of the senior citizens down at the coffee shop were packing heat. I managed to work a good deal with the prosecutor, and Nate and I were back on the road again less than an hour later.

Unbeknownst to me, Nate had been scared to death that he was going to get thrown in jail in Kingman. He didn't want to ask me ahead of time what was going to happen because that would have blown his cool exterior. He was now so giddy that he wouldn't shut up. For the next four hours he talked about music, the Lakers, workout routines, his childhood, gangs, and politics. He had a great sense of humor, especially about himself, and he was brutally honest about everything he had seen and been around. When Nate and I stopped at a 7-Eleven in Las Vegas to get a Coke, people started pouring into the store to meet him and get a picture with him. He stayed and signed dozens of autographs. He was basically shy as a person, but he was not going to disappoint any of his fans.

Several months later we had to represent him again in a case in Van Nuys, California, this time for driving on a suspended license. We immediately started ragging on him about his lack of street cred and how he was never going to get any if the best he could do for a crime was drive on a suspended license. It was a charge that usually did not even involve any jail time. However, when we went into the courtroom, we found out that this was his third arrest for driving on a suspended license, and the prosecutor was adamant about him serving ninety days in jail. The presiding judge was Frank Johnson, a man we had appeared in front of numerous times and who we felt was no-nonsense but always fair and reasonable.

Judge Johnson summoned everyone back to his chambers to discuss the case and we immediately went into our spiel:

"You can't put this guy in jail. It would cause a miniriot. He is a huge hero to these guys. He gets mobbed just going to a 7-Eleven. This is going to cause the sheriff's department major logistical problems. You have no idea how big this guy is."

Judge Johnson looked at us warily and said, "I have never even heard of this guy."

"Neither had we, Judge, but trust us. Do you have teenagers?"

"Two of them."

"Judge, ask them if they have ever heard of Nate Dogg."

The case was continued for a couple of weeks and when everyone came back to court, Judge Johnson called us into chambers again. But this time he couldn't suppress a laugh.

"For the first time since I have been a judge, my kids have been impressed by what I do. They couldn't believe I had Nate Dogg in my courtroom."

We discussed it a little more, and Judge Johnson agreed that putting Nate Dogg in jail wasn't worth it. He decided to let him plead to the court and pay an increased fine.

Nate Dogg was apparently a great rapper, but he was a lousy gangsta. We would represent him several more times, but it was mostly some stupid misdemeanor driving charge or for possessing a small amount of marijuana. Every time we would see him we would accuse him of trying to drive up his street cred with stupid misdemeanors, and he would bust out laughing and just shake his head. Sadly, about three years ago, Nate Dogg suffered a massive stroke and went into a coma. He died on March 15, 2011, at the age of forty-one. We miss him a great deal.

THE MERCHANT OF DEATH

Pat: One day when I was returning to the office after a few weeks trying a case out of town, I noticed a very large man, in excess of three hundred pounds, wedged into a very small IKEA chair that was obviously designed for someone much smaller, near Mark's secretary's desk. The man appeared to be in his late sixties or early seventies, with a big bushy mustache and a shiny bald head. He was asleep. My first reaction was that this must be someone's visiting grandfather. I walked by him and into Mark's office and asked who the big guy was asleep just outside the door.

Mark smiled and replied, "You mean the Merchant of Death? That big guy asleep in the chair was once one of the most powerful men in the world. He is an arms dealer—really THE arms dealer in the world. You could name any war in the last two decades anywhere in the world, and he supplied the weapons—probably for both sides."

After the big guy finished his nap, Mark introduced me to the man known around the world as the Merchant of Death, Sarkis Soghanalian. He started telling stories of world leaders, the Iran-Iraq war, and the many favors he had done for his adopted homeland, the United States of America. After about an hour, he started slowing down, and then he got up, walked back over to his chair, and began to sleep again.

For the next several weeks, Sarkis was a constant presence in our office while Mark worked with the U.S. government to arrange a deal on his latest arrest. He would wander into people's offices, tell them some incredible story about a major world event, and then walk back to his small chair and fall asleep. As a Southerner, I especially appreciate the talents of a truly gifted storyteller. Most Southerners can tell you about sitting on a porch listening to their grandfather or some crazy great-uncle tell stories about the world wars or growing up in Indian territory, stopping every once in a while to give their opinions on what was wrong with the country in the present day. The front porch was kind of a predecessor to blogs.

Like my Southern brethren, Sarkis was a master storyteller. The difference was that where my great-uncle used to tell stories about Aunt Mabel or Grandma Clift, Sarkis's stories tended to be about characters named Saddam, Gaddafi, or George W. The stories were always entertaining, and we especially enjoyed the ones that included some behind-the-scenes look at a famous world leader. Jimmy Carter was a wimp, Richard Nixon would sell his mother for money, and George W. Bush was at one time a huge cokehead. Sarkis

*loved to tell the story about the younger Bush partying with him in a Cancun
bar, at one point alternating between shots of tequila and snorts of cocaine off
the waitress's breasts. He would always end that story by shaking his head and
saying that he never thought Bush would live long enough to be president.*

It is hard to say what an international arms dealer should look like,
but Sarkis certainly did not fit the Hollywood stereotype of the tough,
angry Middle Easterner bent on destruction of the West. It was hard to
imagine that this sweet, schlubby guy had dined at the White House
and slept in palaces around the world, all the while selling billions of
dollars of weapons. Sarkis's stories were fanciful and usually portrayed
Sarkis as a hero or at least a strong moral character. His stories were
fun to listen to, but when you looked at him it was easy to dismiss
them as pure fiction.

Except that they were true. Over the years, through our own research or other corroborating sources, we've been able to confirm just
about everything Sarkis told us. What gave him special credibility
was that he would be periodically arrested by the United States for
some arms deal and then always quickly released—he was obviously
providing valuable information to the intelligence services.

American officials later admitted that Sarkis worked for both the
FBI and the CIA. Sarkis himself also told us that he worked closely
with both the National Security Agency and the Secret Service.
Sarkis could call virtually any person in the world on the phone and
they would take his call. Our favorite quote about him was from an
unnamed American official who said about Sarkis's wild stories that
in the beginning you just couldn't believe them, but "you'd find out
he was telling you the truth, even if he was kind of gilding it in his
favor."

One of his closest American acquaintances was Lowell Bergman,
the former *60 Minutes* and *Frontline* producer who was later portrayed
by Al Pacino in the movie *The Insider*. Right before Operation Desert
Storm, Bergman produced a *60 Minutes* segment on Sarkis in which
Sarkis was grilled about providing weapons to Iraq that might in turn

be used to kill American soldiers. Sarkis laid out how the Reagan and Bush administrations had used him to skirt the embargo against weapons to Iraq, and then, when the United States turned on Saddam, they hung him out to dry. He was angry that he was portrayed as willing to harm Americans when he felt like much of his adult life had been spent providing information to American intelligence agencies and doing them favors. Sarkis very much considered himself an American patriot because he was always doing the United States's bidding, and he was deeply hurt that he would be accused of doing anything to harm American soldiers.

Sarkis grew up and became a ski instructor in Lebanon, where he met and married an American. His first brush with arms trading was during the Lebanese Civil War in the 1970s. The breakthrough sale for him was providing American weapons to the Lebanese military. After the civil war, he expanded his operations worldwide, including helping to arm Argentina in the Falklands War, Gaddafi's army in Libya, and, most important, Saddam's Iraqi army during the Iran-Iraq war.

In 1980, an embargo was placed on the sale of weapons to Iraq, but Reagan administration officials were encouraging Iraq to get weapons from private arms dealers. Iraq turned to Sarkis, who arranged sales of American and French weapons in excess of $2 billion. He also arranged the sale of Iraqi army uniforms from Romania, which he told *60 Minutes* was a deal formulated by former president Nixon, former vice president Agnew, and former attorney general John Mitchell. According to Sarkis, all parties were paid handsomely.

But Sarkis always claimed that his closest relationship with any major American figure was with George H. W. Bush. Sarkis said that he began working with Bush all the way back during Bush's CIA days, and they formed not only a working relationship but also a personal one. But it would end in what Sarkis described as Bush's betrayal. It was the first Bush administration that filed criminal charges against Sarkis in 1991, and then convicted him of six counts of possession of armaments with intent to sell to Iraq. Sarkis insisted that the sales were from a 1983 deal that had had the tacit approval of the American government. It infuriated him that he had done what he felt was a huge favor for the country he loved and was now being punished for it. Sarkis rarely acknowledged that he was paid a large amount of money for these sales and had become quite wealthy because of them. He would constantly refer to how he was helping the American government, and if he made some money from the deal, it was his just reward for helping.

Sarkis was sentenced to six years in prison but was released in less than two years. The story of how he won his early release is our favorite Sarkis tale. While Sarkis was in prison, U.S. law enforcement officials were attempting to find and destroy a huge counterfeiting operation in the Bekaa Valley region of Lebanon. Apparently it was producing nearly perfect $100 bills that were being used throughout the Middle East. Sarkis told one of his friends at the Secret Service to come see him in prison and bring a $100 bill. The Secret Service agent did, and Sarkis took the bill and copied down the serial number. He then told the agent to come back in two weeks. After the two weeks had passed, the agent returned, and Sarkis handed him ten perfect $100 bills, all with the same serial number as the one the agent had shown him. It was a not so subtle way of showing just how much power and influence Sarkis had, even in prison. The government arranged for his early release in return for his help in showing them where to find the counterfeiting ring. But Sarkis gave them a little more information than they wanted. He explained to them that the counterfeiting ring with the mint plates was set up many years ago in Lebanon by none other than the U.S. government, to print money to buy weapons for allies in the Middle East without having to get congressional approval. One of the chief architects of that plan was now occupying the White House. The first part of that story has been admitted by the government—the last part, involving George H. W. Bush, has been denied.

We lost touch with Sarkis over the years but would keep up with his whereabouts on the Internet. As part of our payment, he agreed to assign us the rights to any book we could get written about his life. We frequently talked about doing that but never followed up on it. Sadly he died last year at the age of eighty-two.

MICHAEL JACKSON

We've represented some of the biggest names in entertainment, but none came close to the fame of Michael Jackson. Within two hours of the announcement that Michael was being represented by our firm, the computer system in our office crashed from the volume of incoming e-mails. No sooner would we get it working again than it would crash again. We estimated that we received more than five hundred thousand e-mails in a twenty-four-hour time span, the majority of which appeared to be from countries other than the United States.

On November 15, 2003, we were sitting in a courtroom in Modesto, California. It was the final day of the Scott Peterson preliminary hearing, a proceeding that had lasted a couple of weeks. Around three o'clock, we got a "911" message to call the office. When we called in, we were told that Michael's home at Neverland had been raided by the Santa Barbara County Sheriff's Office using only slightly fewer men than had stormed the beaches at Normandy. They also brought a warrant for Michael's arrest, alleging that he had sexually assaulted a fourteen-year-old boy. Michael was not at Neverland. He was in Las Vegas, and he wanted us to get there as soon as possible. We jumped in a car, drove to Fresno, hopped on a plane, and landed in Vegas at around seven-thirty. That began a cloak-and-dagger affair worthy of a Tom Clancy novel.

We were picked up at the airport by a limo and whisked to Caesars Palace, where we were met by a hotel official who seemed to be totally clueless as to what we were doing there. We waited for about half an hour, and eventually another man showed up and asked us to follow him down an underground labyrinth of halls until we arrived at what we thought was another hotel. We waited in a room off the kitchen for about an hour, until a car arrived at a back entrance. The car took us to a hotel well off the strip, where we were deposited and again told to wait. This time, however, we were allowed to wait in the high-roller blackjack room inside the hotel casino. One hour later, minus several thousand dollars, we were picked up again and driven to the underground garage at yet another hotel. We were then ushered through the laundry room and up the back stairs to a suite of rooms, where we were told to, once again, wait. After a short time, a lovely young woman named Grace came into the living room and introduced herself as Michael's assistant. She then told us she was taking us back into Michael's bedroom, where we would meet him and talk. It was now close to midnight.

We had no idea what to expect. He was obviously a gifted entertainer, but we had heard the rumors of his eccentric behavior and the allegations of drug use. His television interviews hadn't helped his image much, and his physical appearance seemed to be slipping more and more into uncharted territory.

We wound our way through a suite of bedrooms until we arrived at a very small room with a king-size bed, a table, and two chairs. Grace stayed with us the whole time, which indicated to us how important she was to Michael. At the foot of the bed sat Michael Jackson, wearing a white hotel bathrobe with striped pajamas underneath. He stood to shake our hands, and three things were immediately apparent: he was taller than you'd expect; he was much thinner than you'd expect; and he didn't have a nose. In the middle of his face was something that looked like a nose that had melted into his face. The only way to describe it is to compare it to a slab of hard butter that has been left in the sun for too long and is on the verge of becoming pure liquid. The worst part was that there was absolutely nothing you could do except stare at it—it was in the center of his face. The most difficult part of talking to him would be trying to not stare at his nose.

We were immediately taken aback by how fiercely intelligent he was, how quickly he picked up on what was going on, and how good he was at asking relevant questions. He was very lucid, occasionally flashing anger at the charges, but most important he appeared to be totally in control. Whenever we would ask him questions about the circumstances surrounding the case, he would answer them quickly and with authority. Throughout the forty-five-minute meeting he denied all the allegations and seemed determined to fight them.

There was no way this man was on drugs. He was more together than either of us, since we were both bordering on exhaustion and starvation. Far from being erratic or strange, he was one of the best clients we had ever met. He was also very kind, making sure we got some food ordered up and repeating over and over how grateful he was for our help. Although you could hear snippets of the famous quiet, boyish voice from his interviews, most of the time he spoke with a very forceful, deep voice, especially when he was denying the charges.

The more we listened to him the more we believed he was innocent. He was very convincing when he said that he could never, ever harm a child. He talked about his own lost childhood and how he worked so hard to make sure other kids, particularly sick or disadvantaged kids, got to enjoy some of the things he missed. He was especially angry at the idea that Neverland was some type of kid-friendly trap to lure children to him so he could abuse them.

"Every day busloads of kids go up to Neverland and ride on the rides, play video games, pet the animals. Most of the time I'm not even there! And when I am there, I don't even see them."

He opened up a lot, probably more than we were prepared for, about the charges and how he was not going to give in—he wanted to show the world he would not hurt children.

At one point we felt comfortable enough to ask Michael the $20 million question.

"Look, Michael, we gotta ask. It has been widely reported that you paid another kid almost twenty million dollars to make a sexual abuse lawsuit go away several years ago. That is gonna come up in this case."

He shook his head and said, "That was my biggest mistake. Johnnie [Cochran] told me we could beat the case and that we should go to trial. He was convinced we would win. But all my entertainment people kept telling me to settle. They said that with all the horrible things that would be said at trial, that even if I won I would lose. My reputation would be so badly damaged that it wouldn't matter that I won. It was a big mistake and I am not going to do it again. I won't agree to anything."

We explained that we would make arrangements for Michael to surrender to the Santa Barbara County Sheriff's Office the following week. Michael was defiant. As we stood to leave, he said, "I am innocent. I want the world to know I am innocent!"

As we headed back to the hotel bar to discuss what we had just heard, we were overcome from excitement. This was not the guy portrayed in the media at all. He was intelligent, focused, and very businesslike.

A week later we went back to Vegas to take Michael to surrender. He had arranged for a private jet to fly us into Santa Barbara, where he would be booked, fingerprinted, and put into a jail cell to stay until his bail was approved. We had already made the bail arrangements, so it was assumed he would not be in a cell for more than an hour.

We were on the plane as Michael boarded, and we instantly could tell something was different. To begin with it was obvious that he really wasn't sure who we were. He barely spoke. Mark began briefing him on what to expect and how to handle himself, but rather than being engaged in the discussion, Michael seemed to be in a trance. He was not worried, and, in fact, he was remarkably calm for someone about to be arrested in front of the whole world. He asked very few questions and didn't really seem to hear the answers. The Michael Jackson from the previous week was nowhere to be found.

As we drove from the airport to the courthouse, the streets were lined with people cheering, holding supportive signs, or just wanting to catch a glimpse of Michael. When we got to the courthouse, they took us underground to the booking room, where Michael was fingerprinted and photographed. He brought along a makeup artist and she put way too much white base on his face, so in his booking photo he looked a lot like the Joker in *Batman*. He was then taken to the holding cell while we posted the $3 million bail. The entire time he was almost listless, smiling wanly and occasionally shaking hands. It did appear that he was trying to show a strong resolve, but it just wasn't in him. On the trip back to the airport he did not even speak.

A few nights later, we flew back to Las Vegas to meet with Michael. Everyone around him was acting strange, and we were forced to wait for hours to get to see him. Finally, we were told that we would have to wait until the next morning to meet with him. When morning came, we were awakened and told to go to a different hotel. Once we arrived, we were given the lowdown. For approximately three years, Michael's career and his personal life had been run by two businessmen from Germany. Apparently he had no desire to fire them, but he also wanted to avoid them, so instead he just got up in the middle of the night, took his kids, and changed hotel rooms without telling them where he was. They were frantically searching for him, and he was hiding out from them in another hotel. Given the constant circus around him, this did not even strike us as being strange.

In a move that was widely criticized, Michael then brought in a group of men from the Nation of Islam to run his affairs. The leader of that group was Leonard Muhammad. It turned out that this was in fact a very good move: Leonard was intelligent, highly organized, and someone Michael respected. It was becoming increasingly apparent to us that when Michael wanted something, no one said no. At least Leonard appeared to be able to reason with him.

Michael also told us that he was bringing in another attorney to co-counsel on the case, a New York lawyer named Ben Brafman. We had never met him, but we were aware of his reputation as one of the top lawyers in the country and the go-to guy in New York City. When we heard the news, we were not thrilled. The case was not lacking in large egos already, and it is rare that a number of attorneys with large egos can coexist on a case. This turned out to be that rare exception. Ben was not only gracious from the beginning, but his knowledge and intelligence were invaluable. He immediately bonded with the lawyers in our firm and was extremely impressive in how he handled the Jackson entourage. We have worked with a large number of very talented lawyers over the years, but none was more impressive than Ben. His subsequent handling of the Dominique Strauss-Kahn case in New York was textbook. He has remained a loyal and good friend to the firm over the past decade.

As time went on, Michael became more and more detached from the case. Meetings usually consisted of him sitting behind a pair of sunglasses and just mumbling "liars, liars" whenever we would try to talk about the allegations. He would get tired quickly and just leave the room abruptly, sometimes returning, sometimes not.

On one occasion we were invited to a summit meeting at a house he had recently rented in Beverly Hills. Michael had an incredible dinner prepared for us in a dining room that had a glass floor with a large swimming pool beneath us. His children were present at the dinner and were extremely well behaved. It was obvious they had a great relationship with their father as they swarmed around him during the whole dinner. He was very affectionate toward them and seemed much more interested in what they had to say than in what a bunch of lawyers had to say. After dinner he listened quietly to what we all said, but there was none of the give-and-take of our first meeting.

One of the main things we had been preparing Michael for was that first court appearance in Santa Maria, California. The judge who had been assigned the case had a reputation for being very stern. We repeated this over and over to Michael to make sure that he understood there could be no craziness or showmanship. He had to be on his best behavior. The first appearance was going to be a media circus, and we had to make sure it set the right tone. Unfortunately, it did set a tone—but not the tone we wanted.

To begin with, Michael showed up thirty minutes late, causing the judge to warn him to not let that happen again or he would put him in jail. After smoothing things over with the judge and getting a couple of favorable rulings on motions, we headed out of the courtroom. Michael walked slowly, almost feebly, toward the large black SUV that would rush him away from the huge mob outside. He looked like a frail old man trying to cross a crowded street. But as he got to the SUV, instead of jumping inside, Michael took a huge leap onto the hood of the car and then another huge leap onto the roof. He then busted out a few of his trademark dance moves, much to the delight of a screaming crowd and a thrilled media pool.

Pat: I had no idea how to react in this moment. Should I jump up on the roof of the SUV with Michael, bust a few moves of my own like this was normal post-court behavior? I opted instead to stand by, mouthing the words "what the @#%$" and wondering if it was too late to get a degree in accounting.

Not surprisingly, the dancing incident was deemed a disaster, and we were rightly criticized for not having enough client control. The insane part for us was that other than our recent dealings with Michael, the case was going incredibly well. Our investigation had turned up terrific stuff that would make the prosecution look ridiculous, and our interviews with potential witnesses had been stellar. We were confident that there was no way we could lose—the evidence was overwhelming that he never touched this kid, and the entire thing was a huge shakedown by a family that had been involved in frauds before. It was a lawyer's dream case. There was no way he was going to get convicted at this trial.

Michael had been so traumatized by the raid at Neverland Ranch that he refused to go back to the property. But we needed to take a look at it, especially the house where the alleged crime occurred.

One Saturday we drove up the 101 Freeway past Santa Barbara until we hit the heart of the Santa Ynez Valley and the California wine country. Neverland Ranch was located right in the middle of the wine country but well hidden down a long dirt road that went on for several miles. We were swarmed by people who were camping out in front of the ranch in support of Michael. They surrounded the car, yelling at us to please help Michael defeat Thomas Sneddon, the D.A. in Santa Barbara County. Some of these people were so crazed they began throwing themselves on the hood of the car and pleading with us to do something for Michael.

Eventually we got on the property and drove around a number of beautiful fountains until we made it to the main house. The house itself was far from a castle or even a mansion. It was a rather nonde-script Tudor home that could have just as easily been located in a sub-division in Toledo. The inside was nice but nothing special, except for the interior decorating style, which could be described as English castle meets Chinese pagoda meets French whorehouse. Artifacts in-cluded a knight in full body armor, a chair the size of New Jersey, and a bunch of framed Marilyn Monroe movie posters.

Pat: After we left the house, we drove around Neverland and looked at the amusement park, the zoo, and the movie theater. The employees insisted on calling the place "The Ranch," which I had to admit bothered me a little. The Ponderosa was a ranch. LBJ had a ranch. You can't really call a place a ranch if you have a Ferris wheel on it. When we left, I was a bit disappointed. While I am sure Neverland had some appeal for kids, it really was not all that interesting a place. It seemed to be more like a Walmart parking lot when a small carnival sets up shop.

When I drove Mark back to his house that day, there were several un-marked police cars parked down the street and the LAPD bomb squad was in his driveway. Mark's wife, Paulette, had spent several months landscaping the large lawn at their home, and they were still working on it. Near the entrance to the house were a couple of port-o-potties for the landscapers to use while they worked. One of the more observant workers had found an unusual device inside one of the port-o-potties and called the police. It turned out to be a homemade bomb that had been placed there overnight. The bomb would have done very little damage to anyone other than the person inside the port-o-potty, but I took it as a sign that someone was not happy with our representation of Jackson. Death threats are fairly common for us during high-profile cases and are usually totally ignored. This was a different story. For the next few weeks, Mark moved his family to a different location and had security officers at the home on a full-time basis.

On top of all Michael's other legal troubles, a couple of local lawyers in Los Angeles, led by Gloria Allred, had filed a complaint with Child and Family Services asking them to remove Michael's children from the home. Child and Family Services responded by saying they would do a full investigation immediately. We went to the Beverly Hills home Michael was renting and tried to impress on Michael the seriousness of the investigation. They really could take his children. Over the past few months, we had had the opportunity to see Michael interact with his kids. Along with his assistant Grace, they formed a kind of nuclear family that was as loving and as happy as you could hope to see.

Before the Child and Family Services visit, we told Michael that the first thing he needed to do was take down the enormous painting near the entrance of the house that showed him partially dressed in a robe, surrounded by a dozen naked cherubs floating around him. We understood that it was simply a bad attempt at Baroque art, but we were pretty sure that the first thing social workers would see on coming into the house should not be a huge picture of Michael surrounded by naked little kids.

In many ways, we had to spend more time battling side issues like Child and Family Services and Michael's financial issues than dealing with the actual allegations in the case, which were utterly ridiculous. People often talk about Michael's weird behavior and assume that because he "hung around" kids he must have been guilty of the charges. We interviewed a large number of employees as well as a number of kids who went to Neverland. It is true that kids were frequently invited to Neverland to play on the rides or tour the zoo or maybe watch a movie, but they were always in groups and rarely did Michael interact with them more than briefly. Over and over again I heard the same thing from the people who worked there—Michael wanted the kids to have a good time and he would never harm anyone, especially a child. There were times when he would do things that were considered inappropriate, like inviting a group of boys to spend the night for a slumber party. Clearly this was not something a grown man should have been doing, but thousands of kids visited Neverland every year and never alleged Michael did anything sexual to them.

The allegations by this particular family in the Santa Barbara case were so clearly bogus that there was no way the charges should have ever been brought by the Santa Barbara D.A. Tom Sneddon, who had had a running feud with Jackson for years and was looking for any opportunity to try to nail him. Having never found a good one, he desperately jumped on a very bad case.

The public never fully understood the evidence in this case. The furor began when Michael did an interview with Martin Bashir that aired on February 6, 2003. During the interview, Michael stated that he sometimes let kids sleep in his bed. That was the only thing most people heard about the interview, and it set off shock waves of anger. The damage was done and he was back in the headlines.

Several months prior to the interview, Michael had befriended a family whose eldest son, Gavin Arvizo, had cancer. The mother was raising the kids on her own and struggling, so Michael would let them stay at Neverland and live in a house on the property. He was often not there when the Arvizo family was staying there and had only limited contact with the two Arvizo boys. At one point the ranch employees were concerned enough about the Arvizos that they told the ranch manager that this family was demanding things and acting like they owned the place.

The boy who made the allegation admitted that during the entire time up until the interview, Michael had never done anything sexual toward him. He even stated so to Bashir. His allegation was that Michael began sexually assaulting him *after* the TV interview. In other words, Michael had never laid a hand on him until after Michael was being castigated for having inappropriate contact with kids and was under a media microscope. The idea was ludicrous.

It didn't take long for our investigators to poke huge holes in the story. It was clear that right before the allegations were made, everyone at Neverland was tired of the Arvizo family antics, so the Arvizos were on their way out. One of the allegations they made against Michael was that he had essentially kidnapped the family and would not let them off the Neverland property. It did not take much to show that in fact they had access to a driver who took them off the property frequently, and that they came and went as they chose.

The nail in the coffin came when we discovered that the mother had a history of trying to defraud both a private company and the state of California. The case had become such a slam dunk that we doubted it would even get to trial. We would joke that we should let a first-year associate at our office try the case because this was as close to a sure thing as we were ever going to get.

Unfortunately, we did not get to try the case. The people around Michael had been suggesting for some time that they were uncomfortable with us representing Scott Peterson and Michael Jackson at the same time. We told them in no uncertain terms that we were not going to just desert Scott, even for Michael. We have a fierce allegiance to our clients, and even though the Peterson case was a much more difficult case to win, we were not going to give it up. We don't know who made the final decision for the Jackson camp, but at some point his handlers told us that they needed to talk. We agreed to bow out and told them we would help in any way we could.

Mark: I actually ended up testifying for Michael twice during the trial. It was apparent to me that the jurors were not buying what the prosecution was selling. We were not surprised when the jury came back with what was the obvious not guilty verdict—the only thing that surprised us was that it took them longer than fifteen minutes to reach that decision.

Whenever people ask about Michael Jackson, they want to know if we believe he was a child molester. We represented Michael for about eighteen months, and we did not see or hear any evidence at all that he ever hurt children. There is no question that some of his behavior with children was odd. But odd does not necessarily mean criminal. Otherwise we would have jailed half of Hollywood, and Charlie Sheen would be on death row.

What we do know is this: Michael was absolutely 100 percent innocent of the charges brought against him in Santa Maria. What we believe is this: the prosecution was nothing more than a vendetta by Sneddon, a bitter, angry man at the end of his career, who was going to try to get Michael before he quit.

JOAN OF ARKANSAS—SUSAN MCDOUGAL

It has been sixteen years since an unknown young woman from a small town in Arkansas made national news by refusing to cooperate with Kenneth Starr's Whitewater investigation. Susan McDougal chose to spend almost two years in jail rather than make a deal with Starr to implicate President Bill Clinton. As a result, she became a national heroine to a large group of Americans who felt the Whitewater investigation was nothing more than a political witch hunt. In the end, no matter how hard Starr and his people tried to spin it, the Whitewater investigation was a failed enterprise. They were beaten not only in the courts but also in the court of public opinion. No single person was more responsible for that defeat than the woman the press would dub "Joan of Arkansas."

After the Whitewater uproar calmed down, we assumed that Susan would fall into the fifteen-minutes-of-fame category, a Trivial Pursuit question that very few people could answer. That has not proven to be the case. Whenever her name comes up and we start to remind people who she is, they invariably cut us off and say that of course they recall her. She struck a chord with the public that is still ongoing.

Four years removed from the national spotlight, we wrote a book about her life and what had happened to her during Whitewater. Publishers almost unanimously assured us that such a book would be a hard sell that long after the case, and all but one small publishing house passed on it. But the book, *The Woman Who Wouldn't Talk*, shot immediately onto the *New York Times* best-seller list, where it remained for several weeks. Susan is still in demand as a speaker, and even sixteen years later, she still receives letters from people all around the world who have kept up with her.

It would be easy to write the usual theme that Susan was an unlikely hero. Born in small-town Arkansas, raised by a career military father and a Belgian war bride mother, Susan was a religious young woman who attended church regularly and spent four years at a private Baptist college. She married a man fifteen years her senior and began to work with him on his real estate development projects. The only unusual thing in her life was that her husband, a former political aide to Senator William Fulbright, had found a real estate project in northwest Arkansas and convinced his friends Bill and Hillary Clinton to invest in it with him. Susan named the project Whitewater.

But to classify Susan as an unlikely hero would be to grossly underestimate her. The real Susan was hard to know because she hates being analyzed. She is one of the most well-read, intelligent people you will find. She read *The Rise and Fall of the Third Reich* at the age of nine because she was so haunted by the stories her father, who had seen the Holocaust camps, told her. The apartments she lived in always looked like libraries because she would read two to three books a week. She spent more time at the bookstore than the grocery store.

But intelligence is only a part of the package. She is one of the most natural communicators we have ever seen. Susan has the ability to take lengthy diatribes and boil them down into a perfect phrase. When she was preparing to do *Larry King Live* or *Frontline* interviews, we would work with her by grilling her on a number of the questions that would likely be asked. She was horrible at answering them, perhaps because she was disinterested. But the minute she would go on the show and the lights came on, they would ask one of the exact same questions and she would hit it out of the park.

Susan also possessed one other attribute in spades—she could be extremely stubborn. Not your regular run-of-the-mill refuse-to-change-her-mind stubborn. Her stubbornness was the stuff of legend. When she felt she was right, she would not argue or yell as much as she would just shut down. The strange thing was that her stubbornness was usually over some perceived injustice to somebody else. Throughout her life, she was constantly interjecting herself into situations where some David was fighting a Goliath. The circumstances usually involved someone going up against the government or some large company, and Susan would intercede thinking she was going to help even the odds. She despised bullies and any group that picked on someone less fortunate. She would usually begin by approaching the situation in a very cheerful, conciliatory way but would end up getting mad before it was over. And you really did not want her mad. Susan was a force of nature—a one-woman tsunami.

For Susan, Kenneth Starr and his minions were the ultimate bullies. They had ruined the lives of many of her friends, and they had accused her of doing something she hadn't done. To them, she was just a very small person in a much bigger picture. She and her friends were expendable to get to the larger goal.

Susan was up against an enormous battalion of Washington lawyers, an investigation with an unlimited budget, and a prosecutor with the power to coerce witnesses and threaten her friends. She was in a small jail cell with no money and limited phone privileges. It was clearly not a fair fight—anyone who knew Susan knew that the Office of Independent Counsel was way overmatched.

Susan has spent the past decade of her life living in a small town in Arkansas and occasionally venturing out to give speeches about women in jail and the problems they face. She never stopped fighting for the underdog, and now she has a national pulpit from which to do it.

One of the main reasons Susan lives in Arkansas is to take care of her ailing parents. She felt a lot of guilt over their decline in health while she was in jail and wanted to spend time with them in their later years. In 2008 she was invited to give a speech before a group that included chaplains from a number of hospitals across the country. Included in the audience was a group representing a hospital in Arkansas.

After the speech, they talked to Susan about her life taking care of her parents and the problems she was dealing with. They suggested that she take part in a volunteer program at the hospital that would not only allow her to work with people in need, but would also help her deal with her own caretaking issues. She began going to the classes part-time and volunteering at the trauma center one day a week, working with patients who were dying by comforting them and their families. It proved to be meaningful work, something she both enjoyed and was very good at doing. We were ecstatic to find out that she had found something that was both satisfying for her and for which she was perfectly suited.

In 2009, she enrolled in the program full-time and began working at the hospital five days a week. Not surprisingly, with her energy and her communication skills, Susan was an instant success. She graduated at the top of her class, and, remarkably, the hospital offered her the chance to become the head chaplain at one of the largest and most prestigious trauma centers in the United States. She loves the job, calling it the most fulfilling thing she has done in her life. When asked how she is able to handle working with people dying and to deal with tragedy all day, she says that this is her method of redemption. When she was in trouble and hurting in jail, more than fifty thousand strangers from all over the world wrote letters to her, supporting her and trying to lift her spirits. This is her way of repaying that debt.

WILL LYNCH

Pat: In late May 2010, our receptionist, Aja Matelyan, buzzed me in my office and said there was a phone call from a prospective client that I should take. His name was Will Lynch. It was unusual for Aja to ask me to speak to a potential client directly—usually our calls are screened by our young associates in order to weed out the cases that we are not going to take. But she was insistent I talk to this guy, and I knew she had good instincts, so I picked up the phone and asked Mr. Lynch how I could help him.

"The police are at my house and I am hiding in the back bedroom. What should I do?"

"Well, that depends. What exactly did you do?"

"I think I may have killed a priest!"

Two years later we were sitting in a courtroom in San Jose, prepared to go to trial in the case of the *People of California v. Will Lynch.* Lynch was charged with beating up a Catholic priest living at a retirement home for Jesuit priests near San Jose. The priest had not died from the beating, as Will had originally thought, but he was injured enough that the Santa Clara County D.A. decided to charge Will with two felonies, one for assault and one for elder abuse (the jury would also be given the option to vote for lesser charges, i.e., they could choose to vote for either or both counts as a misdemeanor). As we prepared for trial, we knew that if the evidence just focused on the day of the assault, we would lose. Instead, we had to somehow bring up events that had occurred almost forty years before.

In 1976, seven-year-old Will and his five-year-old brother went with their parents on a camping trip with several other families, in a park in the mountains surrounding the Silicon Valley. The families had met through a loosely affiliated religious organization, and they had invited a priest to come along and say Mass on Sunday morning. The priest's name was Father Jerold Lindner.

One night, Lindner lured Will into his tent, which was set well apart from the rest of the camp. Once Will was in the tent, Lindner proceeded to force his penis into Will's mouth while choking Will around the neck with both hands. Lindner then turned him around and began to anally rape him, at which point Will passed out. When Will woke up, Lindner cleaned him up and told Will that if he ever told anyone, he would kill his parents and peel the skin off his sister. Will left the tent too terrified to speak to anyone about what had happened.

The next night was even worse. Lindner had gotten Will's brother into his tent and made Will join them. He then forced the two young children to have oral intercourse with each other. While Will was performing oral sex on his brother, Lindner sodomized him again. The feeling of helplessness that Will had when his brother looked at him with terror in his eyes was something Will had nightmares about his entire life.

After that camping trip, Will's life changed dramatically. The happy, outgoing young boy became sullen and withdrawn. By the time he was twelve, he was experimenting with drugs and sex. He was rebelling against any authority figures, whether it was teachers, police officers, or his parents. Finally, when Will was twenty-seven years old, his brother told his parents, who were horrified and guilt-ridden, about what had happened. After an initial angry reaction at his brother, Will decided to face it and go after Lindner. He called all the local police and sheriff's offices, as well as a number of district attorney's offices in Northern California, to tell them the story and see if they could arrest Lindner or at least investigate him to see if he was still harming children. His persistence was met with the same reaction from every agency: there was nothing they could do because the statute of limitations had run out on Lindner's rape of the two boys.

Will then hired a lawyer and sued Lindner and the Catholic

Church. The Church, which knew much more about Lindner than they let on, settled quickly. But Will wanted more than just money. As part of the settlement he wanted the Church to promise to take Lindner away from children (he was teaching at a high school); he wanted Lindner to acknowledge what he had done, and he wanted to know where Lindner was living at all times. None of those terms were met.

As Will was going through the process, he learned that he and his brother were not the only victims of Lindner. He learned that Lindner's nieces and nephews, children of family friends, and even Lindner's younger sister had all accused him of sexually abusing them. A number of these cases were eventually featured in a 2003 article in the *Los Angeles Times* that detailed Lindner as one of the Catholic priests most frequently accused of molestation. The article pointed out that over the years, the church has paid out millions of dollars to victims of Lindner's abuse.

An increasingly frustrated Lynch went into serious therapy for the first time in his life, but he continued to want to confront Lindner and make him admit what he had done. Several years later, he learned that Lindner had been removed from teaching and placed at a retirement home for priests known as the Sacred Heart Jesuit Center, in Los Gatos, California, about thirty miles south of Will's San Francisco residence.

Over the years, Lynch tried to get up the courage to confront Lindner. He drove down to Los Gatos on several occasions, but each time his fear of Lindner caused him to turn back. But on May 10, 2010, Will got up the nerve to walk into Sacred Heart and ask to meet with Lindner. He was taken to a small private room and told to wait. When Lindner came into the room, he did not recognize Will, who then looked at him and said, "You should remember the kids you raped." Will then stepped over to Lindner and told him to take off his glasses. He then began to pummel him. Lindner fell to the ground and covered up his head, which had the effect of deflecting many of the blows. After about thirty seconds, a woman walked in and pleaded with Will to stop. Will then got up, left the room, and as he was exiting Sacred Heart, he screamed back at Lindner, "You made me fuck my own brother. Turn yourself in or I will come back and kill you."

Several months later Will was arrested and he called us. From the very beginning, he said that he was not going to deny that he beat up the priest. He also said he was not going to plea bargain; he wanted to go to trial. He wanted to expose Lindner and the Jesuit center where he was living. We explained to him that the likely outcome of admitting his guilt on the witness stand in front of the jury was that he would go to jail. He said he understood that but was willing to risk it if it meant he could use the publicity surrounding the trial to make sure the community knew who Lindner was and what he had done.

The publicity part proved to be a huge success. At every court appearance, Will had twenty to thirty supporters, some of whom were victims of Lindner, stationed at the entrance to the courthouse. They carried large signs with Lindner's picture and name on them in huge letters, next to the words "rapist" and "child molester." The press had a field day with the supporters, repeatedly photographing and videotaping them and planting Lindner's name and face all over the news. By the time the trial started, Lindner was afraid to show his face in public.

Leading up to trial, the D.A., the judge, and even the press were trying to get us to reveal what our defense was, but we refused to reveal it. The reason we refused to reveal it was simple: we had no defense. We were going to go to trial, admit Will committed the crime, and then hope for jury nullification. A jury nullifies a case when the jurors choose to ignore the law and the court's instructions and decide to vote not guilty based on their own sense of justice. The problem with jury nullification is that under the law, its existence is not to be acknowledged. The lawyers are not allowed to argue it, and the court cannot tell the jury it has the right to do it. If the jurors ask about it, the court is to tell them that it goes against their oath as jurors. In short, we were going to trial with a client who was going to admit to the crime, and the only defense we had was one we could not mention.

Then it got worse. Two weeks before the trial started, the judge ruled that we would be limited in how much of Will's story we could tell. The judge ruled that Will could testify that Lindner molested him, but he could not discuss any details about what happened during the camping trip; nor would Will be allowed to talk about what had happened in his life since that trip. The jury was not going to get to hear the story that was our only chance at jury nullification. Our best hope now was to convince the jury that the priest's injuries were minor and thus they should vote for a misdemeanor assault instead of a felony assault charge. That would lessen the amount of time Will would have to spend in jail.

But just when it seemed that the case had gone from difficult to impossible, we were rescued—by the prosecuting attorney. All attorneys make mistakes during trials, but rarely do they make enormous strategic blunders. The Santa Clara County D.A.'s Office didn't make just one incredible blunder, it made two, both of them in the opening statement. The D.A. began by telling the jury that the victim in the case, Father Lindner, was going to lie. He was going to commit perjury by denying that he had ever sexually molested Lynch. The prosecutor then went on to say that she believed Will had been molested and in a particularly horrific manner. Apparently she believed that telling the jury this was a clever way to get out in front of the issue and attempt to soften the blow. Instead, it solved one of our biggest problems. Since the judge had limited Will's testimony so drastically, to the point where he could say only that he was molested, we felt there was a real chance some of the jurors might believe that this was a minor incident, perhaps even a misunderstanding, since Lindner was never arrested. The prosecution's verifying that it was a horrible assault solved that problem for us. It also allowed us to repeatedly jump on the prosecution for putting on a case where they admitted they were going to allow their star witness to commit perjury. On the one hand, they were saying they had to prosecute Will because the rule of law must be followed no matter what, but on the other hand, they were going to allow their witness to break the law by committing perjury and that was okay. It made them look silly.

➤ That was only the warm-up act. At the end of the opening statement, the prosecutor showed a ten-minute video interview of Will that had been done the week before by a local media outlet. The video showed an emotional Will going into detail about the rape as well as its aftermath and how it had changed his life. The video was gut-wrenching (at least one juror was spotted wiping away tears), but showing it did something important for our defense—it opened the door for us to go into all of Will's past, including his efforts to have Lindner arrested. After the video was shown, we immediately went into chambers with the judge and pointed this out to him. The prosecutor looked stunned, as if she had never even considered this possibility. The judge admitted he was mystified as to why the prosecution would do this, and then he ruled that we could now tell the full story.

A trial that was bizarre to begin with took another unexpected turn on the second day of testimony. On the first day, the prosecution called Lindner to the stand, where he testified for forty-five minutes on how badly he had been beaten. Then, as the court was about to finish for the day, the prosecution asked Lindner a final question:

"Did you molest Will Lynch?"

"No!"

As the prosecutor had predicted, Lindner had now lied under oath, and done it in front of the Santa Clara County D.A.'s Office.

The next morning, before Lindner got back on the stand, an attorney showed up and told the court that he represented Lindner and that Lindner was not going forward with his testimony. The attorney told the court that he felt that his client was being set up for perjury charges and that he was going to take the Fifth Amendment the rest of the way. All hell broke loose, with the judge eventually deciding that Lindner could take the Fifth, but that the judge would tell the jury that all his previous testimony would be stricken (i.e., they would be told to ignore it as if it did not happen). They would also not be told why Lindner had suddenly disappeared. We were livid, screaming that Lindner had gotten to testify to what the prosecution wanted out, and now we would not get to cross-examine him. We asked for a mistrial, which the judge denied.

Pat: Eventually the case got to the closing arguments. Since I could not mention jury nullification, I had to come up with creative ways to suggest to the jury that they could do whatever they wanted to do, and there was nothing the prosecution or the court could do about it. On numerous occasions I got close to the edge and the prosecutor objected and the judge admonished me. But I was sure that after everything they had heard, this jury wanted to nullify—I just wasn't sure they knew that they could.

On the second day of jury deliberations we found out exactly what they knew about nullification. The jury sent a note to the judge asking, "What are the rules of law of jury nullification and what exactly is it?" This jury question set off another round of heated arguments. We kept arguing with the judge that he had to tell them that although they might not have the right to nullify, they had the power to, which is exactly the phrase used in a Supreme Court decision. The judge disagreed and eventually sent back an answer to the jury that was almost word for word what the prosecution had proposed. In essence, the judge's response told the jury that they could not nullify and it would be against their juror oath to do so, suggesting they could get in legal trouble if they did.

We were devastated. It felt like we had won the case only to have it taken away from us by what we believed was an incorrect ruling by the judge. A few hours later the jury announced that they had reached a verdict. It was obvious to us that the judge's answer had pushed the jurors to convict Will of something. Apparently the D.A.'s office felt the same way: a lineup of twelve to fourteen district attorneys strode through the courtroom single file and took seats right next to the jury box, from which to hear the verdict and take a victory lap.

They left very disappointed. The jury found Will not guilty on both felony counts and on the misdemeanor elder abuse case. On the misdemeanor simple assault, which is what we had admitted he was guilty of, the jury had hung 8–4 in favor of guilt. Despite the judge's warning, four jurors had voted to nullify anyway. In post-trial conversations, a number of the jurors admitted they wanted to nullify but were scared by the judge's order.

Will was stunned and ecstatic. He had made preparations to be taken to jail after the verdict and was now adjusting to the fact that he was not going to be a convicted felon. In the midst of the post-trial celebration, we were talking with Will's mother when she said, "This is the first time since he was a seven-year-old boy that I have seen him smile like this. This has given him his life back."

SCOTT PETERSON

On the day the verdict was to be announced in the Scott Peterson trial, hundreds of people gathered at the San Mateo courthouse hoping to hear that the jury had found Scott guilty. Across the country, TV viewership spiked as millions tuned in wanting to see that he would be convicted of murdering his wife. When the court clerk read the word "guilty," a celebration broke out outside the courthouse that would have rivaled anything at Mardi Gras. One woman interviewed by a local TV station stated that this was the best day of her life, surpassing the birth of her son. As the jurors were escorted out of the courthouse to their waiting bus, they were cheered like conquering heroes. All that was missing was the confetti.

Every day in America, approximately forty-five people are murdered. Elderly women, middle-aged businessmen, teenage girls, even small children are killed both by accident and sometimes in brutally horrific manners. We mourn for the victims and seek justice for the killers, most of whom are captured and ultimately convicted. Other than from the direct participants in each case, very few cases attract attention or are even noticed by outside observers.

So how do you explain that a nice-looking, likable salesman from Modesto, California, would end up becoming the most hated man in America after being accused of murdering his wife? What made this case so different from the thousands of other murders every year in the United States? How is it possible that this unknown middle-class kid with no prior criminal history would become a national obsession? Why would a person consider the day of this man's being sentenced to death to be a happier one than the day she gave birth to her child?

For years we have struggled with those questions, and we have yet to come up with a definitive answer. In retrospect, it seems that it was a number of factors that converged to create the storm that was the Scott Peterson saga. One of those factors was certainly the charisma and appeal of the victim, Scott's wife, Laci. By all accounts, Laci was a firecracker, a beautiful young woman with a radiant smile and a fiery personality to match. Her charisma shone through in the numerous pictures of her, many of which also showed a cute, rounded pregnant belly. It was unfathomable looking at those pictures to think that anyone would want to hurt her.

But there was more to the equation than just Laci's beautiful persona. As we came to learn during our representation of Scott, he had become a symbol for a lot of women who had been cheated on or lied to by a husband or boyfriend. We began to notice that the people who would argue most vociferously for Scott's guilt were women between the ages of eighteen and fifty. They could quote every rumor and false story circulated in the media, no matter how far-fetched, and would insist that these stories proved he was obviously guilty. When we would explain how these stories were wrong and that the facts were actually much different, the response was strikingly similar: "Oh well, I hate him anyway. He reminds me of my ex-boyfriend!"

This was clearly part of the equation. Scott became a symbol for every wronged woman who wanted to see her ex rot in hell.

But an attractive young woman as victim and a cheating husband as defendant would not have been enough to propel this case beyond the city limits of Modesto.

What made it a national story was a growing twenty-four-hour cable cycle that was desperately looking for stories that might resonate with the American public. In particular, the angry blond white women were just beginning to emerge as more than occasional guest commentators on cable shows, and they needed someone to demonize. Every hero or even perceived hero needs a nemesis. Superman was boring without Lex Luthor. Batman was nothing without the Joker. Scott Peterson proved to be the perfect foil.

Within days of Laci's disappearance, the feeding frenzy started. The angry blond white women were commenting on his demeanor, his lack of obvious emotion, and his going fishing on Christmas Eve with a pregnant wife at home. That frenzy snowballed when it was revealed that Scott had a mistress he had met the month before. Every single night some new rumor surfaced about Scott, and each one pointed to his guilt. Furthermore, whatever action he took was interpreted as further evidence of his guilt. When he smiled, he was criticized for being callous and smug. When he didn't smile or seemed dazed, he was criticized for not caring.

The campaign against Scott Peterson began in January 2004, and it continued unabated for almost two years. TV executives loved it because they finally had a ratings bonanza that came close to rivaling O.J. Virtually every single night, commentators like Larry King and Greta Van Susteren devoted whole hours or at least partial segments to that day's Scott Peterson news.

Another thing about the Scott Peterson case that has always puzzled us is the widespread, almost unanimous opinion that Scott was guilty before one piece of evidence was introduced. If you examine every high-profile case of the past two decades (O.J., Michael Jackson, Casey Anthony, Robert Blake, the Duke lacrosse team, Dr. Conrad Murray), you'll see that every one of the defendants had some group or constituency that argued on behalf of their innocence. But Scott Peterson didn't. When we took over the case, we soon found out that it was considered an accepted fact that he was guilty. In other cases we had done or commented on, people would often ask us if we thought our client "did it." In this case no one asked because they assumed we knew that he had. Instead we were asked, "Do you think you can get him off?" When we tell someone that we have sincere, honest doubts that Scott murdered his wife, you can just see that it is the equivalent of telling someone that Elvis is alive and working at a Piggly Wiggly in Arkansas. The most common response is "And I suppose you think O.J. is innocent too?" Since the end of the trial, we have refrained from arguing the result—it is simply a subject you cannot approach.

We understand why some people think Scott Peterson is guilty; it's difficult to understand why *everyone* thinks he is guilty. In a country that breeds contrarians on virtually every subject, no one of note has suggested Scott is innocent. This is especially troubling in light of the fact that the actual evidence against him was questionable at best and certainly not beyond a reasonable doubt.

Here is the case against Scott Peterson: He was cheating on his pregnant wife with a woman in Fresno when his wife disappeared. He had seen this woman a total of four times. He lied to the woman about having a wife, and he lied to the police about his affair. Four months later the body of his wife washed up in a marina near where Scott had told the police he had gone fishing the day she disappeared. That is the case against Scott Peterson. Period.

Everything else you heard on television or read in magazines— escapes to Mexico, disguises, selling the house, selling Laci's car, hiding the boat, etc.—is ridiculous hyperbole, and all of it was torn apart at trial.

Could you convict Scott of murder because he was having an affair and because the body washed up near where he had been fishing? We couldn't, but we do understand that people could make a legitimate argument for his guilt based on these facts. If they had put on these two pieces of evidence as their case, we could have respected that. And given the hysteria surrounding his trial, they might very likely have won. But the prosecution didn't do this. Instead, the prosecution spent months introducing ridiculous evidence, much of which had originated in the tabloid media.

Pat: When we were first approached about taking the Scott Peterson case, we were split: Mark was willing to take a chance on him, but I didn't want any part of the case. We were riding high on the tail of a number of successes, the firm was growing by leaps and bounds, and Mark was one of the most popular lawyers in America. If we were to represent Scott Peterson, we'd immediately become the most hated lawyers in the country. But Mark had a good argument for taking the case that eventually carried the day:

"This is what we do. We are defense lawyers. We represent people who are not popular. That mob that gathered outside the Modesto jail was ready to lynch him. The day we quit taking cases because the defendant is not popular is the day we shut the firm's doors."

Having been properly shamed into agreeing, I nevertheless bowed out of working on the case until approximately three months after we had been hired. The attorney in our office who was assisting Mark was so media crazy that he was leaking materials to the press and telling them that we were going to blame Laci's death on a satanic cult. Publicly Mark covered for him, but privately he was seething and removed him from the case. He asked if I would move to Modesto to work the case while he was tied up at a trial in Los Angeles. Over a three-month period, I spent eight to ten hours a day with Scott, going over the evidence, quizzing him about Laci's disappearance, and trying very hard to break him down. Mark and I cross-examined him and pushed him hard, even yelling at him at times. We would go over the same stories again and again, and we would look for contradictions or inconsistencies. During the three months, he never once changed his story or contradicted himself, even on small

details. It was truly amazing. I told Mark that I just did not think it was pos-
sible for Scott to have killed his wife and not get tripped up even once on his
story or a piece of overlooked evidence, like a cell phone record or credit car re-
ceipt. A guilty person would make a mistake over months of grilling, but he
never did.

After reviewing all the evidence with Scott, our biggest fear in
the case was not the evidence. Our biggest fear was jury selection.
Finding twelve people without a negative opinion of Scott was impossible. We knew that. It was going to come down to trying to find
twelve people who would admit they didn't like him but who we felt
would be fair and listen to the evidence. As with any media circus
trial, we also needed to be wary of people looking to get on the jury
for their fifteen minutes of fame writing a book or doing TV interviews.

The results from the jury questionnaires given out to prospective
jurors were not promising. There is a fairly substantial Buddhist population in the San Mateo area, and one of their principles is opposi-
tion to the death penalty. When we received the first batch of
questionnaires, two Buddhists said they would make an exception for
Scott. One man tried to fill out the questionnaire, but he was illiter-
ate. He wrote only one word on the front of the form—GUITY. A
poll released before the trial showed only 3 percent of people questioned believed Scott was innocent. In the same poll, 6 percent said
the moon landing was staged. The questionnaires seemed to bear that
out. Overwhelmingly, the prospective jurors trashed Scott in their
answers. It got so bad that when a prospective juror did not say something negative, we became immediately suspicious that that person
was lying to get on the jury.

We decided early on that our best bet for jurors would be highly
educated professionals, particularly those who analyze facts for a living, such as lawyers, engineers, and computer analysts. But there were
two major problems in getting them on a panel. First, the trial was set
to last six months, and very few professionals could take time off from

work for that length of time. A lawyer or a doctor who leaves a practice for half a year is likely to come back to half a practice. Second, this was a death penalty case, which meant the jurors had to be "death-qualified." A death-qualified juror must be willing to state that he or she is not opposed to the death penalty and can vote for it if it is warranted. A large segment of the public does not believe in the death penalty under any circumstances, and they are automatically excluded from serving on a death penalty case. Furthermore, studies show that those who oppose the death penalty are overwhelmingly the higher-educated people we were trying to get on the jury.

From jury selection it just got worse. The tabloid media put forward a number of crackpot theories that were picked up by the prosecution. Here's a selection:

A month after Laci disappeared, Scott contacted a real estate agent about selling their house, which, according to the prosecution, showed that he knew she wasn't coming back. In actuality, it showed just the opposite—he thought she was coming back. Of course he was going to sell the house. If his wife came back, do you think he'd ask her and a newborn baby to stay in the house she'd been abducted from while he was on the road with his job? Do you honestly think Laci would have stayed there for one minute? He was actually planning as if she were still alive, looking for a new area for his family to move to.

The prosecution also argued that Scott dyed his hair blond so he could escape to Mexico and then lied to investigators when he told them his hair had turned blond from swimming in a pool. In actuality he dyed his hair with a kit he bought in a grocery store to help him avoid the media that was hounding him everywhere, including at his job, before he'd been arrested or charged. The dye turned his hair lighter but with more of a red tint. The next day he went swimming in his friend's pool, and the chlorine mixed with the bad hair dye, turning it a lighter shade of red. He explained that to the police, who only wrote down that Scott said his hair changed color from swimming. As for using it as a disguise to escape to Mexico, that would have made a better story if he hadn't met with police *after* he had dyed his hair and grown a beard. We actually had a picture of him meeting with police with the alleged disguise he was going to use to avoid police.

Another sure sign of his guilt apparently was that Scott had traveled to the San Francisco Bay to watch police search the bay for Laci's body. The theory was that since he knew he had dumped her there, he was scared they would find her body and he was watching to see if he needed to flee. What was not discussed in the media was that Scott also went to several other lakes and rivers where the police were searching, to see if they had any luck finding her. Why would he do that if he knew she was in the bay?

These are three examples of what came to be known as the "he didn't act right" evidence. The vast majority of the evidence in the case had nothing to do with the murder of Laci Peterson. Instead, it focused on how Scott acted after her disappearance and argued that he didn't act the way an innocent man should.

In particular, his stoic demeanor really set the naysayers off. Throughout the ordeal, Scott was portrayed as an emotionless psychopath, some sort of sick bastard who didn't even cry when his pregnant wife disappeared. During the trial a next-door neighbor testified how in the privacy of her home he broke down and inconsolably cried with her when talking about Laci. But Scott's problem was that he did not put on a show for the media that followed him relentlessly, trying to get a response from him. It has now become expected that every person in a tragic situation needs to run and find a TV camera and then cry uncontrollably while being interviewed. A dramatic, public display of emotion in a tragic situation is not only expected, it is apparently necessary as proof of lack of guilt.

This is a recent phenomenon. For most of the twentieth century, the image of a strong man was Gary Cooper in *High Noon* or John Wayne in any John Wayne movie or Clint Eastwood as Dirty Harry.

Stoic, calm, focused—you were never going to catch one of them crying when a problem arose. Men didn't show emotion in public—they solved problems.

Scott's father, a truly wonderful man named Lee Peterson, was definitely raised that way. Born of Norwegian ancestry and raised in Minnesota, Lee was the definition of a man's man. He was quick with a joke and had a big, easygoing smile, but Lee was not a man who wore his emotions on his sleeve. His son Scott idolized and emulated him. When a problem arose, they approached it the same way. Instead of standing around talking about it or complaining about how unfortunate it was, both men would check their emotions and begin systematically looking for a solution. That is exactly how Scott went about trying to find his wife. To many, it appeared to be cold and calculating, but Scott was just not going to hang around the search headquarters crying.

But of course Scott had a bigger likability problem than his demeanor: he'd been cheating on his pregnant wife with a thin, blond massage therapist named Amber Frey. Scott met Frey on one of his many trips to Fresno, and he told her he was not married. They spent the night together at a hotel on their first date, and subsequently he saw her three more times within the space of about one month. It was a largely sexual relationship on Scott's part, but it was more than that to Amber, who quickly became infatuated with Scott.

The prosecution's theory was that Scott began to premeditate Laci's murder after his first date with Amber, but that seemed rather far-fetched since he made no attempt to hide his dates with Amber, charging the dinners and hotels on his credit card and even attending Amber's friend's Christmas party, where he was photographed repeatedly with her. If he was plotting to murder his wife, it would have been prudent to at least try to obscure the fact that he had a mistress.

When Laci disappeared, the media had gathered at Scott's house by the next day, and his face was plastered all over television. The only person who did not know about Laci and Scott Peterson was

Amber Frey, because she did not own a TV. It was obviously just a matter of time before she found out about Scott, but for the time being he would call her periodically to see if she knew anything. For him, it now became a race against the clock to find Laci. He knew that sooner or later Amber Frey was going to realize who he was and go to the police, and Scott would instantly become not only the prime suspect in the case but the only suspect. He knew that his lying to Amber was eventually going to hurt him, but if he could just keep her in the dark for a little while longer, until Laci was found, the worst thing that would happen would be that he would have to explain his infidelity to Laci.

But Amber was playing her own game. She did find out a few days after Laci disappeared, and she did go to the police. Instead of confronting Scott, she acted in concert with the police to record her conversations with him. The police even taught her how to try to get information from him. He would call Amber, unaware that she knew he was lying, and continue to lie, sometimes in ridiculous fashion. He told her he was in Europe watching fireworks bursting over the Eiffel Tower or that he was headed to Spain for a business meeting. But lying during an affair is not exactly uncommon. It was his phone demeanor that was ultimately his undoing at trial. At times he seemed absolutely giddy on the phone, laughing and joking with Amber. At other times he was sweet and caring. It was hard to listen to this and believe that he was concerned about his missing wife. Eventually, Amber told Scott that she knew about Laci and began quizzing him about her disappearance.

Pat: When we got the written transcripts of the recorded phone conversations, we pored over them and then let out a sigh of relief. In the transcripts, Amber tries repeatedly to get Scott to admit to things and Scott repeatedly denies any involvement in Laci's disappearance. He is adamant in his denials and eventually tells Amber he is sorry but that he really loves his wife. When we read the transcripts, we could not find one single thing that seemed to indicate his guilt.

A few days later, we received the actual audiotapes of those conversations. I was taking a flight to New York for the weekend and took the tapes on the plane to listen to them. When I got back to L.A., I walked into Mark's office and said, "We are so screwed. When you hear him on the tapes, it is one hundred times worse than reading the transcripts. He sounds cavalier and carefree. I know he was trying to put on an act for Amber, but it comes across really bad. This jury is going to hate him!"

The tapes were played after the midpoint of the trial. Lost in all the post-conviction celebrations was the fact that before the tapes were played, the case had been an utter disaster for the prosecution. Witness after witness for the prosecution was made to look foolish, including one of the two main detectives who was caught hiding evidence in his reports. The local newspaper in San Mateo published an editorial suggesting that the prosecution might have to drop the case if things continued to go as they were going. One of the jurors was removed from the panel and promptly told the media that he would have found Scott innocent. The prosecution's biggest advocates in the media were alarmed at how badly the trial was going.

Then the courtroom listened to Scott laughing with his mistress on the phone. We could already hear the prosecution's closing argument. "And while his wife and unborn son lay dead at the bottom of the cold, dark ocean floor, Scott Peterson giggled with his mistress while pretending to the rest of the world that he was busy searching for his wife."

The anger and hatred in the courtroom, already palpable, jumped to a new level. The jurors who already wanted to find Scott guilty finally had something to hang on to. The entire mood of the trial changed although there were still another six weeks of witnesses. In the end, the fact that "he didn't act right" would be his downfall.

Scott is sitting on death row at San Quentin. His appellate lawyer, Cliff Gardner, one of the best in the business, has just recently filed his appeal, and it will likely be heard sometime in 2013. For anyone who has spent any time with Scott, it is impossible to reconcile this image of him as the devil with the man who is always smiling and refuses to this day to say anything negative about any of the witnesses against him or the jurors who convicted him. Shortly after his conviction, he moved on from what had happened at trial and began methodically working on the appeal.

Over the past eight years, we have taken a lot of grief for believing that Scott did not murder his wife. We lived this case for two years—we knew it better than any human beings on the planet other than Scott himself. We will sometimes tell people that if they give us ten minutes we will convince them of Scott's innocence or at the very least create a doubt in their minds. So far, every person who has taken that challenge has walked away with serious doubts about his guilt. Most are surprised to learn that the stories they heard were just not true. But none of that matters now unless his appeal is granted and he gets a new trial. Otherwise, it is very possible that the state of California will put an innocent man to death.

CHAPTER FOUR

Prosecutors—
Being a Prosecutor Means
Never Having to Say You're Sorry

Mark: In late 2011 I sat in the lobby at one of the branches of the Los Angeles County District Attorney's Office waiting patiently for a two-thirty appointment with the supervising D.A. in that courthouse. Every courthouse has a number of assistant D.A.s who handle the large volume of cases that flow through the courtrooms every day. They answer to a supervisor who generally does not go to court but sits in the office and directs them on their cases. The supervisor has the ultimate say about a case in that courthouse, so we sometimes set up meetings with them if we can't resolve the case with the assistant D.A. On this particular day, I had a rather unusual case involving an assault with a deadly weapon that led me to request the meeting.

I have participated in hundreds of these types of meetings during my career, but a lot has changed over the years. Twenty, maybe even ten years ago, I would have just dropped by the office around lunchtime and invited the supervisor to go grab a sandwich. We would have walked to somewhere nearby and gossiped about what judge was sleeping with what clerk or who was thinking of running for head D.A. in the next election. When lunch was done, we would walk back to the courthouse and I would tell him about a case I needed his help resolving. The D.A. would agree to help resolve it or explain why he couldn't. Either way the meeting would end amicably and we would agree to get together for dinner soon. There was always a mutual respect for each other and our jobs even if we disagreed about the proper resolution.

On this day, however, I waited for forty-five minutes before the door opened and I was ushered down a series of hallways to the supervisor's office. When I entered the office, the D.A. arose from behind an obscenely large desk and gruffly shook my hand. I had known this particular D.A. for at least fifteen years and had gone up against him in court a couple of times but did not have an opinion on him one way or the other. Before I could congratulate him on his promotion or even compliment his tie, the D.A. launched into a diatribe against my client that sounded more like a closing argument than a discussion. He informed me that he was not open to discussing the case and that there was no point talking to him about it. When I finally did start to speak, he picked up a file from another case and started glancing through it while I talked. The entire atmosphere of the meeting was that I was expected to grovel and offer fealty to him. I am not above a little necessary groveling for my clients, but this was beyond ridiculous. I quickly excused myself before he asked me to kiss his ring. I was afraid what I might tell him to kiss in return.

We have come to accept that a major part of getting older is looking back and seeing the past through rose-colored glasses. But the change in prosecutorial attitudes and tactics in the past twenty years is not simply a product of wistful longings for our youth. A growing number of prosecutors now see themselves as moralistic crime fighters, Batman in a coat and tie. It is an attitude that is largely prevalent among D.A.s with less than ten years' experience, who grew up watching shows like *Law & Order*. All cases are black-and-white, good versus evil, and they are the only thing standing between a civilized society and the social anarchy that defense lawyers hope to create. To negotiate with a defense lawyer would be like negotiating with a terrorist.

When we started out as defense attorneys, it was not unusual for legal organizations to hold monthly functions where new D.A.s and defense attorneys could mingle and get to know one another. In L.A., we even had a tradition where defense attorneys, D.A.s, and a few judges would spend one weekend every year in Arizona watching spring training baseball. This was not simply for social purposes. Developing relationships meant that it would be much easier to work together when the time came. What should have been a very clunky, overloaded system actually moved somewhat smoothly due to those relationships. There was a mutual respect for one another and the roles that each party played in making the system work. When there was a disagreement, it was not personal. Both parties would put it in front of a judge or jury and let the judge or jury resolve it, then meet for a drink later to swap stories.

This was the system we grew up in. There was always a lot of trash talking and telling war stories, but at the end of the day we were serious about the work. After gaining a few years of experience, both sides had a pretty good idea what a case was worth, and the two estimates were usually close enough to get the case settled. The idea was to come together to see if we could work it out. If not, we would agree to go to trial. Back then it was extremely rare to ever get into a shouting match or personal argument with a D.A.

Remnants of those days still exist. We can still walk into most any courtroom in California and run into a D.A. who we have had a long-term relationship with. Also, it would be unfair to classify all young D.A.s as uncooperative and full of themselves. Some still have a strong understanding of their role as a prosecutor and conduct themselves professionally. It is just that they are becoming fewer and fewer.

Mark: Recently I walked into a courthouse in downtown L.A. and with my daily files went up to the D.A. sitting at the counsel table to discuss a possible plea deal. It is a routine I have practiced thousands of times before. As I approached him, the D.A. barely even raised his head up and just sneered out of the corner of his mouth, "What do you want?"

He looked to be in the twenty-five- to thirty-year-old age range, and this was almost certainly his first job out of law school.

"What do I want? Really, what do I want? Let me tell you what I want! I want to deal with a D.A. who doesn't look like he is just starting puberty, a D.A. who doesn't think he is Wyatt Earp, a D.A. who won't piss in his pants the first time a jury walks into the room."

As I turned to walk away, the D.A. managed to spit out, "Yeah, well, we'll see what the judge has to say about that."

A few minutes later the judge walked into the courtroom and started to get on the bench. She spotted me sitting in a chair near the bailiff and immediately made a U-turn and waved me forward to give me a big hug. She was a woman I had known for more than twenty years, from her days in the D.A.'s office, and had socialized with often—she had even stopped by my house for Christmas once. The D.A. looked sick, but when the case was announced, he still started on a rant about how I had insulted him. The judge just waved her hand at him to stop. "I worked with Mr. Geragos on at least fifteen or more cases when I was a D.A. If you can't work with him, then you can't work with anyone."

That case had a happy ending—most do not. That's what drove Pops crazy and led to him limiting his court appearances. By the end of his career, he had no patience for a pompous D.A. If a D.A. acted like an ass, Pops would just yell at that D.A. unmercifully. It was not unusual for him to yell at a D.A. who had been disrespectful to "Sit down and shut up!" The judges all knew Pops, so they gave him a wide berth, plus I think they also enjoyed watching him operate.

Today you see many D.A.s treat defense attorneys with thinly disguised disdain, knowing that, with the power they have, they face very few repercussions. With the backing of the large portion of society that feels the system is soft on crime, they can present themselves as the ultimate moral authority, the only ones concerned about right versus wrong.

Not too long ago in a federal courthouse on the East Coast, we had a case arguing a motion where the law was clearly on our side. After we made our argument, the U.S. attorney stood up and, instead of addressing the issue or even making a pretense of a legal argument, began to recite his résumé and the résumé of his fellow U.S. attorney who was assisting on the case. The implication was not even subtle. His entire response was based on the assumption that he was a career prosecutor and therefore on the side of truth and justice. Fortunately the judge in that case was more interested in the law than the prosecutor's résumé.

Television has played a large role in developing this pervasive hubris. Prosecutors used to be portrayed as nebbishy, vanilla personalities. Usually they were not even the main nemesis of the defense attorney. The prosecutor in *Perry Mason* was always the same man in every episode, yet no one can even remember his name. Today's prosecutors in shows like *Law & Order* are ethical, brilliant legal minds whose courtroom skills surpass any real trial attorney's. In a typical episode the heroic prosecutors fret over ethical dilemmas while the high-priced Armani-clad defense attorneys break enough ethical rules to be disbarred ten times over. We actually enjoy *Law & Order*, but then again we used to enjoy *Fantasy Island* as well, and that was probably a little more realistic.

But it's not all in the prosecutors' heads. They actually do have more power today than ever before. The prosecution has always had the sole power to charge a person with a crime, as well as to decide what crime and how many charges to bring. It is the prosecution that sets the terms of the plea bargain and can in fact decide whether to even negotiate. It is also the prosecutor who makes the first offer. And, finally, it is the prosecutor who can dismiss a bad case. That is why a prosecutor with common sense and good judgment can do more for the defendant than any ten defense lawyers.

Prosecutors have added to their advantage in recent year as judges have ceded power to them. Two decades ago, judges were not going to get defeated for reelection unless they, to quote Edwin W. Edwards, the former governor of Louisiana, "were caught in bed with a dead girl or a live boy." That is no longer the case. More and more judges across the country face heated reelection battles. And the way you run against an incumbent judge is to declare the judge soft on crime and to drag up court cases where it appears the defendant got an easy sentence from the judge. It is a foolproof tactic to accuse a judge of handing out a light sentence in a case, because the opponent knows that in a thirty-second sound bite the judge cannot likely explain why he or she gave that sentence. As a result, we see more and more judges simply deferring to the prosecutor as a way to provide themselves cover.

THE ROLE OF THE PROSECUTION

The most common misconception about prosecutors is that they have the same role as the defense attorney, only they represent the victims and the defense attorney represents the defendants. That is not the case. The simplest way to describe a prosecutor's job is "to do justice." They're supposed to both investigate a crime to try to discern the truth and at the same time be an advocate for the alleged victim. They need to both find a guilty party and be sure that they don't charge an innocent party with the crime. A smart and strong prosecutor can toe the line in balancing these two duties, but we are seeing more and more young prosecutors who ignore the first duty to investigate and jump right to the second duty of advocacy.

Most defense attorneys understand and respect the high-wire act that the prosecutor must perform. It is also fair to say that the majority of prosecutors take this balancing act seriously and genuinely try to do the right thing. During our many years of practice, we have been involved in hundreds of cases where the prosecutor has dismissed a case outright or lowered the charges against the defendant because it was the right thing to do. A few years back we had an arson case with a very good trial prosecutor, Mike Cabral. After the first witness in the case backtracked from his original story, casting doubt on the prosecution's entire version of events, Cabral asked for a recess, which the judge granted. The prosecutor promptly returned, stood up in front of the jury, and dismissed the case. Cabral was a very good attorney and might have won anyway, but when he began to have doubts about the case, he was not going to risk convicting an innocent man.

This is not as easy as it sounds. Many times the prosecutor has the victim yelling in his ear or, worse, yelling in his supervisor's ear, complaining that the prosecutor is giving away the case. Complaining victims frequently have an inflated idea about what a case is worth. For example, they assume that a person caught breaking into their house and stealing some jewelry must be looking at twenty years or more. When the prosecution settles the case for three years, they become angry and feel they have been cheated by the system. Many of them are very vocal about it to the D.A.'s office, their local newspaper, or their councilman. Prosecutors have to have very thick skin because they know a particular plea or a dismissal will result in them catching hell from the complaining victim. Indeed it is hard to fault those who have been the victim of a crime, but not every crime deserves a max sentence, nor is every crime worth the expense of a trial.

And once a trial begins, it is very difficult for a prosecutor to fold his or her hand and admit that the prosecution has charged the wrong person or that they don't have sufficient evidence to convict. Instead many prosecutors these days will never admit a mistake. They'll go forward on virtually all cases, no matter how ridiculous, and at least try to get some sort of plea out of them. We have had two instances in the past year where we've gone to court ready to start a trial only to be confronted by a D.A. who said that he too was ready to go to trial, but was also willing to let our client plead out to a much lower charge than had previously been offered. In both cases, suspicious of the D.A.'s sudden generosity, we said no thanks. And in both cases the D.A. then admitted that his chief witness had recanted his story and that he was going to have to dismiss the case. These particular D.A.s knew that they had no case and that the defendants were very possibly not guilty, but they chose to go ahead anyway and try to trick us to get a plea to something. This is outrageous, unethical behavior. For these D.A.s, it was more important to never admit a mistake than "to do justice."

The curious case of a woman we represented two years ago provides the perfect example. The woman was a forty-seven-year-old widow who lived in a house in a marginal neighborhood in South Central Los Angeles. The district attorney's office charged her with two separate felonies of assault with a deadly weapon. The first one allegedly occurred when she pulled a gun on two young men who were walking on the sidewalk in front of her house. The second assault charged involved her hitting one of the young men with her truck.

From the very beginning the case seemed upside down. The defendant was a small woman in her midforties, recently widowed, who lived alone in her house. The two supposed victims spent a great deal of time hanging out in the street in front of her house, smoking dope and causing trouble. At some point, they began harassing her. They would periodically egg her house, vandalize her yard, and stand on the sidewalk and yell obscenities at her.

The assistant district attorney who handled the case was Ashley Rosen. She was someone we had worked with before on numerous occasions. Ashley was very pleasant, reasonable, and an excellent lawyer. In our opinion she was one of the better young D.A.s in L.A. County. The bit about the two victims vandalizing the defendant's house wasn't just supported by the defendant's testimony—we had video of it, which we showed to Ashley. At the very least, the video showed that the victims were far from innocent (as they claimed) and that there was a lot more going on here than simple assault. A few days later, Ashley got back to us and told us that she was proceeding with the prosecution. We could only assume that she was being instructed by people upstairs who hadn't tried a case in this millennium.

The case did go to trial, and on the second day one of the alleged victims took the stand. His testimony was not just bad—it was ludicrous. He contradicted everything he had said in the police report and lied with every answer. During a break, he got off the stand laughing uproariously and went over to Ashley and tried to give her a high-five. At the end of the day, the judge called us to the bench and suggested to Ashley that she tell her supervisor what was happening and that they should consider dismissal. Ashley said she would. The next day she came back and said that her office wanted her to go forward.

This case is a classic example of the evolution of the D.A.'s office in the past two decades. There is no way in hell the D.A. would have proceeded on a case like this fifteen years ago, especially with the judge suggesting a dismissal. At the very least, the D.A. would have realized that the case was no longer winnable and would have dismissed for those reasons.

Instead the case went forward. By the third day, the D.A. had learned that the second alleged victim had been observed in the witness room of the D.A.'s office bragging to a girl about his gang affiliations and flashing gang signs. We also learned on the third day that the first alleged victim had a prior arrest for beating his mother. Again, Ashley went to her superiors and again she was told to continue. The case just kept getting worse and worse. It finally got to the jury after six days. They took less than half a day to return a verdict—not guilty on all counts. The entire trial had reached a point of absurdity, but it apparently fit into the new philosophy of the D.A.'s office. They would rather waste the court's and the jurors' time trying a case they know they will lose than admit they are wrong and dismiss.

A month after that case, we did a trial in Orange County involving a police officer who claimed he was threatened by our client during an arrest and was also kicked by our client's daughter during that same arrest. Our client denied he had threatened anyone and in fact said he was mistreated by one of the police officers. Shortly before trial, the assistant D.A. handling the case found out that not only were two of the police officers in the case contradicting each other about what happened, but one of the police officers was actually suing the other officer over the incident. The one who was suing claimed that the other officer had forced her to go after our client or else face being isolated by her coworkers. By the time all the interviews of the police officers and witnesses were over, three separate and totally different stories had emerged, with each officer calling the other a liar.

We assumed that when all this came out the D.A. in Orange County would dismiss. As a general rule it is never good for the prosecution when their police officers are actually suing one another. The assistant D.A. was a young guy, but he seemed to be reasonable and very smart. We had a hard time believing he was going to go forward with this loser of a case. But on the day of trial, he just shrugged his shoulders and called his first witness. Not surprisingly, our client was found not guilty, and then we subsequently sued the county on his behalf for the false arrest and treatment. The county quickly and quietly paid him a large settlement. All of this was predictable, which made it seem even more remarkable that they had gone forward with the trial.

A couple of weeks later we ran into the assistant D.A. again in the courthouse, and he told us he had just been promoted. We asked him rather bluntly if he was being promoted because he had been willing to try that dog of a case. He just smiled. I don't blame him personally—he was acting on the orders of his supervisors, and he was not authorized to drop a charge on his own. But it is absurd that taxpayer dollars and court time were being wasted on these cases. It is even more absurd that D.A. offices are teaching young D.A.s that it's part of their job to take highly questionable cases to trial.

PROSECUTORIAL MISCONDUCT

The problems go beyond pursuing shaky cases and wasting resources. There is an epidemic of outright prosecutorial misconduct. The more powerful prosecutors have become, the more they see themselves as above the law. Hiding evidence, putting on witnesses they know or strongly suspect are not truthful, and programming witness testimony have become rampant. Winning at all costs has trumped their duty to do justice—and why not? Winning is rewarded—even if it is at the cost of doing the right thing. No one is going to complain. There are just not a lot of defendant advocate groups out there. The public is happy because a supposed criminal is off the street. The head D.A. is happy because the D.A.'s office can point to this as yet another example of the D.A. being tough on criminals. The D.A. assigned to the case is happy because he or she advances in the office. The only loser appears to be the defendant, who nobody gives a damn about anyway.

But there is another loser—the criminal justice system. Every time the rules are bent or broken to accommodate the prosecution's push to convict, the constitutional rights the system is based on are eroded a little more. It also becomes a little easier to use whatever means necessary to convict the next guy. The problem is that the next guy may be innocent.

If all this sounds like the hyperbolic whining of a couple of defense attorneys, let us offer as Exhibit A a trial we did in 2007. The defendant was a man who was being accused of traveling to a foreign country to engage in sexual activities with boys in the age range of fourteen to eighteen years old. The legal age for consent in that country was fourteen, but the United States government had passed a law preventing U.S. citizens from going overseas to participate in sexual activity with anyone under the age of eighteen. The idea was to try to help limit the international sex trade in foreign countries, most notably Thailand.

The assistant U.S. attorney assigned to the case had the ethics of a Somali warlord. At the outset of the case, he failed to turn over important discovery that several of the boys who were alleged victims had gone to court in that country and sworn that nothing happened to them. It got worse: the attorney we had hired in that country had produced a wealth of important information that was extremely helpful to our case. He was obviously going to be the chief defense witness. The prosecutor's solution: he issued an arrest warrant in the United States against the attorney. He conjured up some charges accusing him of trying to interfere with the government's witnesses, an accusation that was later ruled to be totally unfounded. The warrant had its desired effect. There was no way the attorney was going to set foot in America and risk being arrested.

When the judge in the case heard about what the prosecution had done, he blew a gasket, calling it "stupid, stupid, stupid." He was wrong. There was nothing stupid about it—unethical, yes. Against both the spirit and letter of the law, absolutely. But not stupid. The assistant U.S. attorney knew exactly what he was doing. He knew it would work. And indeed over our objection the judge allowed the case to move forward. The judge at least promised that after trial there would be a hearing on prosecutorial misconduct.

After the trial concluded and our client had been convicted, the judge set a hearing to determine if misconduct had occurred. The hearing lasted the better part of a day, with the prosecutor's own witnesses doing him the most damage. The prosecution tried to put together a rather lame timeline that would show that the arrest warrant was not issued in retaliation, but that timeline quickly fell apart under cross-examination. At the end of the hearing, the judge announced his decision. The prosecutor was found to have committed prosecutorial misconduct for using the arrest warrant to dissuade a witness from testifying.

U.S. attorney's offices across the country are very familiar with the charge of dissuading a witness or interfering with a witness—they charge defendants with it all the time. Usually such a charge involves a minimum of a year or two in federal prison. When one of their own was found by a federal judge to have committed the very same action that they have accused so many others of, we assumed they would want to make an example of this assistant U.S. attorney so that other U.S. attorneys would understand the repercussions of this type of behavior.

The Department of Justice did choose to make an example of the prosecutor—it promoted him to become the interim head of the U.S. Attorney's Office in that city. When the prosecutor left the hearing that day, after being found to have committed prosecutorial misconduct, he was laughing with one of his colleagues. It was a joke—he could do whatever he wanted, and the U.S. Attorney's Office would back him up. The message they sent was loud and clear: win at all costs, including committing misconduct.

Years ago we had an extortion trial in L.A. in which, midway through the trial, the complaining witness, whose testimony was essential to the prosecution, was on the stand and, during the direct examination by the government, his answers started to seem a little too rehearsed. His testimony conveniently filled in holes in the prosecution's case, even though the police reports on the case had none of the things the witness was now testifying to. On cross-exam, we very strongly suggested that his testimony was rehearsed at best and perhaps even fed to him by the prosecution.

When the prosecutor got up on redirect, he leapt to his feet and began his questioning with a strong sense of outrage over the insinuation that the witness had been programmed.

"Did anyone tell you what to say today?" he asked, his voice booming throughout the courtroom.

There was a brief pause, about four seconds, and then a very confused-looking witness looked back at the prosecutor and replied, "Yes."

A good lawyer knows to never act surprised by an answer, but the prosecutor was clearly stunned by the witness's response. He had dug a hole with no way out. He could ignore the answer and not ask the obvious follow-up (i.e., just pretend that it was no big deal). But that would mean that the jury was going to see that he was afraid of the answer, and they would wonder exactly what it was that he was so afraid of hearing. The other option was to just ask the question with-out knowing the answer and hope for the best. He opted for the latter approach.

"Who told you what to say today?"

The witness looked even more confused, but this time he didn't hesitate, "Well, you did!"

The whole courtroom erupted in laughter. It was hard to not laugh at such a bizarre turn of events, but it was also maddening. A major government witness had just admitted under oath that he had been told what to say by the prosecution. If the shoe had been on the other foot and it had been a defense witness who had just made that admission, we would have been looking at a contempt hearing and probably state bar discipline. But since it was a prosecution witness, the judge did not even blink an eye, except to wipe away the tears of laughter.

This win-at-all-costs attitude has resulted in some rather original practices. For example, prosecutors will put anyone on the stand now. One of their new tricks is something they've picked up from the ranks of the civil attorneys: hire experts who are willing to say anything. One stands above all others: Park Dietz, who is the current go-to prosecution expert in any case where the defense may claim the ac-cused was insane at the time of the crime. He has testified at the trials of John Hinckley Jr., Jeffrey Dahmer, Joel Rifkin, and Andrea Yates among many others. He almost always takes the prosecution's posi-tion and testifies that the defendant was sane. Jeffrey Dahmer tried to dig up a corpse to have sex with it. Dahmer drilled holes in the heads of some of his victims while they were unconscious and attempted to inject boiling water into their skulls with a turkey baster. He tried to create zombies for sexual gratification. He also ate some of his vic-tims. Dietz testified, however, that he was not really insane, just a sexual deviant. He won over the jury with his knowledge and easy-going manner. They found that Dahmer was not insane at the time of his crimes, and he was subsequently sentenced to prison. As one observer put it at the time, "Exactly how many people do you have to eat in Milwaukee before they conclude you're mentally ill?"

Increasingly we are seeing that when prosecutors decide that someone has committed a crime, nothing will stop their quest for conviction. In the past, they would weigh and consider whether the suspect put forward by the police had actually committed the crime or whether the evidence was strong enough to go forward on a case. A prosecutor would get a case file with police reports and would analyze it for weaknesses or have the D.A. investigator check out the witnesses and verify their stories. Today, the police report is almost never questioned. From the very first court appearance on a case, no effort is made to investigate if the report is wrong—investigators are used only to bolster the police report.

But by far the worst by-product of the win-at-all-costs approach is the willingness to hide evidence that could potentially help the defense. The Supreme Court ruled in 1965, in a case called *Brady v. Maryland*, that the prosecution is responsible for turning over what is known as exculpatory evidence to the defense before trial. Exculpatory evidence is any evidence that would clear or tend to clear the defendant. The defense does not have to make a motion to have the evidence turned over—prosecutors are required to turn it over if they have it or if their agents (police, investigators, etc.) have it.

But turning over evidence helpful to the defense is not a great strategy for prosecutors who are only concerned with winning. Especially since it's a near certainty that they won't be punished for failing to turn over the evidence. There's the simple fact that if a prosecutor hides evidence, there is only a very small chance the defense will ever find out it exists. And even if by some stroke of luck the defense does find out about withheld exculpatory evidence, the courts rarely give the prosecutors more than a simple slap on the wrist. For example, the Innocence Project found that between 2004 and 2008 in the state of Texas, 91 prosecutors had been found by courts to have committed prosecutorial misconduct. Not a single one was disciplined.

In California, an even more extensive study showed that betwe
1997 and 2009, 707 prosecutors had been found by a court to
committed prosecutorial misconduct. Only 6 were disciplined.

The tide may be turning a little bit on this issue, as m
more examples of hiding evidence are being brought to lig
cially in high-profile trials. In the Texas case of Michael N
featured on *60 Minutes*, Morton spent twenty-five years in prison
before DNA testing determined that he was innocent. An alarming
amount of evidence that would have bolstered the defense case had
not been turned over by then-prosecutor Ken Anderson, who is currently a district judge (same old story—win cases, get promoted). But
Anderson is now facing a rare "court of inquiry" that will determine
if his actions violated criminal statutes.

In another high-profile case, Senator Ted Stevens of Alaska was
convicted in an influence-peddling case, only to have the conviction reversed because the United States attorney had withheld evidence. Likewise the United States Supreme Court overturned a
conviction in Louisiana based on eyewitness identification when it
was determined that the prosecution failed to turn over evidence
that the alleged eyewitness had originally told the police he could
not identify anyone. (The vote was 8–1 for overturning the conviction with the only dissenting voice being Clarence Thomas. This is
the same Clarence Thomas who screamed bloody murder that he
was being figuratively lynched at his confirmation hearing because
of false evidence being brought against him. Apparently he has little
trouble with other young men and women being figuratively
lynched.)

There is no single solution to stopping prosecutorial misconduct,
but as Professor Robert Schuwerk of the University of Houston Law
Center put it during an interview in the *Austin Chronicle*, "There must
be a culture change within the prosecutor's office. . . . What needs to
happen . . . is they need to have a different conception of what justice is."

We agree wholeheartedly. A few years ago a former prosecutor who was a friend of ours dropped by the office for lunch. One of our clients, who was charged with embezzling, was at the office as well, so we invited him to go to lunch with us. The client and the former prosecutor struck up a conversation about a number of things and seemed to genuinely hit it off. After the lunch, the former D.A. sat down with us and seemed sincerely surprised that the client was not a monster and in fact was a pretty good guy who had made a mistake. We could tell that this lunch had been a revelation to him—he was so used to demonizing defendants that it had never occurred to him that he could actually be friends with one.

Back in the sixties a proposal was floated that every few years the D.A.s and the public defenders would switch jobs for a year or two so that they could see what the other side was like. Although it would never work logistically, it would probably do both sides a world of good to stand in the other side's shoes for a while.

FALLOUT FROM BEING TOUGH ON CRIME

The public clearly supports prosecutors in their attempt to get tough on crime. After all, who is in favor of crime? It is politically easy to run on a platform of making sure criminals are off the streets for longer periods of time. Any wannabe politician can research and find a case where the defendant got a lighter-than-expected sentence or got out of jail early and committed another crime, and then use that case to claim that our justice system needs to clamp down on crime—despite the fact that violent crime has drastically declined in this country over the past three decades.

We see this constantly in cases where our clients have to plead out. In years past, we could negotiate down sentences with D.A.s, avoid a trial, and give someone a chance to get his or her life back in order. But today when the prosecutors have anything close to a solid case, they often refuse to negotiate at all. Negotiation has become the prosecution telling you what they will offer. Why? Because they can, and they know there are no ramifications. Crimes that used to get you six months in jail now get you two or three years. A crime that was routinely settled at three years now is going to be a minimum of eight years. Prosecutors are convinced that more jail time is always better. And the public is convinced as well.

It is probably fair to assume that many people do not have sympathy for the defense attorney's position. In fact, when we try to explain what is occurring, the general reaction is "So what. Quit whining! Good for them."

However, these changes are having a very dramatic effect on people's lives, and not just in California. The criminal justice system must have balance. When the balance of power shifts too dramatically in the criminal justice system to one side or the other, it affects everyone. It may initially sound good that a criminal got a much stiffer sentence than in the past, but there are many predictable—and undesirable—results.

California is suffering many of the results of a tough-on-crime attitude in the criminal justice system. By declaring that everyone who has committed a crime, even nonviolent minor crimes, should spend years in prison, prosecutors have crowded the jails so much that there is simply not enough room to house inmates. The state budget, already pushed to the max, cannot build more prisons and cannot even afford to staff some of the prisons the state has. The federal government has had to step in and order that a large percentage of the prison population in California, perhaps as much as 20 percent, be released in the upcoming year because the overcrowding has reached epic proportions. Nonviolent prisoners are serving less than 50 percent of their sentences and in some cases as little as 10 to 20 percent. And while California is leading this trend, most of the larger states—and even some smaller states, like Connecticut—are experiencing similar difficulties as well.

Given the current situation in California, you would assume that the district attorney's offices statewide would take a different approach from the one that got us into this mess, making sure that nonviolent criminals, especially those involved in low-level drug crimes, serve less time so they don't take up prison space that would be better used to house violent criminals.

But that is not what is happening. Recently during one week, we had three separate cases involving nonviolent offenders charged with vandalism and drug-related possessions that did not warrant jail time. In all three cases, the D.A.s asked for considerable jail time and refused to budge. Their attitude is pretty simple: overcrowding is not their problem. The truth is that it is very much their problem because they largely created it. They can pass the buck all they want and still try to run on their tough-on-crime mantra, but they created the problem and they refuse to address it. Ironically, the result in many cases is that prisoners end up being released earlier than the sentence that even the defense attorney tried to negotiate for.

The classic example of how this mentality has failed is Riverside County, California. Riverside County is in the middle of what is often referred to as the Inland Empire. Part suburb of Los Angeles, part manufacturing center, and part desert, Riverside has long been considered a conservative, law-and-order county. In 2006, the county bolstered that reputation by electing Rod Pacheco to head the district attorney's office. Pacheco promised that he would push for the maximum sentences possible for lawbreakers. While he served in the assembly, several fellow Republicans reported that he once repeated a favorite line of win-at-all-costs prosecutors: "Any prosecutor can convict a guilty man, but it takes a great prosecutor to put an innocent man in prison."

Pacheco's campaign was pandering at its very worst, but at least he kept his campaign promises. Once elected he ran the D.A.'s office with an iron fist. Offers made to defendants were so out of the norm that his own deputies began complaining. Instead of listening to them, Pacheco would suggest they find other employment. He would offer defendants ridiculous plea bargains and then refuse to negotiate—they could go to trial if they didn't like it. He talked tough and gave the public exactly what it wanted. If ever there was a symbol of being tough on crime it was Rod Pacheco.

Four years later, Pacheco ran for reelection, a foregone conclusion for most D.A.s who have not been involved in some type of scandal. Pacheco, however, was beaten in the primary election by his opponent. How was it possible that a D.A. who ran on a platform of being tough on crime could lose an election for doing exactly what he promised in a county with a law-and-order reputation? Once again unintended consequences came into play. During Pacheco's tenure as D.A., defendants had no reason to plead, because even if they lost at trial they were likely to end up with a better sentence from the judge than what the D.A. had offered them in negotiations. The defendants were better off rolling the dice at trial—there was no downside to losing.

Predictably, the courts became jammed, and if you could get a courtroom there was a good chance that there would not be enough jurors. The chief justice of the state supreme court actually created a strike force of judges to try to reduce the crushing backlog of cases that had crippled not only the criminal courts but paralyzed the civil court system as well. Retired judges were brought in from all over California to cover the overflow of cases. Defendants who had a right to a speedy trial were refusing to waive that right because they knew the D.A.'s office was swamped and unprepared. Cases that were usually won were being lost because inexperienced prosecutors were thrown into trials over their heads or because they didn't have time to prepare. Civil cases were often taking five years or more to get to trial. Child custody cases and other urgent family law matters could not be heard because there were no judges and no courtrooms. And through it all, Pacheco bragged to his constituents about how he was not "coddling criminals."

The Riverside experiment has played out to a lesser extent all over the state of California. D.A.s running for election or reelection drag out the same stale slogans and the same tired speeches about locking away criminals and making the streets safe. We all know the truth now. Not only has this policy made the streets less safe, it has sent a message to criminals: come to California to commit a crime, because we cannot afford to house you any longer. The rest of the country looks at California and wonders how it is that whatever current Hollywood "it girl" gets in trouble and is sentenced to jail, she instead ends up at home within days of sentencing. Why? Because California is tough on crime.

D.A. SCHOOL 101

There is a misconception that D.A.s are not very good trial lawyers. This is a belief held not only by members of the public but often by other lawyers as well. Since our office does civil work as well as criminal, we frequently find ourselves facing civil lawyers from big firms who will challenge us by saying that if we go to trial against them, we will not be facing some low-paid, punk prosecutor who graduated from some C-list law school. It is hard to not laugh in their faces. We have yet to meet an A-list lawyer who is half as good in trial as the prosecutors we go up against every day.

The prosecutor's role at trial can be misleading. It is not flashy; nor is it, in our opinion, nearly as much fun as the defense attorney's job. It requires discipline, patience, and a very steady hand. But to downgrade their ability because of the nature of the job is to make a serious error in judgment. Their job is to present an easily understandable recitation of facts that detail all the elements of the crime, which sounds easy, but it's not. It can be extremely challenging.

Imagine being a prosecutor and finding out one hour before trial that your chief witness for the day is suddenly unavailable, and that the police officer you are also putting on has just been suspended for disciplinary reasons. Or imagine that your chief eyewitness just admitted under cross-examination that he really didn't see what he told the police he saw. Or that your victim tells you over lunch that she has exculpatory evidence that is likely going to result in a mistrial. These things happen to prosecutors every day. Not only do they have to adjust immediately, they have to figure out how to salvage a case that may be beyond repair. It is not an easy job, yet many of them are great at it. In fact, the best trial attorneys we have faced in our careers have all been prosecutors.

Part of the reason that prosecutors tend to be effective is that most D.A. offices put their lawyers through a great deal of training both in and out of the courtroom. Every case is different, but there are common elements in almost all cases, and prosecutors are drilled in how to handle them. For example, there are certain procedures they follow for questioning cops and certain procedures they follow for questioning a coroner. Experienced D.A.s follow these patterns, which allow them to jump from case to case smoothly, sort of like a horse jockey working a day at Churchill Downs. The horses are different for every race, and the jockey has to adjust to each horse's foibles, but in the end he relies on a basic blueprint for every race.

While that makes it easier for prosecutors to operate, it also provides an advantage for the defense. After doing trials for a number of years, you learn that D.A.s have relied on the same seven basic arguments since Cain went on trial for killing Abel. They use some variation of one or more of these arguments in every trial.

Argument #1—Beyond a Reasonable Doubt Is Not That High a Standard

The great fear of all prosecutors is that they can prove a case, just not beyond a reasonable doubt. Thus the solution is to try to get the jury to lower the standard for reasonable doubt in their minds. They do this by explaining that everything in the world is open to some doubt; an old saw is to claim that there can be some doubt as to whether the earth is round. This now frames the very notion of "doubt" as some-thing that the jury needs to, well, doubt. Especially because the jury only has to worry about *reasonable* doubt. Clearly all jurors are reason-able people, are they not? The argument is simple and brilliant, and prosecutors use it all the time when their evidence is shaky.

Argument #2—The Defendant Refuses to Take Responsibility for His or Her Actions

The claim that people need to take "personal responsibility" for their actions is a common one these days, and prosecutors have latched on to it. The way this works at trial is that the prosecution argues that the defendant obviously committed the crime but is so unwilling to take responsibility for it that he or she is wasting everyone's time with the trial. A more accurate statement of what is really meant by this argument would be to say that the defendant has refused to roll over and admit guilt and has actually got the nerve to insist on his or her innocence and go to trial to prove it. Those "excuses" the prosecu-tor accuses the defendant of making are actually alibis that can help prove the defendant's innocence.

Argument #3—The Defense Is Attacking the Victim

No matter how much the defense attorney patty-cakes around the vic-tim during questioning, the D.A. is going to argue how despicable it is that the defense is attacking the victim. He or she is being victimized all over again. The apparent essence of this argument, which is heard in almost every closing argument, is that the alleged victim can get on the stand and trash the defendant, accusing him or her of all kinds of horrible things, but any suggestion that the alleged victim may be wrong or not telling the truth will bring out howls of "How dare you attack the accuser!" This argument questions the right of the defense to cross-examine the victim, which is a bedrock constitutional right. This is infuriating, especially because it so often works. Apparently what we are supposed to do when it comes time to cross-examine the victim is to stand up and thank that person so much for coming into court and for taking the time to testify against our clients.

Argument 4—The Defense Is Attacking
That Poor Police Officer Who Is Neutral in This Case

This argument usually takes the form of a question: Why would the cop lie? The defense suggests the cop is not telling the truth or has added false testimony. Why would this hardworking police officer come into this courtroom and lie about a case? The truth is that police officers are far from neutral witnesses and the D.A. is well aware of it. Their reputation, future promotions, and competency are all on the line when they testify in a case. This is discussed in more detail in Chapter 6.

Argument #5—The Defense Case Is Smoke and
Mirrors Designed to Confuse and Muddy the Waters

At least this argument has the advantage of being true. Yes, the defense is trying to muddy the waters and cast doubt on the prosecution's case. That is how the system was designed—the defense is *supposed* to inject doubt into the proceedings. But according to this argument of the prosecution's, attempts to show that someone else may have committed the crime, evidence that the defendant was at another location at the time of the crime, testimony that the defendant had no motive to commit the crime, cross-examination that shows that the alleged victim has a history of lying are all examples of smoke and mirrors. (On the defense side, we have another name for these things: evidence.) Prosecutors hate the inconvenience of the defense putting on a defense.

Argument #6—The Defense Wants You to Believe
That It Is All a Huge Conspiracy Against the Defendant

In this argument the prosecution lists all the people who testified for them during the trial and then says that, according to the defense, all these people, many of whom don't even know the defendant, are wrapped up in some grand conspiracy with one another to convict this defendant. They *all* lied just to convict this person. Thus the defense is equated with those who believe that 9/11 was planned by the U.S. government or that the moon landing was faked.

This is perhaps the most disingenuous argument of all. First of all, many of the witnesses have little or nothing to say about the defendant—they are just foundational witnesses who are there to get evidence admitted. No one is accusing them of lying. Second, of those witnesses who do testify against the defendant, much of the time we are not accusing them of lying or being part of a conspiracy to get the defendant; we are simply arguing that they are wrong. People make mistakes. There is ample evidence about the unreliability of eyewitness testimony. No one is saying they are lying—we are just pointing out how and why they may have been wrong. The only time this prosecutorial tactic is understandable is in situations where a defense attorney has to accuse more than one or two people of actually lying. And those cases are extremely rare because a good defense attorney will likely not proceed with a case where the defense has to prove a conspiracy.

Argument #7—The Prosecution's Witnesses Can't All Be Saints

In many cases the prosecution witnesses are convicted criminals themselves or have acted despicably. It is not unusual for the D.A.'s chief witness at trial to have been a co-conspirator in the actual crime. Thus the prosecution has to explain to the jury that in criminal trials there will be some witnesses who aren't exactly saints. We always love this argument because they are in a sense apologizing for their own case, which is exactly what we tell the jury. It's a hard argument to make well because if the D.A. has to stand up in front of the jury and apologize for the prosecution's witnesses, then maybe, just maybe, the D.A. has his or her own doubts about the case.

The above tactics aren't the only ones a D.A. has available, however. One of the biggest weapons in the prosecution's arsenal comes in closing arguments. In closing arguments, the prosecution gets to argue first. The defense attorney then gets to do a closing, but the defense attorney gets to address the jury only once. After the defense sits down, the prosecutor gets to argue again, in what is called rebuttal or the closing closing. The law allows the D.A. the last word because the prosecution has the burden of proof. Defense lawyers hate rebuttal because they have to just sit there and not respond, which goes against their DNA.

There's a way for D.A.s to turn this setup even more to their advantage: sandbagging. Here the D.A. gets up and gives a very lukewarm, passionless closing, oftentimes focusing on jury instructions or laying out the elements of the crime in a relatively bland manner. The idea is to not tip the prosecution's hand as to what they are really going to argue. Then, after the defense attorney has finished closing, the D.A. gets up in rebuttal and, like an evangelical preacher at a tent revival, tears into the defendant as if the defendant is the devil incarnate, knowing the defense attorney cannot say a word. And because the D.A. didn't give any indication of what he or she actually intended to argue, the defense attorney's closing didn't address the real substance of the prosecution's argument.

This is not only a perfectly acceptable tactic, it is also an effective one. Sandbagging is now so common that we anticipate being sandbagged at every trial. We tell the jury that when we sit down, here is what they will hear from the prosecution and here is why it is wrong. Furthermore, we often tell the jury that since we can't get up again and rebut the prosecution's argument, we want them to act as defense attorneys and try to see through the holes in the arguments.

EMOTION VERSUS EVIDENCE

As much as we like to goad D.A.s about their robotic, podlike presentations, the truth is that the most dramatic innovation of the past decade is the prosecution's increasing reliance on emotion over evidence. Specifically, we're referring to attempts by the prosecutors to get the jury to make a decision based on how they feel about a case rather than on the facts presented to them.

These are always the shakiest cases, and more and more of these are brought to trial. In the past, the D.A. would not try a case where the prosecution did not have hard-core evidence and instead had to rely on emotion alone. This is not to imply that D.A.s haven't always used emotion in trials to help sway a jury. It is just that they rarely relied mostly or even only on emotion—there was always also a strong evidentiary basis to back it up.

That has changed dramatically. Many trials not only rely heavily on emotion, but the prosecution counts on that emotion to get a conviction because they lack the evidence. For example, if you watch a murder trial today, a pretty good rule of thumb for assessing the strength of the prosecution's evidence is to count how many times they show the picture of the murder victim. The more times they show the picture, the weaker the case.

Take the Conrad Murray case in Los Angeles. It was a tough case because the prosecution was asking jurors to convict a doctor for negligence, rather than for harming his patient intentionally. The prosecution did a very good job presenting the evidence and destroying the defense witnesses, but it was interesting that in the closing arguments they spent a great deal of time focusing on the fact that there were now three children without a father because of Michael Jackson's death. While that is certainly true, it was not evidence of Murray's guilt. The D.A. was likely nervous about getting the conviction, and to make sure he got it, he relied heavily on the three orphaned children. Nothing wrong with that, but this is a recent development in how prosecutors try cases.

And it is a problem in what we call the "he didn't act right" cases. This was the crux of the case against Scott Peterson—he didn't act right for someone whose wife was missing. A defendant's behavior after a crime has been committed has always been fair game for the prosecution. But it is no longer just a part of their case—in many cases it *is* their case. The "he didn't act right" prosecution is now center stage. Major prosecutions are going forward not based on the evidence of a crime, but rather based on the demeanor of the defendant after the crime.

The beauty of this prosecution style is that once the police have identified a suspect, that person's actions—no matter what he or she does—can be presented to the jury as an indication that the suspect committed the crime. It is really quite easy. First, you put a police officer on the stand who has had years of experience investigating crimes. Then you ask if, based on the officer's years of doing investigations, the officer noticed anything unusual about the way the defendant acted. Well, as a matter of fact the police officer did. . . . And then they are off to the races. A subdued, quiet, withdrawn suspect is uncaring and sociopathic. A hysterical, crying, out-of-control defendant is obviously acting out to avoid suspicion. A suspect who won't talk to the police has something to hide. A suspect who talks to the police has a guilty conscience. A suspect who volunteers information must have knowledge of the crime. A suspect who doesn't volunteer information is uncooperative and suspicious.

In short, there is not a single action or reaction a suspect can take or have that cannot be twisted to indicate guilt. And as long as the police officer is willing to get on the stand and testify that the defendant's reaction was unusual or out of the norm based on the officer's experience, then the prosecution gets to argue that the suspect didn't act the way an innocent person would; therefore the suspect must be guilty.

There is no book on how to act, but the prosecution tries to appeal to jurors who will think, "Well that's not how I would react." Maybe or maybe not—you can't know until you have been put in that situation. Of course people can never know for sure how they would react in extreme circumstances, but all the same, jurors are likely to buy arguments that a defendant's behavior seemed "off."

A great example of this was the case of a marine's murder in San Diego. Cynthia Sommer had been married to her husband for approximately seven years when he suddenly died of a heart attack, leaving her a widow with four children. He also left her a $250,000 life insurance policy. According to prosecutors, very shortly after her husband's death, Ms. Sommer began a spending spree that would have been beyond her means before she had the life insurance policy. Most prominently featured in the spending spree was surgery for breast enhancement. According to the prosecution, Ms. Sommer proceeded to spend the grieving period for her husband entering wet T-shirt contests, letting random guys feel her new breasts, and sleeping with a number of young men in a very short time. She was the very definition of a "merry widow."

Unfortunately for Ms. Sommer, a toxicology report came back that indicated that her deceased husband had unusually high levels of arsenic in his liver. She was immediately arrested and charged with poisoning him for financial gain. The prosecution introduced the toxicology report at the trial, but their main focus was not on the science—which was weak—but on the "she didn't act right" evidence. Witness after witness was brought in to testify on her apparent celebration of her husband's death and the fact that she had money to finally live the life she wanted. Front and center to the prosecution's case was the breast augmentation surgery. Cynthia Sommer did not act like a grieving wife should have—therefore she must have killed him. The jury agreed, and she was subsequently convicted of having murdered her husband.

It turned out that the toxicology report had a number of issues with it, not the least of which was that the arsenic in the deceased's liver seemed to be at odds with the tissue samples. A new attorney hired after the conviction, Allen Bloom, arranged for additional testing, and before long it was determined that the toxicology report was dead wrong—it had apparently been contaminated. The deceased was in fact never poisoned and had died of a heart attack as originally thought. After more than two years in jail, Ms. Sommer was released, free to engage in life, liberty, and the pursuit of wet T-shirt contests.

She had been convicted for one reason and one reason only—she didn't act right. Ms. Sommer is a drastic example of the "he didn't act right" syndrome, but go into virtually any courtroom, watch a trial, and you will see examples of the "he didn't act right" syndrome. There is no handbook on how to react if you have not committed a crime—we all react differently to stressful situations. That is why it is ridiculous that prosecutors are allowed to rely heavily on testimony that the defendant didn't react the right way to a tragedy.

CHAPTER FIVE

Judges—At Least Get It Wrong for Both Sides

The most admired judge in America doesn't sit on the Supreme Court, has no real record of jurisprudence, and isn't even a real judge. What she has, though, is ratings. Judge Judy has been ruling from her TV courtroom for more than fifteen years, and for many Americans she symbolizes what the courts should be. She makes her rulings based on good old-fashioned common sense and doesn't have to deal with any pesky lawyers, unpredictable juries, and troublesome things like the law. She is sharp-tongued, theatrical, and able to render a decision after only fifteen minutes of testimony, including commercials. Her judicial philosophy is summed up in the title of her book *Don't Pee on My Leg and Tell Me It's Raining*. It is safe to say she did not plagiarize that from Oliver Wendell Holmes.

Is it silly that she's America's leading judge? Of course. But her show is pretty harmless, other than that it convinces a few of her viewers that when they go into real court they will get a speedy disposition. The very fact that she is the most recognizable judge in the country is actually a positive because real judges should remain obscure—it allows them to rule without fear of being skewered on the front page of the newspaper.

Up until recently, judges in this country did their job in virtual anonymity. Only serious court-watchers or people who got into trouble consistently even knew who their local judges were. But this is rapidly changing. The politicization of the criminal justice system has given rise to judges having to look over their shoulders for fear that even the most innocuous ruling could backfire and produce a front-page newspaper article or a mention on television that would be run over and over in an election campaign against them. For example, setting bail used to be one of the simplest, most formulaic procedures for a judge. In some jurisdictions, the courts have even created what are known as bail schedules that list a recommended bail for each crime (e.g., $250,000 for arson, $500,000 for attempted murder, etc.). The bail schedule acts as a guideline, because all cases are not alike, and there are extenuating circumstances that call in some cases for a lesser amount of bail and in some cases for a greater amount of bail. Requests to increase the bail are frequently made and frequently granted. But these days, granting a request to lower bail below the schedule is a much rarer occurrence. A judge just can't risk that the defendant will make bail and proceed to go commit another crime. The victim's picture would be on the front page of the paper right next to the article detailing how a judge set this person free to go terrorize the community. We call that the *L.A. Times* test: "What would happen if this defendant commited another crime and I landed on the front page of the *L.A. Times* tomorrow?"

That scenario actually plays out one time in ten million, but it is at the forefront of a judge's brain. Why? Because judges have been forced to behave more like politicians, concerned about public opinion and worried that every decision could later be scrutinized and second-guessed if things go wrong. In case they do forget the possible political ramifications, they have the prosecutors there to remind them that this particular defendant could be the one that comes back to haunt them. Frequently the prosecutor's office itself will run one of their own prosecutors against the judge and accuse him or her of being "soft on crime."

We agree that judges should be held accountable—just not by voters. Virtually every state has a judicial performance board that serves as a watchdog for judges whose behavior is inappropriate. It has the power to remove the judge if the behavior is serious enough. For example, in California in the past few years, a judge was removed for fixing traffic tickets for his relatives and friends, while another one was removed for improper sexual contact with a witness. Most judicial governing bodies have a better handle than voters on situations where a judge has gone over the line. In addition, they hopefully understand that being a judge is not a popularity contest.

It pains us to say it, but a judge should not be removed from the bench just because the judge does not agree with us. Nor should a judge be removed if he or she is not the smartest judge in the world or has a nasty judicial temperament. All lawyers have certain judges they would like to see removed, and any lawyer who has practiced long enough has had fantasies about either running against a particular judge or running someone else against the judge.

But a judge should be ruling on a case based on the law, not polls. The founding fathers understood this and made federal judges appointees for life. Some states follow that lead and appoint state judges either for life or for a set term. Some states have a combination system where you are appointed and then you run for reelection in a few years. But a number of states have systems that only provide for the popular election of judges. In those states, it takes two things to win. One is money so that you can afford to put on a campaign to get some name recognition going. The second thing is getting your name listed the right way on the ballot. Since most people walk into a voting booth with no idea who to vote for in a wide-open judicial race, they tend to look at the title of the people listed on the ballot. For example, let's say a ballot lists the following candidates for judge:

> Assistant District Attorney John Baldwin—
> career gang prosecutor
> Assistant Public Defender Judy Johnson—
> ten-year public defender
> Attorney James Pope—corporate lawyer
> Former Assistant District Attorney Sam Watters—
> recently disbarred prosecutor

Who is going to win this race? If you said John Baldwin, then you have obviously been paying attention. Of course the gang prosecutor is going to win—people like electing prosecutors like him to judgeships. Their background is not in coddling criminals, and if you're a prosecutor, you've already shown you don't like criminals. The irony of this is that it means the judiciary in most states is filled almost exclusively with ex-prosecutors. And when people rant and rave about the weak-kneed, crime-loving Marxists who dominate the judiciary, they are actually talking about former district attorneys who have spent most of their legal careers putting away criminals.

The bigger question is who will come in second in our fake ballot. The answer is Sam Watters. After all, he was once a prosecutor, which again goes back to the whole argument that at least at some point in his life he hated criminals. The fact that he was disbarred is irrelevant. Maybe he was disbarred for taking bribes or maybe he was disbarred for shooting his neighbor. Doesn't really matter. As long as the prosecutor label is attached, he is going to pick up a lot of votes.

You might think second place would go to Judy Johnson, the public defender who has spent a lifetime in court and likely knows the law. Yeah, right. A defense attorney—a criminal coddler? Seriously? Even her relatives are voting for the other guys. She would be better off changing her name to Joseph Stalin and running under the flag of the Communist Party. The last president who was a criminal defense lawyer was Abraham Lincoln. If he ran today, he wouldn't even get out of the primary.

The third spot would go to the corporate attorney, although he is not going to receive very many votes, because his candidacy raises way too many suspicions. Why would a corporate attorney be willing to take such a drastic cut in salary? He is either not a very good corporate attorney (e.g., he doesn't drive a Mercedes) or he is just really squirrelly. Either way, he is not judge material.

Once elected, getting reelected used to be a sure thing for judges. A sitting judge is listed as "Judge" on the ballot. People who saw that label in a voting booth figured that if they had no idea who the judge was then he must be doing a pretty good job. People generally vote the status quo on races they know little about. That is why very few people who carry the label "Judge" were ever defeated.

But times are changing. Judges are under greater scrutiny as television, blogs, and newspapers increase their coverage of courts. Greater scrutiny only forces judges to be timid and to find ways to rule that match public opinion. If a judge is going to be challenged in an election, there is only going to be one issue: Was the judge tough enough on crime? Did the judge let someone go who then killed or raped someone? It is the only issue that resonates with voters in a judicial election; potential opponents are going to scour the judge's record and find a case or two where the judge appears vulnerable to the "soft on crime" charge and then repeat that charge over and over. That is how you beat a sitting judge.

In fairness, not all judges concern themselves with reelection. Some don't give a damn and make it a point of pride to dare someone to challenge them. Usually you see this more in the older, established judges who have set their career path. In Los Angeles, we often tell young lawyers and law students to go spend a day watching Judge Elden Fox in Beverly Hills, or Judge Janice Croft or Judge Larry Fidler in downtown Los Angeles. When you watch them in action, you quickly realize that they never think for a second about how they are going to look in the press. And every one of these judges has a single trait you look for in a judge: a very dry wit. There is a definitive correlation between a dry wit and judicial excellence.

Appointing judges and letting them serve until they choose to retire (subject to periodic board review) would create a much fairer system than elections. This would not be a perfect system, of course. In some states the governor makes the appointments, and instead of looking for the best and brightest, the governor is looking for the most well connected. Judicial appointees in these states are sometimes the people who raised money for the governor's campaign, or they are close friends of the people who raised money for that campaign.

Judges appointed to the criminal courts by the governor tend to be mostly prosecutors as well, since that is the safe political move. On occasion, a governor will appoint a public defender, but only after receiving assurances that the public defender will not try to overthrow the government. Interestingly, ex–public defenders often turn out to be the judges who are the most hostile to the defense. This could be because they have dealt with really hard-core criminals for so many years that they've become jaded and burned out. From that point on, every defendant is just another gangbanger, and every story a defendant tells is just another excuse. That doesn't make for a very sympathetic judge. One of the few judges ever removed from the bench in California for misconduct, Judge Robert Furey, was an ex–public defender who was cited for consistently being "punitive and vindictive toward defendants." You really have to go a long way to be removed from the bench for harsh treatment of defendants.

On the flip side, prosecutors often make very good judges. For almost all judicial appointees, putting on that black robe means something. It carries with it a great deal of responsibility and a sense of doing justice that they are acutely aware of. Some of the most rabid and relentless prosecutors become some of the most measured and thoughtful judges. If you ask a group of L.A. attorneys who the best prosecutor they ever saw in front of a jury was, a number would probably answer Harvey Giss. He was a tough-as-nails, take-no-prisoners D.A. (with a great head of hair of which the authors are both extremely jealous). Many believed that he should have been the prosecutor in the O. J. Simpson trial. But when Giss was appointed to the bench in 2001, his entire demeanor changed, and he is now widely respected by both sides. He has an excellent judicial temperament, tries very hard to be fair to all sides, and seems the antithesis of a hard-charging prosecutor.

When they put on a robe, many prosecutors make a very determined effort to be fair to both sides. They are always going to have a prosecutorial bent—they're unlikely to change that after they have been programmed that way for most of their legal careers. But as long as they are willing to listen to the defense, display a little compassion, and try to be fair, we can live with their prosecutorial past.

CAREER PATH

When judges are first appointed or elected in a large city, the likely starting point is some type of misdemeanor arraignment court in some godforsaken dilapidated courthouse at the farthest outreach of the county. The daily docket in one of these courts is usually quite large, with fifty or seventy-five cases a day to be dealt with. There is not a lot of legal analysis or in-depth research being done in these courts. Chaos is actually a goal to strive for. The judge just has to get through it all and try to maintain a semblance of order, because at this level the judge is more like a ringmaster at a circus; his or her performance is based on the ability to keep chaos to a manageable level. The biggest job for the judge is to make sure it all gets done before 5 P.M., which is, not coincidentally, when happy hour begins at most bars.

After a couple of years of crisis management, a judge may get moved to a midlevel position where the chaos is a great deal more controlled. The calendar is reduced to fifteen to twenty cases a day, including some felonies, and some actual law is practiced. Various motions may be filed at this level, and the court may hear several preliminary hearings a day. Preliminary hearings are brief; they often last an hour or less, but they do involve the judge making rulings from the bench on objections, as well as the ultimate decision whether to hold the case over for trial. The last part is not really that difficult, since the standard for holding a defendant over for trial seems to be if he or she appears to be breathing.

If the judge completes a successful stint at this midlevel position, he or she may eventually be promoted to being a trial judge. A successful stint is usually defined as being on the bench for a few years without being arrested or suffering a nervous breakdown, and of course no headlines about having released a killer.

Trial judges have a much lighter calendar, maybe as few as five or as many as fifteen cases a day, because they are often in trial for the majority of the day. For most of the country, trials begin at 8 or 9 A.M. and go until 5 P.M. In California, we take a much more civilized approach. Most trials won't begin until 10:30 A.M. at the earliest in a calendar court, followed at noon by a one-and-a-half-hour lunch break that can often bleed over to nearly 2 P.M. If everything goes well, the court may get another two hours of actual trial time in the afternoon. That doesn't include the twenty-minute afternoon break. California believes that trials, like the wines we produce, need to age a little bit. Lawyers from other states are often shocked to see the length of our trials. We, on the other hand, mock Texas, where a death penalty case is shorter than most California traffic ticket trials.

|||||

A defense attorney looks for three traits in a judge: fairness, a good temperament, and intelligence. Despite the screwed-up system for electing judges, there are a surprising number of judges who embody at least two of these attributes, and sometimes they have all three. We complain among ourselves a lot about judges, but the truth of the matter is that most judges are good at what they do.

Take the Scott Peterson case, which was presided over by Judge Alfred Delucchi. Judge Delucchi was handpicked by California State Supreme Court Chief Justice Ronald George to preside over the case. Judge Delucchi had technically retired in 1998, but he had continued to work, including handling a number of death penalty cases.

Pat: Although Judge Delucchi knew the law, it wasn't his intellect that made him a good judge. He was an old-school judge who based his rulings on an innate sense of fairness and his instincts from having been around for so many years. He was a very kind man who treated everyone with respect, including the defendants, but he also possessed a wicked sense of humor that he loved to use on lawyers who challenged him. He encouraged attorneys to congregate in his chambers to trade insults and stories. He could get angry quickly, but it passed just as quickly. We vehemently disagreed with a number of his rulings in the Peterson case, especially the removal of two jurors. At one point in chambers, he and Mark got into such a bad screaming match that it looked like they were going to come to blows. By the afternoon, they were laughing and talking like nothing had even happened.

He and I would gather in chambers at the beginning of each court day to discuss a very weighty matter: the Oakland A's and the Texas Rangers, our two favorite baseball teams. We would exit chambers, and a number of commentators would make remarks about whether it was appropriate for a judge to be socializing so much with one of the lawyers. But anyone who knew Judge Delucchi knew that such a relationship would never alter his decisions. He loved the camaraderie of the courtroom and the lawyers; they made him come alive.

After the Peterson trial we had several cases in the courthouse where he was sitting, so I often dropped in to say hello. As soon as he would see me in the audience, Judge Delucchi would call a recess and invite me back to chambers. We would never discuss the Peterson case other than me telling him how badly he had screwed it up and that it would almost certainly get overturned on appeal. He would laugh and say that I may be right and that hopefully this time the defendant would get some competent lawyers. We remained friends until he died of cancer in 2008 at the age of seventy-six, four years after the Peterson trial. At his funeral one of the speakers said it best—he was a good judge but a better man.

It is the rare judge that does not embody at least one of the three attributes. Most people might assume that of the three, the one we would covet most would be intelligence. While intelligence is important, it is the sense of fairness that we value most. We are happy with a judge who may not be the most even-tempered or is not the most intelligent judge around, as long as the judge is getting it wrong for both sides.

There are a number of judges who possess nothing more than a pleasant judicial temperament, and frankly there is a lot to be said for that. Walking into a courtroom on a daily basis is stressful enough— you are dealing with difficult issues and nervous clients. If the judge is pleasant and accommodating to all parties, it makes the entire experience go much smoother. Many court appearances just involve dealing with procedural issues, which usually have to do with scheduling. Sadly, there are a few judges who can take a hearing on the simplest scheduling issue and turn it into an exercise in showing they are in control.

That's why a judge with a great demeanor makes such a difference, even if that judge is not the smartest or even if you know that judge has not granted a defense motion in fifteen years on the bench. Such a judge will listen intently to your argument, smile a lot, nod, and then tell you what a fine job you did arguing and how lucky your client is to have you. Then the judge will rule against you. It can be frustrating because you know the ruling is incorrect, and you know the judge doesn't understand the law, but you can't be really mad at judges like that, because they are just so darn nice about it.

The ones that drive us nuts are the judges who are smart, know the law very well and understand how it should be applied, but seem to have an agenda. They twist the law to reach a disingenuous result. Nothing upsets a defense lawyer more than a judge who pretends to be listening, asks a number of relevant questions that indicate he or she knows the law, and then issues a decision that is clearly not based on the law but rather on the judge's fear of being in the newspaper or of alienating the D.A.'s office. The intellectually dishonest ones are the judges who drive us crazy. We would have a lot more respect for a judge who skipped the pretense and instead just called us to the bench, looked us in the eyes, and told us that he or she couldn't afford to find in our favor and have it backfire.

And then there are the judges who are just nasty from the minute you walk into the courtroom. Unpleasant, controlling, and condescending, these judges scare the hell out of young lawyers and send them scurrying back to their cubicles vowing never to enter a courtroom again. We have seen judges reduce lawyers to tears—and even cause one lawyer to be carted off in an ambulance.

Pat: When I was just starting my legal career, at the Nashville Metropoliton Public Defender's Office, my supervisor Laura Dykes and I had been sitting in a courtroom together watching a particularly nasty judge insult a trio of lawyers, and I was next on the chopping block. Laura leaned over to me and went through the list of all the things judges could legally do to a lawyer—yell at you, insult you, embarrass you, stare menacingly at you, and tell you to sit down and shut up. She then went over the list of things that judges couldn't do—beat you or have you beaten, maim you, imprison your family, disbar you for incompetence, or make you stay after court and write on the blackboard. The point was clear: the worst single thing a judge can do is to wound your ego a little and make you walk out of the courtroom a little embarrassed. Once you realize this, it becomes possible to tune them out when they try to bully you— the best thing to do is just smile at them and not engage. (Luckily, I have noticed that as my hair has gotten grayer, judges are a lot more reluctant to raise their voices at me. Sort of a court version of a senior citizen discount.)

Some lawyers do get into shouting matches with judges, mostly as a natural response to being yelled at. The problem about getting into a fight with the judge is that the lawyer is always going to lose. Last year I was in front of a judge who wanted to revoke my client's bail for no good reason he was capable of articulating. I began arguing that the evidence against my client was flimsy and that there was absolutely no reason to lock him up when a reasonable bail had already been set. The judge refused to listen and I got madder and madder. After twenty minutes of heated back-and-forth, I shut up, very satisfied to have gotten the last word. Except that I hadn't. The last word was the judge, having waited for me to stop talking, then ordering my client to be handcuffed and taken into custody.

Cranky judges frighten many lawyers, but we take a more nuanced view. We don't care if the judge is cantankerous or a curmudgeon or slams us, just as long as he or she is an equal opportunity slammer. If a judge is going to light into us for doing something the judge considers wrong, that judge better darn well do it to the prosecutor if the D.A. makes the same mistake. What infuriates us is a judge who plays tough guy with the defense and then rolls over for the prosecution like a dog wanting to get its stomach scratched.

Several times a year, this will happen over the issue of continuances. If either side wishes to delay a preliminary hearing or a trial, they ask the judge to continue the matter (i.e., they ask for a continuance). For the most part, continuances are granted routinely, but sometimes we run into judges who take these requests as a personal affront or a sign of some sinister plot by the defense. They will do a two-minute rant about the defense and how there will be no more delays and how this is a defense tactic that will not be allowed. The funny thing is that judges don't always know which side asked for the continuance. It is always amusing to see a judge rant about the defense stalling by asking for a continuance and then be informed that it was in fact the prosecution that asked for the continuance. At this point an amazing transformation takes place that rivals Saul on the road to Damascus. The heretofore nasty judge suddenly becomes docile and gently inquires of the D.A. how much time the prosecution needs to get ready and if there is anything else the D.A. requires.

One of the great curmudgeonly judges of all-time was Leslie Light. Judge Light played no favorites—he yelled and screamed at everyone: prosecutors, defense attorneys, defendants, jurors, victims—it didn't matter. He was an incredibly bright judge who knew the law well, but he had little patience for lawyers and would frequently interrupt them while they were questioning a witness and begin asking the questions he wanted to hear.

Judge Light was also party to one of the most unintentionally funny moments we've ever seen in a courtroom. He was the judge in the first Susan McDougal trial in Santa Monica, and he was determined to maintain control within his courtroom even though it was a circus outside. When the trial began, Susan had just been released from jail, having served twenty-two months for being in contempt of a federal court order.

During this highly emotional trial, her emotions frequently got the better of her, and she would make inappropriate facial gestures, get into verbal arguments with the prosecutor, or just act out. Judge Light exhibited great patience and repeatedly warned her on two or three occasions to temper her behavior or face the consequences. Finally, about midway through the trial, Judge Light had seen enough. On this particular day Susan had become angry at something the D.A. had said, and she slammed the palm of her hand down on the counsel table, the noise reverberating throughout the courtroom. The judge was furious. He sent the jury back to the jury room and then began screaming at Susan. He got increasingly angry and then issued the ultimate threat. If she did one more thing, he was going to find her in contempt of court and put her in jail for twenty-four hours.

Right after he made the threat, he took a brief pause to let it sink in. As he did, a wave of muffled laughter began rising in the audience. It soon began to grow, and eventually most of the crowd in the courtroom was laughing out loud. It didn't take long for Judge Light to realize what was going on. This was a woman who had just spent twenty-two months in jail for contempt. Twenty-four hours was not much of a threat. As the laughter in the courtroom increased, Judge Light put his head down on the bench and kept it there for a good ten seconds. It was hard to tell if he was laughing or crying.

As a postscript, we volunteered to bring a cattle prod to court and zap Susan every time she got out of line. It was obvious from the look on Judge Light's face that this idea held some appeal.

One of the more amusing things to watch in court is when a judge with a less than sunny disposition magically turns on the charm when jurors walk into the courtroom. It borders on bipolarity. Within thirty seconds of dressing down one of the attorneys, the judge will have the jury ushered in and instantly assume the role of genial father or mother figure as well as wise mediator. Sort of a judicial Ward or June Cleaver. The attorneys sit with a bemused smile as the judge, who had been impatient with both sides, now patiently, almost lovingly, lays out the procedures, answers questions, tells the usual jokes, and gives a short, patriotic speech on jury duty. In return, jurors almost universally love judges. They laugh at even the bad jokes (as do smart lawyers), and they hang on every word the judge says.

This is why we instruct younger attorneys to always treat the judge with ultimate respect in front of the jury and to not appear to be at odds with the judge. Jurors often look at the judges for clues as to which way they are leaning, because they are sure that judges know what is really going on. By antagonizing the judge in front of the jury, not only do you look as if you are on the opposite side, but you appear to be picking a fight with Ward or June.

JUDICIAL MISCONDUCT

Given the wide spectrum of possibilities for misbehaving, there are actually remarkably few incidents of judicial misconduct. Donning the robe does have an effect on people—there really is a sense of greater responsibility that we believe most judges feel. Judges are held to a very high standard by judicial commissions across the country, and on the whole they act accordingly. A prosecutor or defense attorney can get away with things in court that a judge cannot, because the judge is the neutral party. For example, a prosecutor or defense attorney can make a sarcastic remark about a witness in front of the jury. A judge making the same remark will likely get into trouble.

When judges go off, though, they make it count. Judge Richard "Deacon" Jones of Nebraska was removed from the bench for throwing firecrackers into a colleague's office and for signing court orders with names like Adolf Hitler and Snow White. He was also alleged to have set bail for defendants at amounts like thirteen cents or a zillion penegots. This is why we love being trial lawyers—you just can't make this stuff up.

In Lakeland, Washington, a judge was presiding over a driving while intoxicated trial. While the jury was deliberating, he went out and bought a twelve-pack of beer. After they reached a verdict, he invited the jury into chambers to have a drink with him. As he left to get into his car that night, someone suggested that maybe he shouldn't drive, to which he is alleged to have said, "I always drink and drive."

Another judge we used to regularly appear in front of never offered any of us beer, but he did not hide that he was imbibing. He had a cooler under the bench, and every so often you would hear the top of a beer can being popped open and shortly thereafter a cup would appear on the bench. He would appear to go through more than a dozen beers a day. Amazingly, he was still smarter at a .20 blood alcohol level than most of the attorneys who appeared before him.

On the more serious side, judicial misconduct can take the form of abuse of authority. This covers a lot of potential bad behavior, from being exceptionally belligerent with attorneys to having sex with defendants in exchange for lesser terms. The latter accusation was made in a famous case in Los Angeles involving a judge, George W. Trammell III, whom we had been appearing in front of for years. Judge

Trammell, a twenty-six-year veteran of the bench, was presiding over a criminal case in Pomona in 1996 against alleged gambler Ming Ching Jin and his wife, Pifen Lo. Ms. Lo eventually pled guilty to charges of counterfeiting and money laundering and was sentenced by Judge Trammell to five years' probation, a sentence the prosecution felt was too light. A few months after she pled, a jury convicted Jin of kidnapping and he was facing life in prison. As Jin was awaiting sentencing, Judge Trammell brought Ms. Lo into his chambers and suggested that the best way to get her husband's sentence reduced was to have sex with the judge. Lo consented, which began a months-long sexual relationship through the sentencing process. However, at some point Jin found out what was going on with his wife and the judge and reported it. Judge Trammell quietly resigned from the bench before the judicial commission could hear the case. But that was not the end of Judge Trammell's problems. Federal officials stepped in and used an obscure mail fraud statute to charge Trammell with the use of the mail to execute a "scheme to defraud the people of the state of California of their intangible right to his honest services as a judge." Trammell ultimately pled guilty and was sentenced to eighteen months in a federal prison.

The most common occurrence of judicial misconduct, however, is entirely banal: ticket fixing. Judges inevitably have to face friends and family members asking them to fix a traffic ticket. Incredibly, despite the fact that a number of judges have been removed from the bench for doing just that, every year you read about another judge somewhere who just couldn't resist.

CHAPTER SIX

Police Officers—
to Preserve, Protect, and to Lie

Cops lie. Every day in courtrooms across America, police officers raise their hands, swear to tell the truth, and then lie. Everyone in the court system knows it, but if questioned about it they will vehemently deny it. It is as much a part of the proceedings as the judge's black robes. Harvard law professor Alan Dershowitz even coined the phrase "testilying" to characterize the practice. It's an open secret that no one wants to talk about because we all appreciate our police officers and their willingness to put their lives on the line for us every day. No one wants to call cops liars.

So why is a system that relies on the truth willing to overlook police officers lying in court? The reason is simple. Cops are not lying for personal gain, nor are they lying to be malicious. In fact, it is just the opposite. They are doing it because they see it as the right thing to do—lying in court is morally justifiable if it helps take a criminal off the street.

And we should not be surprised that cops lie. When they arrest someone, they do it because they feel that person has committed a crime. To question that arrest is to question their ability and integrity. Yet that is exactly how our system works—a defense lawyer is going to get up and question why the cop did one thing instead of another, why the cop thought this instead of that, and why the cop wrote down one thing in a report and said another thing on tape. A cop on the stand believes that he or she arrested the right person, and the cop knows that getting this person convicted is for the public good. But now the cop has to sit on the stand and listen to a defense attorney— who has no idea what it's really like on the streets—question his or her judgment and recollection? It is even more tempting if it appears that the case that seemed so good on paper does not look so good in the courtroom. What can it hurt to throw in a couple of extra facts or to "remember" something suddenly? After all, the defendant is a scumbag, and even if the defendant did not do this crime, the scum-bag has no doubt committed others. The main thing is to get the criminal off the streets—isn't that what the cop's job really is?

Most cops don't much care for a process that allows non-cops to second-guess their work. They sure don't like it when some smart-ass lawyer questions them about what they did and didn't do during their arrest and investigation. Imagine being an accountant and having your audits dragged into court, subjected to questioning by a skeptical attorney, and ultimately judged by twelve non-accountants. Most cops signed up for the job to fight crime (while getting to carry a gun and drive a car really fast), not to have their work ridiculed in court. Thus, if they can clean up any problems with their investigation by adding a few previously undisclosed facts to a case during their testimony, they feel they are justified in doing so.

The smart cops merely fudge the facts a little. For example, the prosecution will question an officer about what he or she saw or heard at a crime scene or during its aftermath. The defense attorney will then get up and try to test the cop's testimony. The easiest way to poke holes is to point out certain things that the officer failed to write in the police report. Obviously an officer can't write down everything in a report or it would resemble a Tolstoy novel. But sometimes officers leave out important details in the report, and a good defense attorney will pounce on that.

That is when the magic of what we refer to as police memory syndrome, or PMS, appears. Confronted with a gap in his or her written record, the officer will have a sudden memory of the criminal act or witness account. Even though the cop is often being asked about events that took place more than a year prior and with hundreds of cases in between, a police officer under the spell of PMS will be able to magically fill in all the gaps in the prosecution's case. (We should note that this doesn't happen just with cops—watch any divorce proceeding to see how aggrieved spouses can magically recall picture-perfect details while fighting over who gets custody of the Crock-Pot.)

For example, an assault with a deadly weapon case we did turned on whether the defendant actually pointed a gun at the victim. When the victim was first interviewed by the police, she never mentioned that the gun was pointed at her. In fact, her memory was that it wasn't pointed at her. Later on down the line, when interviewed by the D.A., the victim remembered that the gun was pointed at her, so the D.A. charged the defendant with assault with a deadly weapon. The problem was that the police officer's initial report didn't say anything about the gun being pointed at the victim. Not to worry, though, because the officer's memory was about to improve:

Pat: Officer, isn't it true that the witness never told you that the gun was pointed at her?

Officer: No. That is not true. The witness did in fact tell me the defendant pointed the gun directly at her.

Pat: Officer, can you please show us where in this rather detailed six-page report you wrote that the witness told you the defendant had pointed the gun at her?

Officer: It is not in the report, but I have a vivid memory of the victim telling me that the defendant pointed the gun at her.

Pat: C'mon, Officer! Wouldn't that be a rather important detail to have written in your report?

Officer: In retrospect, I should have, but I can tell you that as I sit here today I know that she told me the gun was pointed at her.

Pat: Isn't it true that the reason you have such a clear memory today is because the prosecution needs you to remember it that way in order to make their case?

Officer: No, sir. That is not true.

The cop didn't lose any sleep over his testimony because he viewed the defendant as some scumbag who pulled a gun, so he should be in jail. The D.A. wasn't going to challenge his sudden memory because it benefitted the case. We harped on the PMS in the closing statement, but a lot of times jurors don't really care at what point the cop came up with the memory: the main thing is that he has the memory.

Cops can start building a case for the prosecution before it gets to trial. Most interviews are not recorded, so we have to rely on the police version of what the person said. Oftentimes the written record left by cops leaves a lot to be desired, especially if they are looking to slant a report against a defendant they believe is guilty. That is why we tell clients that they should never talk to the police. The police are trained to be really nice and helpful, especially to naïve suspects, while they are simultaneously busy screwing them over.

As an example, let's take a fictional case where a man has been accused of robbing a bank. He denies it and is interviewed by a skeptical police officer who is already convinced of his guilt:

Question One

> **Police officer:** Where were you at 2:35 P.M. last Tuesday?
>
> **Suspect:** Gosh, that is a while ago. I think I was either eating lunch at the diner or I was shopping at a jewelry store looking for a present for my wife.
>
> **Officer writes in report:** Suspect cannot confirm whereabouts at time of robbery.

Question Two

> **Police officer:** Have you ever been to the Bank of America on Third Street?
>
> **Suspect:** Sure. I used to have an account there, but I shut it down about six months ago when they started charging five dollars for use of debit cards. I couldn't afford that because I am living on a tight budget and I thought it was unfair.
>
> **Officer writes in report:** Suspect admits to having animosity toward the bank over past dealings and left the bank very upset. Furthermore, suspect reports being in desperate financial straits. Appears to have strong motives for bank robbery and for targeting this particular branch.

Question Three

> **Police officer:** Have you ever robbed a bank?
>
> **Suspect:** Good Lord, no! The closest I have ever come to robbing a bank was watching movies about bank robberies. I like some of those old heist movies. I wouldn't even know how to rob a bank other than what I have seen in the movies.
>
> **Officer writes in report:** Suspect apparently spent a substantial amount of time researching bank robberies and plotting the crime. Admits that his research has aided him in learning how to pull off robbery.

Question Four

Police officer: Sir, do you use drugs?

Suspect: No, not at all. I smoked some pot in college and tried cocaine at a party once, but that's it. Nothing in the past fifteen years.

Officer writes in report: Suspect has a history of drug usage.

So what the prosecutor now has and what the jury will hear is that the suspect/defendant has no alibi, has a strong motive, researched the crime, and is a drug abuser. The poor sap is headed for three to five years in state prison. If you think this example is exaggerated, ask anyone who has ever been interviewed by a police officer what they said and then read the report.

It would leave a false impression to say that cops lie in every situation. Some cases don't need that extra push. Or frequently experienced cops who have testified many times also understand how to best handle cross-examination without using PMS. They know what looks good to a jury. Whereas a younger cop will often try to match wits with you or fight you over every detail of a report and add in a little PMS, an older cop knows that the best testimony often concedes the defense attorney some points while focusing on the big picture. Juries like cops who are willing to admit that a mistake or two was made. A smart cop knows that mistakes are made at every crime scene, and a good defense attorney will point it out to the jury. The cop looks best if he acknowledges the mistakes. Just because mistakes are made does not mean the defendant did not commit the crime, and the smart cop makes sure the jury understands that.

We understand why cops lie, and interestingly it sometimes backfires and ends up helping the defense. It's difficult to keep a lie straight on the stand, and there's nothing better for the defense than catching a cop in a lie. Of course the D.A. doesn't want the jury to even consider the possibility that a cop isn't telling the truth, so in almost every case we'll hear a version of this line:

"The defense is essentially saying the cop is a liar. Now, why would this police officer, an eight-year veteran of the LAPD, lie about this matter? He doesn't know the defendant—he has no personal grudge against him. So ask yourself, why would he get on the stand and lie about something that makes no difference to him?"

Of course, this is total BS. If a cop makes an arrest, that cop is invested in a case. People in general don't like to be shown they made a mistake on the job, and it can be particularly humiliating when it's revealed in front of twelve people sitting in judgment and a packed courtroom. Second, a police officer's career advancement depends heavily on his or her ability to make a strong case and present it in a courtroom to obtain a conviction. A cop who loses in court repeatedly is a cop with very little advancement potential. Finally, cops are every bit as competitive about a case as the attorneys. They want to win—we all do. Just like the attorneys, they believe in their case and they believe they are doing the right thing. It is incredibly disingenuous for the D.A. to act as if a cop has no investment in the case—they know better.

A classic example was a truly bizarre case we had involving a lesbian cop, a hate crime allegation against a high school principal, and the stealing of some lawn sprinklers. Our client was a high school principal with an impeccable reputation whose career had been on a meteoric path. He lived at the end of a cul-de-sac in the quiet suburb of Santa Clarita in Los Angeles County. Across the street was a lesbian couple, one of whom was a police officer. At some point they got into a dispute about where he parked his cars, so the couple turned their lawn sprinklers on his vintage car, ruining the paint. He retaliated by taking their lawn sprinklers and discarding them, which they videotaped and turned over to the police.

The sheriff's department assigned one of their best police officers to the case, Detective Todd Anderson. Detective Anderson is a stand-up guy with a good reputation among attorneys for being very professional. If the alleged victim had not been an LAPD officer, there is no way a detective, especially one of his caliber, would have been sent to investigate this silly neighborhood dispute. Under normal circumstances the police would have told the couple to fill out a police report and quit playing around with sprinklers.

But the case took on a life of its own. First, Detective Anderson interviewed the principal and the two men developed a mutual dislike for each other almost instantly. Second, he interviewed the LAPD officer and was not all that crazy about her either. But Anderson filed his report and sent it to the D.A. Somehow it ended up in the Los Angeles County District Attorney's Office Hate Crime Unit. Incredibly, taking the sprinklers (which the principal never denied) had been elevated to a hate crime punishable by up to a year in jail. After the news of the principal's arrest for the hate crime hit the papers, his career was over. No school district will hire a guy charged with hate crimes.

As the case headed to trial, we spoke to Anderson a lot and could tell he was not overly enthusiastic about the case. But when the trial started he locked in and fought us every step of the way. He was competitive, and he wanted to win even if it was not his favorite case. He had also invested a lot of time and energy into putting the case together and interviewing witnesses, so it was not as if he didn't care what happened with the case. Of course he cared—cops always have a dog in the fight.

After hearing the evidence and especially after seeing the testimony of the alleged victim, it took the jury about ten minutes to acquit the principal of the hate crime. As a postscript to the case, he asked us if he could sue the neighbors for malicious prosecution. We advised him against it and told him to pick up the pieces and try to go on with his life. One day after telling him that, our office received notice that the next-door neighbors were actually suing him, asking for several hundreds of thousands dollars. We were stunned that after getting beaten once they wanted to go back for round two. So we decided to countersue them and tee the case up again, this time in civil court. On the eve of the civil trial, the judge took both parties into chambers and tried to get them to settle. The judge told us that we should just pay them $5,000 in nuisance value for the case to go away. He further explained that juries in that particular courthouse did not award large fees, especially in a countersuit.

Despite his warnings, we took the case to trial. Amazingly, the couple partially blamed the loss in criminal court on Detective Anderson and the L.A. County D.A.'s Office, both of whom had gone to bat for them in the criminal case. The jury came back with an award of $600,000 for the principal, the largest award for a countersuit in that courthouse's history. The money was certainly nice, but his neighbors had effectively ended his career and nothing could give that back to him.

WHAT POLICE OFFICERS REALLY DO

The reality of police work is a great deal different from what most people imagine or what is portrayed in the media. In most cases, police don't solve crimes as much as they write reports. If you want a reality check, call the police when your car or laptop gets stolen. If you have watched *CSI* for several years, you may assume that the police will show up and start by taking photos of the crime scene. After that, they will begin dusting for fingerprints and searching the floor for any possible DNA-related materials. Then they will bring out the ultraviolet light to make sure there is no other evidence present. After they leave, they will scour the neighborhood interviewing witnesses. Then they will take the collected evidence back to the police lab, where they will process the information through a series of computer programs until they produce a list of potential suspects. The suspects will be interviewed until the cops determine which one is the culprit, at which point that person will be arrested and charged.

In reality, when you call the police about the theft, they will likely tell you to just come down to the station and fill out a report. No one will be showing up at your home with fingerprint kits and light shows. If they do come to your home, they will stay for about ten minutes, long enough to get the basic facts and write a report. They will then leave and tell you that if they hear anything they will call you. They are blowing you off. Much like the time the European model in the bar took down your phone number and then said she would call you, you are getting the kiss-off. Except the odds are actually better the European model will call.

This is not to suggest that police work is not dangerous—it is. In fact, some of the smaller cases can be the most dangerous. A call to a domestic violence situation can result in the police being attacked by one of the participants, sometimes fatally. Likewise, even a simple traffic stop can turn into a life-threatening situation if the driver of the car has an outstanding arrest warrant out and is determined to not go to jail.

Cops spend their time and resources focusing on larger crimes, usually the ones involving violence and a threat to human life. However, in the past decade, more and more cities are going to a concept called "community policing," where police try to assign officers to the smaller crimes, such as prostitution, graffiti, and vandalism, as a way to improve the quality of life in a community. It will be interesting to see in the years ahead if this is just a passing fad or a new wave of police work.

When a complicated investigation is necessary, cops have a go-to move: arrest them all and let the courts sort them out. Often when the cops arrive on the scene of a fight or other dispute, there are a number of witnesses there all eager to tell the cops their story. The stories rarely match up and are usually contradictory, so the officers will go around and question a number of the people to see if they can get a clear picture. Having failed to do that, they will just arrest all the main players on both sides. The courts will take it from there.

The same can also be true of a large white-collar corruption investigation. If it is unclear who is responsible, the thinking is again to just arrest anyone connected and let it get sorted out by the lawyers.

People assume that because of our cross-examinations of cops we must hate them or that we and the police are enemies. Not at all. They have a tough job and we respect them for it, and we tend to get along well with the vast majority of cops we deal with on a regular basis. We are often invited to speak at police conventions and have even been asked to work with officers to help train them in what to expect on cross-examination. In fact, young defense lawyers are often surprised by the amount of cooperation that goes on between the defense and the investigating officers on a case. In a case we did in San Francisco concerning the San Francisco Zoo (discussed in greater detail in Chapter 8), it was the lead investigating officer who contacted our office and told us the shenanigans that the zoo officials were up to in trying to frame our clients. San Francisco police inspector Valerie Mathews, a terrific example of courage and honesty, refused to go along with what she was being told to do but instead called our office and told us what was happening. The result was that we prevented the zoo from pressuring the D.A. to file a case against our clients.

POLICE MISCONDUCT

When people think about police misconduct, things like the Rodney King beating come to mind. But gratuitous abuses of power like that are not that common. The most common form of police misconduct is forced confessions. Without a doubt the single best piece of evidence a prosecutor can have in a case is a confession. An eyewitness may be a full house in a trial, but the confession is the royal flush. It is the rare jury that will find a defendant not guilty after they learn he confessed to a crime. And why not? Why would someone admit to a crime he didn't commit? In fact, most lawyers won't even go to trial with a client who has confessed—it is a lost cause.

Yet, in the past few years, the Innocence Project has used scientific evidence (mostly DNA typing) to free more than 295 men who were wrongly convicted of crimes ranging from rape to murder. In an astounding one-third of those cases, the defendant confessed even though he was not guilty. Most of these men were not scared kids or first-time offenders—they were full-grown men who knew their rights. In the opening chapter of this book, we detail the case of the Norfolk Four, the tough navy seamen who all confessed to a rape/murder that they knew would put them away for the rest of their lives.

Why do people confess to crimes they didn't commit? It comes down to police interrogation techniques. Police certainly have a right to question a suspect, and they have a right to grill that suspect very hard. But that is different from what happens when an officer coerces a confession from a person.

To begin with, most people are intimidated by police officers and the power they have. Combine that with being taken by one or two police officers into a small windowless room, and the suspect is already at a huge disadvantage. If the person asks about getting a lawyer, the cop often says, "Why do you need a lawyer if you didn't do anything? Only guilty people need lawyers." People feel that if they ask for a lawyer they are in a sense confessing, which is rather ironic when you consider what is about to happen.

After a few minutes of questioning to see whether the suspect will confess easily, the cop then turns to his best weapon—lying. Cops are allowed by law to lie to suspects, and they will use this to the fullest. The most common tactic is to tell the suspect that the police have already piled up other evidence of guilt. An eyewitness has identified the suspect. A video at the scene shows the suspect prominently in it. The smart thing for someone in this position to do, the cops will say, is to just admit to committing the crime, and the cops will promise to help. They will talk to the D.A.'s office and tell them to go easy on the suspect because he or she was so stand-up about the whole thing. Conversely, if the suspect doesn't confess, then the hounds of hell will be released and there is nothing the police can do.

This doesn't go on for fifteen minutes and stop. It goes on for hour after hour after hour. Sometimes you get a little food, sometimes you don't. You are not allowed to sleep no matter how tired you get, and these interrogations often go late into the night or early morning. People are alternately yelling at you and trying to reason with you. They are telling you that you may get the death penalty or rot in a horrible prison for the rest of your life unless you cooperate. It seems it will never end. However, it will end if you just do one thing—sign the confession. It takes an extremely strong person to stand up to twelve or thirteen hours of this kind of mental torture. As one senior deputy put it, "Give me enough time and I'll have 'em confessing to a crime that was committed before they were born." By the end of the night, a lot of people just sign the confession to get out of there, assuming they can correct it later.

The other most common form of police misconduct is planting evidence. This is a little less insidious because, at least in California, jurors are aware that there are bad cops planting evidence. There have been a number of high-profile cases in the newspapers and on television where rogue police officers were nailed trying to frame defendants. The most famous of these cases is known as the Rampart case, which rocked the city in the late 1990s. Rampart was the name of a police station and was a street near downtown Los Angeles. A newspaper investigation brought to light that a number of cops were running wild in the streets there, planting drugs and guns on people they didn't like or whom they could extort. There were even allegations of contract killings and horrible beatings.

As with PMS, evidence-planting is often done with what the cop views as the right intentions at the time. Cops are not planting evidence on shoplifters or DUI drivers. They are planting it on gang members or drug dealers because, frankly, they can't catch them committing a crime. An experienced drug dealer is not going to be stupid enough to do something that a cop can easily see or record. So the cop simply pulls him over and looks in the trunk, where, as it turns out, there is a ton of cocaine ready to be sold. It is not hard to tell cases where the evidence has been planted. In that example, everyone knows the drug dealer is not going to be dumb enough to drive around with the drugs in the trunk. But the cop knows there is very little the dealer can do. He can protest, but who is going to believe some sleazy drug dealer?

On more than one occasion, we have represented a person accused of being a major drug dealer who was either a very low-level pot salesman or not even selling drugs at all. Drug busts draw headlines and cops get promotions, so it is very easy for them to jump the gun or see what they want to see. Our experience is that every major drug bust announced by the FBI and local law enforcement has turned out to be considerably less than what was announced on the day of the bust. Sometimes it has turned out to be nonexistent.

There is no question that police administrators take police misconduct investigations more seriously than in the past, but the code of silence among rank-and-file officers prevents most misconduct from ever being reported. If a cop plants a potential defendant's face in the concrete because he didn't like the guy's attitude, his partner is not going to contradict the ensuing police report that states the defendant struggled with the officers and then accidentally fell face-first into the sidewalk. The code of silence among officers is widespread and virtually impenetrable. Ironically, law enforcement officials have for decades complained about organized crime and the cultural attitude known as "omertà," wherein members of the mob refuse to snitch on anyone to law enforcement even if they are falsely accused of a crime. But the mafia code of omertà pales in comparison to the police "blue shield."

We get hundreds of calls a year from people claiming to have been physically abused or sometimes sexually abused by police officers. Many of these calls are clearly from people with overactive imaginations, but even with the ones that are credible, there is often very little we can do, since the accusation usually boils down to the word of the accuser (oftentimes someone who has a criminal record) versus the word of a police officer. District attorneys work very closely with police officers, and unless there is substantial evidence against the officer, they are going to roll their eyes at any accusation.

In 2008, we got a firsthand look at how the blue shield works in a case the international media dubbed "the Japanese O.J." because of the insane amount of media attention it had garnered in Japan. The defendant's name was Kazuyoshi Miura and he was a well-known businessman in Japan. In 1981, Miura and his wife were visiting Los Angeles as tourists and were snapping pictures of buildings in an alley in downtown L.A. A car came down the alley and a gunman began shooting. Miura's wife was hit in the head and went into a coma she stayed in for almost a year before she died. Miura was shot in the leg but survived. After the incident, he flew back to Japan, where he was featured prominently in the Japanese media complaining about how dangerous L.A. was.

In the mid-eighties, media stories began to circulate suggesting that Miura had arranged for his wife to be murdered. It was discovered that he had taken out a large insurance policy before her death, and a former porn star came forward who alleged she had been his girlfriend and had solicited him to kill his wife. Finally, in 1994, he was charged with conspiracy to murder his wife. The case, which already had extensive coverage, exploded in the media. There were reports that as many as fifteen articles a day were being written about Miura, including what he was eating at every meal. After weeks of testimony, the court convicted Miura of the conspiracy to commit murder and sentenced him to life in prison.

But his saga was just getting started. Four years after the conviction, the Japanese appeals court overturned the decision, and shortly thereafter the Supreme Court of Japan affirmed that decision. The Los Angeles Police Department, which had investigated the case, had come to believe that Miura did kill his wife, and was not happy with this turn of events. But there was little they could do. Japan, like many countries, will not extradite to the United States its citizens charged with murder, because they do not support the death penalty. As long as Miura stayed in Japan, he was safe for life.

Either by accident or ignorance, Miura did not stay in Japan. In February 2008, he decided to take a trip to Saipan, an island off the Asian coast that is a U.S. territory. To make matters worse, he discussed his upcoming trip on his Web site. When he got to Saipan, LAPD was there to greet him with an arrest warrant, for conspiracy to commit murder, and to begin extradition proceedings. Through their lawyer William Cleary, the family contacted us from Japan and asked us to represent Miura. We agreed and quickly realized that the Japanese High Court dismissal of the murder charges was the same as a not guilty verdict. There was a code section in California that provided that an acquittal in a foreign jurisdiction barred prosecution in California. We filed the motion to dismiss and asked that Judge Steven Van Sicklen allow us to litigate the issue without bringing Mr. Miura from Saipan. Judge Van Sicklen agreed, and we did an all-day hearing with Mr. Miura attending from Saipan by closed-circuit television. At the end of the hearing, the judge agreed with our analysis and dismissed the murder charge. However, he ruled that he did not have enough evidence yet to determine whether under Japanese law the other count of conspiracy would be barred as well. We were elated. We felt that even though Mr. Miura would have to travel to the United States, he would now only be facing a conspiracy charge, and we felt confident that we could get that dismissed without trial as well.

Shortly after the murder count was dismissed, Mr. Miura was brought to the United States and placed in a holding cell at police headquarters in downtown L.A. When he left Saipan, we spoke with his lawyer there. We were told that he was very upbeat and determined to fight and win the lone remaining charge. His family told us that he was excited to leave Saipan because he hated the food in jail there. Within twelve hours of Miura's arriving in L.A., the Japanese consulate sent two representatives to meet with him in jail. They arrived early in the morning and later reported to us that Miura appeared normal and healthy and did not seem the least bit despondent or even nervous about the charges. He had asked them to contact our office to send a lawyer over to see him.

At approximately 1:30 P.M., we sent a young associate lawyer from our office to see Miura since we were overseas on a case at the time. The young associate arrived at the jail and met with Miura. He reported back that Miura appeared to be in good spirits and his only complaint was that he had an allergy to fried foods. Our associate discussed the case with Miura, who was very pleased that he was no longer facing a murder charge and confident that the conspiracy count would be dismissed once we could show that the Japanese court had already ruled on that issue and found in his favor. Miura was also excited about seeing his wife and child, who were flying over from Japan.

Within a few hours, Miura was dead. According to the police report, a detention officer found him in his cell hanging from the top bunk, his shirt used as the noose. An autopsy was performed by the county coroner, who concluded that Miura had committed suicide.

Miura's family was suspicious of the coroner's findings from the beginning. His wife told us that he had an abnormally low threshold of pain and would never do anything intentionally that would cause himself pain. When this fact was combined with how upbeat Miura had been, she felt that we were not getting the whole story and asked us to investigate. But therein lay the problem. It is difficult enough to investigate potential police misconduct when it occurs out on the streets or in public, where there might be witnesses. It is next to impossible to investigate an incident that allegedly occurred inside the LAPD jail.

As a first step we hired a well-respected pathologist, Dr. David

Posey, to do an independent autopsy of the body within a week of the death. His findings were alarming. Posey's preliminary conclusions were that Miura's body, particularly the lower back, was severely injured from blunt force trauma before his death, which indicated he had been badly beaten before the hanging. He recommended the coroner take a more extensive look at the soft tissue hemorrhaging and that the police open an investigation.

We provided the police with Posey's findings and asked that they follow up on his conclusions. The result was that the police circled the wagons and refused to cooperate in any manner. Even a basic request for records and potential witnesses was ignored. At that point we explained to the Miura family that doing a full-scale investigation of the incident, including getting the courts involved, would be costly. And even if we were able to penetrate the blue shield, there was no guarantee that we would find that misconduct had occurred. One of the strange things about organizations like the police is that they often cover up things even when there is no wrongdoing. Old habits die hard. We decided to not go forward.

The problem with cover-ups is that eventually they may surface, and since they have never been dealt with, they tend to blow up into much bigger problems. For example, three years after the Miura case it was discovered that a number of the L.A. County sheriff's deputies were routinely beating up prisoners in jail, in some cases just for sport. Some of the guards had actually formed gangs inside the jail, complete with tattoos and gang signs. Instead of reporting what was going on, jail administrators had turned a blind eye—the blue shield was there to protect them. It took a very brave chaplain and a lucky piece of videotape to eventually pierce that shield.

|||||

The above are examples of willful misconduct, but one way cops consistently go wrong is to make a mistake and then refuse to admit it. Everyone makes mistakes on the job. At some point we have all misread a situation or made a bad character judgment. It's part of being human. Of course cops are going to make mistakes. The problem is that the consequences can be so severe. If a waiter makes a mistake, you may get a steak medium instead of well done. If a gardener makes a mistake, you may have brown grass instead of green. If a police officer makes a mistake, though, your life may be totally turned upside down.

The criminal justice system is a whole lot better when we freely admit that cops make mistakes and that a trial is simply one way of seeing whether the cops made a mistake in a particular case. That was the idea when the founding fathers set up a system in which they felt the best way to the truth was subjecting witnesses to vigorous questioning. If it is the truth, then it should hold up. If the cop has made a mistake, then hopefully cross-examination will reveal it.

But the angry blond white women brigade wants to destroy that part of the system as well. They scream and holler at the very suggestion that a cop may have gotten something wrong. They hide behind the totally irrelevant axiom "They put their lives on the line for us every day." We get that, but it does not mean they don't make mistakes, sometimes serious ones where the person ends up on death row or in prison for life. In order to help prevent those types of mistakes, we need to get over the idea that questioning a cop is akin to questioning motherhood, the flag, and apple pie. They are big boys and girls—they can take a little tough questioning. If they are right, then it should not be a problem. If they are wrong, then hopefully we don't send an innocent person to jail.

For example, one of the most common mistakes we see in police investigations is that they fall prey to tunnel vision. Police officers are trained to investigate a case and to look at all angles and possibilities. But more often than not a police officer very early forms an absolute opinion about the case and who the perpetrator is. Later on in the investigation, if evidence is discovered that contradicts the cop's opinion, the officer either ignores the evidence or invents some crazy

scenario where the evidence fits his or her story. Officers pride themselves on their instincts, so getting them to change their minds after
they have reached a conclusion is almost impossible.

You may recall the case of the father accused of throwing his
daughter off a cliff as detailed in Chapter 2. Cam Brown was accused of
the horrendous crime of throwing his four-year old daughter into
the Pacific Ocean in order to get back at the child's mother, whom he
disliked. The case was assigned to a veteran detective, Jeff Leslie. He
interviewed Cam the night of the incident, and even though Cam vehemently denied throwing the girl off the cliff and told Leslie it was an
accident, the detective immediately determined that Cam was guilty.

From that point on, every piece of evidence in the case was filtered
through the prism of Cam's alleged guilt. When it appeared that he
didn't cry at the scene that night, the investigators concluded that he
didn't care about his daughter's death. But when a later report came
in that he was in fact crying at the scene, they determined he must
have been faking to hide his guilt.

They collected the physical evidence from the scene and gave it
to a leading expert on falling accidents, but when they did not get the
answer they wanted, they chose to ignore that expert. Finally, they
found an expert who was willing, for the right amount of money, to
say that the physical evidence showed the child had been thrown.

As the red flags kept popping up all along the way, the investigators chose to ignore them. One of their biggest arguments was that
Cam took his daughter on an arduous one-hour hike the day she
died, a hike that no four-year-old would ever take unless forced.
They even brought in an expert who re-created the hike with the officers and testified that no young child could possibly take that hour-
long hike. Except it was not an hour-long hike and they knew it.
When the expert and the other deputies took their walk, they stopped
at numerous places, backtracked at times, took photographs, and even
took a wrong route. When we took the video they had shot of that

alleged hour-long walk and had our expert edit out all the stops and backtracking, the hike became a very easy twenty-six minutes. Despite the new evidence, the detectives and the D.A. continued to insist it was a one-hour hike.

Argument after argument in their case was shot down, but they still continued to claim that Cam had thrown his daughter off that cliff. They were so totally invested in their theory that they could not look at any other possible scenario. The truth was that Cam loved his daughter very, very much, and there were a number of witnesses, including a therapist who met with the couple during the child custody issues, who testified to that. Cam was the consummate outdoorsman: surfing, mountain-bike riding, hiking, etc., and had even lived in a cabin high in the hills of Colorado where he had to hike two miles through the snow to get to work. He had never had a child before and did not get visitation until his daughter was three, so he had no idea the limitations of a little girl. He took her on a hike to a beautiful spot overlooking the ocean and was showing her the spectacular views. He made the huge mistake of not holding on to her, and as she walked around she slipped and fell over the side. It was irresponsible and stupid, but it was not intentional.

The case has gone to trial twice, and both times the jury has hung. Only two jurors in the first trial voted for the prosecution's theory of first degree murder, and none voted for it in the second trial.

Despite the fact that only two jurors out of twenty-four in two trials have supported the theory that Cam threw his daughter off the cliff, Detective Leslie refuses to budge. He made a gut decision that first night, and now, almost ten years later, he refuses to even look at the other side, despite the fact that the evidence that came out at trial strongly supported the defendant's position. Detective Leslie is a good police officer—we like him a great deal personally—but he has tunnel vision when it comes to Cam Brown. This happens a lot with cops and is the number one reason that innocent men and women are sitting in jail.

But occasionally it goes beyond wrongheadedness. Some cops actively and knowingly commit misconduct. Are there cops who write false police reports? Are there cops who plant evidence on potential defendants? Are there cops who beat the hell out of a suspect? Sure there are. Just as there are bad lawyers, bad doctors, and bad teachers, there are also bad cops. Are we talking a lot? No. Most do their jobs as best they can and the worst thing they do is commit a little PMS. But there are some cops who cross the line between mistake and malice. These are the cops who coerce confessions and plant evidence. Sometimes it's because they're convinced someone is guilty and they want to get that person off the street. But sometimes they simply want someone—anyone—to be convicted of the crime.

Our office ended up in the middle of a case where an innocent young man spent nine months in jail due to the actions of the Glendale Police Department. The name of the defendant was Edmond Ovasapyan. The case began in October 2009, when a young man was shot in his home by two intruders. His mother had seen the killers but managed to escape.

The police arrived at the house about fifteen minutes after the murderers had fled. They briefly interviewed the distraught mother, and she told them that one of the intruders resembled a young man who had laid down some tile at her business. Within hours, the police found out that the young man's name was Edmond Ovasapyan.

Over the course of the next twenty-four hours, the police interviewed the mother several times. They pulled Edmond's driver's license picture and showed it to her to identify him. She looked at the picture and told them very emphatically, "It looks like him, but it is not him." Over the course of that interview, she told the police no fewer than five times that the boy in the picture, Edmond Ovasapyan, was not one of the two boys who broke into her house.

But the Glendale police were anxious to solve the case and solve it quickly. Glendale is a small community with very few murders, and it looks bad for the whole department if there are murderers running loose. As a result, the mother's repeated denials that Edmond was one of the killers were ignored. They needed a suspect and they needed one fast. Edmond was found and arrested. He was then sent to the worst jail in L.A. County, where he was put on murderers' row and awaited word whether he would be subject to the death penalty. Meanwhile, Glendale police issued a press release naming Edmond as the killer and congratulating themselves on having arrested him within twenty-four hours.

It wasn't just the mother's testimony the police ignored. They talked to Edmond and his cousin and determined that Edmond had an alibi. He and his cousin had been laying tile at a house several miles away that morning. At the time of the murder, Edmond had gone to a local fast-food restaurant to get them some lunch. He then came back, and they ate the lunch before Edmond left again to go to Home Depot to get some more supplies. The police were able to get the video from the Home Depot. Sure enough, approximately forty-five minutes after the murder, Edmond was standing calmly in line buying supplies. He was also wearing a totally different outfit from the one the mother had described the killer wearing. Detective Arthur Frank, the lead detective assigned to the case, explained that he could have committed the murder, gone home, and changed clothes and then gone to Home Depot. Which of course made perfect sense, because most people who have just committed their first murder in front of a witness and fled in a panic like to go buy bathtub caulk within an hour after the killing.

The police continued to search for evidence to pin the crime on Edmond, but the more they tried, the more it backfired. Evidence was collected, interviews were conducted, and records were subpoenaed— an enormous amount of effort was expended to prove Edmond had committed the murder. None of the evidence collected pointed toward his guilt. In fact, it kept pointing to his innocence.

After we received the discovery from the prosecution, we found out that they had another piece of evidence that overwhelmingly pointed to his innocence. When Edmond was arrested, he had a cell phone on him, so the police subpoenaed his phone records in the hope that he had made a call during or shortly after the murder that would place him at the scene. The records showed he had indeed made a call, at almost the exact time of the murder. We got the phone records and the cell tower records, which showed that the call was made from the area where Edmond and his cousin had told the police they were working. We had our investigator drive the route between where they were and the crime scene to see how long it would take. The drive time was twenty to thirty minutes. It would have been physically impossible for Edmond to commit the murder and then get to the work location to make the phone call.

But the Glendale Police Department had an answer for that as well. Their new theory was that Edmond planned the whole thing. He left the phone on purpose at the work location, drove to the crime scene, and had someone make a call while he was murdering the victim so that he could later use that as an alibi. This completely ignored the fact that the police had earlier agreed that the murder was not planned but had only occurred when the victim happened to come home and get in a fight with the intruders.

Thus, the police and the district attorney were going forward on a case in which the victim specifically ruled out the defendant during an identification, where cell phone records showed he was at a totally different location, where they had video of him shortly after the murder in different clothing calmly buying Home Depot supplies, and where, despite massive amounts of time and effort, they couldn't find one piece of evidence implicating the defendant. To make it even worse, he was charged with special circumstances first degree murder, which meant that the death penalty was an option.

Before a defendant can be taken to trial on a felony charge, he or she must be given a preliminary hearing in front of a judge. The standard of proof at these hearings is very low. Prosecutors have to show a judge that they have some evidence, even a minimal amount, to hold the case over for trial. They usually do this by putting the victim on the stand to tell his or her story or by putting the investigating cop on the stand to testify what the cop was told by the victim (hearsay is allowed by a cop at a preliminary hearing). As with many things, the preliminary hearing has now become nothing more than a perfunctory rubber stamping of the prosecution's case. When we began practicing, a prelim was often a pretty good chance to get a dog of a case dismissed. Not so much anymore.

Mark: Despite all that, I looked forward to the opportunity to do the preliminary hearing for Edmond Ovasapyan because I felt I could at least convince the judge to take a hard look at this case. There was no evidence, and the main thing the prosecution was pointing to was an identification that never happened. Even the worst judge in L.A. would have to take a hard look at this case. Unfortunately that is just what we had: one of the worst judges on the bench.

We went inside to start the prelim, prepared to do everything we could to get the case dismissed. As I walked into the courtroom, I was stunned. I had assumed that the prosecution would do a hearsay prelim, which would have meant that Detective Frank would testify instead of the mother of the victim. I had repeatedly told both Detective Frank and the deputy district attorney that they had the wrong man. The cell records proved it. In addition, when the mother was shown a picture of my client before his arrest, she was unequivocal that he was not the murderer. She even stated that she "didn't want to do to another mother what had been done to her" (i.e., take her son away from her). All of which was captured on tape. Unfortunately, after she made that statement the cops told her not to worry, that the D.A wouldn't file the case based on her identification alone, and they encouraged her to make the identification anyway.

When I saw the mother seated in the courtroom, I instantly realized that they were going to put her on the stand and have her do an in-court identification of my client, the wrong man. I walked over to the D.A. handling the case,

Susan Navas, whom I had known for years, and pleaded with her, "Please tell me you did not bring her here to identify Edmond in court."

"That is exactly why I brought her here."

"Susan, for God's sake rethink this. Of course she is going to identify him—she has no choice. He is sitting in the courtroom in an orange jumpsuit sitting next to me and the sheriff. Who else would she identify? Step back and think for a second. Once she identifies Edmond, whenever you find the guy who actually pulled the trigger, you will have screwed up this case."

For the next hour I begged and pleaded with both her and Detective Frank to please take another look at this case and not go down this road. But nothing worked. They were determined to go forward with the preliminary hearing and the in-court identification. Many D.A.s and cops no longer feel as if they have to listen to the other side. Better to go full speed ahead, looking tough and emphasizing law and order. The public has shown that they will overlook a D.A. who jails an innocent man. What they won't overlook is a D.A. who lets a possible murderer go because the evidence is not strong. If that murderer kills again, the D.A. and the D.A.'s career are toast. Once upon a time we were taught in high school civics that the American system of jurisprudence was based on the concept that it was better that ten guilty men walk free than that one innocent man be wrongly convicted. That saying now seems arcane, almost cute in its naïveté. Now the feeling is that it is better that ten men be wrongly convicted than that one guilty man walks free.

Later that morning they brought out the mother and asked her if she could identify the killer. She paused and then quietly pointed a finger at Edmond. That was all it took for the judge to set the case for trial.

But a case that already had several twists and turns was about to experience the biggest twist of all. When the assailants fled the scene, one of them had lost a New York Mets baseball cap in the house. The cap was sent away for DNA testing, and nine months later, the testing came back with a positive hit—a young man who was already serving time in state prison on a violent crime. Detective Frank drove to the prison to interview the young man and to confront him with the evidence. He also was sure that the young man would implicate his partner in the murder—Edmond Ovasapyan. The prisoner did indeed break down and admit that he had been involved and stated that they had never intended to murder anyone. He also admitted something else—he had no idea who Edmond Ovasapyan was. They were not even passing acquaintances.

Not totally convinced, Frank continued to investigate and discovered that it was true—there was no connection. He was also able to conclusively determine who the other intruder from that day was, and it was not Edmond. The problem was that, as we had pleaded with them to avoid, they were now going to have trouble charging the two actual intruders because the victim had been forced to give a false I.D. A defense attorney would have a field day with the prior identification. To this day, neither of the men who actually did the killing has been charged for the murder.

Remarkably, Edmond's release was not immediate. The D.A. insisted on keeping him in jail for another three weeks, until they could put together a lineup with the new suspect in it. That made us even more furious because they had not used a lineup to put Edmond in jail, but now they were insisting on one to get him out. Eventually that was arranged, and for the first time since the day of the murder, the mother saw the man who killed her son. She promptly vomited all over the floor and became distraught. She had told the police she did not want to be forced into falsely identifying the wrong person because she did not want another mother to lose her son. Now, as she saw the real killer, she realized that that was exactly what she had been forced to do.

After more than nine months on murderers' row in jail, Edmond Ovasapyan was released. This time, the Glendale Police Department did not issue a press release. All the people who had read that Edmond was a killer never heard one thing from the police or the D.A. saying that they were wrong. Nor did they ever apologize to Edmond. Remarkably, not only did Detective Frank not apologize, he insisted that Edmond should be grateful to him for solving the case. He actually took credit for Edmond being free!

A year later, our office filed a civil lawsuit against the Glendale Police Department and Detective Arthur Frank and Lieutenant Ian Grimes, his supervisor, asking that they at least reimburse Edmond for having spent almost a year in jail. We asked for $400,000 in damages, which seemed like a low figure, but Edmond wanted to move on with his life. In a totally knee-jerk reaction, the Glendale City Council not only rejected our offer but told us that we needed to go to trial and be taught a lesson.

Pat: Shelley Kaufman, a terrific lawyer and one of the deans of the Civil Rights Bar, who has been with Mark for fifteen years, and I tried the case, and Mark was actually a witness. Amazingly, Detective Frank continued to refuse to apologize and kept insisting that Edmond should be grateful to him. He demonstrated a large amount of hubris when I cross-examined him, never realizing that his attitude was sealing the deal for our case. When I asked him if he thought he at least owed Edmond an apology, he curtly said, "No." In the end, the jury awarded Edmond $2.1 million, which was later reduced to $1.3 million.

The Glendale City Council, apparently not content with the lesson we had been taught, went crazy and voted to appeal the verdict. Since the beginning of the case, we had asked to address the city council so they could understand the facts of the case. They kept getting a distorted picture from the police department, and they were sure that this was a runaway jury whose verdict would be overturned on appeal. It wasn't. The appeals court voted unanimously to uphold the verdict. The City of Glendale ended up writing a check to Edmond for $1.7 million (interest had accumulated while they appealed), and the taxpayers of the City of Glendale had absolutely no idea that they were being forced to pay for a case that could have been resolved if they had bothered to listen to us. But voters want law-and-order candidates at even the city council level, and no one wants to be "soft on crime" or be perceived as anti-police. Here, the police not only took the wrong person off the street, they virtually assured that the real murderers will never be brought to justice.

VETERAN COPS

The public often assumes that the young cops do everything by the book while veteran cops will bend the rules—think of movies like *Training Day*. However, the opposite is often the reality.

Pat: Early in my career I did a ride-along with two police officers one summer night. One of the cops was a thirteen-year veteran and the other was just beginning his second year. During the course of the evening they talked about a lot of different things. I shared with them some ideas about surviving cross-examinations, and they talked to me about what being a street cop was like. After a while, the two cops got into a friendly argument about planting evidence. The young cop saw nothing wrong with it—he thought it was a valuable tool of law enforcement, especially when dealing with the scummier elements. The older cop kept telling him that it was stupid and reckless. When they stopped at a 7-Eleven, the young cop went inside to get a drink. The older cop leaned back and started laughing.

"I used to be just like him when I started. Gonna clean up the streets single-handedly. After a while you learn. You just learn. You get too old to do that shit anymore."

Is it okay to break the law sometimes in order to enforce the law? It is a conversation that we have had frequently with other lawyers and with several cops. There is no definitive answer, but we do know that it happens often. The cops have to deny it for public relations reasons, but they know it happens a lot as well.

CHAPTER SEVEN

Jurors—Nobody Knows Anything

Pat: *Ask fifty lawyers what the most important part of a trial is and you will likely hear all fifty say it is jury selection. There is not even a close second. Yet no part of a trial is more confusing, more mistake-prone, and more misunderstood than jury selection.*

In my first year as a public defender in Nashville, I had to try a case where my client was accused of driving while intoxicated. It was my first time picking a jury, and I was more than a little nervous. The voir dire process where attorneys question potential jurors is for the lawyer a little like being a host of a dinner party where many of the invitees are strangers. As I asked questions—like what do you do for a living, how do you like your job, how many kids do you have and what do they do, have you ever been on a jury—I became more confident. This wasn't so hard.

It got even better near the end of the questioning. Seated in chair number six was an attractive brunette woman in her midtwenties, with big green eyes and a huge smile. She lit up at my questions, making sure to mention that she was single and throwing what I was sure was a come-hither look.

But my good fortune did not end there. In seat number twelve was another attractive young lady, in her midthirties, with a bob haircut and a flower-print dress. When I asked her questions, she was even more outgoing. The flirting was so obvious that I was sure the prosecutor was going to exercise his right to remove her from the jury, but surprisingly he didn't.

After questioning, I sat down with great confidence, convinced that I was already truly becoming a stud lawyer in every sense of the word. As the trial progressed, I would occasionally glance at the two women, and my glances would almost always be met with smiles. During closing argument, I focused a large amount of attention on the two women to ensure I would get at least two votes.

As jury deliberations began, I actually felt very good about how the case had gone. But then jury deliberations stretched all day and I began to get worried. Finally, the call came that the jury had reached a verdict. I was scared but didn't panic because I was sure I had at least the two votes.

After what seemed an eternity, the clerk stood up and announced the verdict—not guilty! I had won my first trial. After I exited the courtroom, the jury foreman was waiting for me. He told me that he thought I had done a good job and he wanted to get my card because a friend of his was in some trouble. I took this opportunity to quiz him on a number of things about the testimony and witnesses, trying to find out what worked and what didn't. And then I asked what was foremost on my mind:

"Why did it take you guys so long to reach a verdict?"

The foreman shuffled his feet a bit and appeared a little uncomfortable, but finally he told me that from the very beginning the vote had been ten to two for not guilty, but the two guilty voters were very stubborn and would not change their minds. I pushed further and finally found out who the two guilty voters were—the two flirtatious women.

I was floored, so I blurted out, "I'm really surprised it was those two women. Are you sure it was them?"

"Yeah. It was them. It wasn't so much the evidence as that they didn't like you very much."

Legendary movie screenwriter William Goldman was once asked to sum up what he had learned about making movies in his many years in Hollywood. His reply was simple: "Nobody knows anything." The same can be said of lawyers picking juries.

Every year law professors and legal experts spend thousands of hours studying jurors and juror behavior and then writing law journal articles detailing their findings. Every year corporations and white-collar criminal defendants spend millions on jury consultants to advise them about jury selection, and every year researchers spend even more millions working with focus groups to predict how a jury will react to a particular case. This data can be helpful to use in your approach to juries, but in the end jury selection is just not a science—it is an art form.

When you put twelve strangers in a box and question each of them in public about themselves for less than five minutes, you're not going to learn very much. A handful of people will spill their guts in their five minutes, but it's extremely rare. Most people are reluctant to discuss their personal lives and beliefs in a public forum. So lawyers fall back on profiling juries based on things such as age, sex, and race. This leads to problems because stereotypes are easy to assign but hard to change. The country is becoming too diverse and too complex to choose a jury based on one such criterion. For example, for years it has been accepted wisdom that African-Americans and Hispanics make great defense jurors. But today African-Americans and Hispanics in higher crime regions, while suspicious of the police, have seen the effects of crime firsthand and as a result are now often pro law and order. Yet lawyers will still fall into the trap of writing off every black or Hispanic juror as a pro-defense vote, which often leaves them very disappointed when the jury comes back with a verdict.

Every trial lawyer can tell you a story about profiling gone awry. We were once suing on behalf of a family whose son had been shot by two police officers in what we felt was an unjustified shooting. One of the prospective jurors identified himself as a former police officer in New York who had moved to Long Beach and had been in law enforcement there as well. It turned out that his father, brothers, and uncles had also been in law enforcement. During the jury selection process, each side has a number of "preemptory challenges" they can use to have a juror removed from the pool. You can also have a juror struck for cause, which doesn't count against your number of preemptories. But to do that you need to have a juror basically admit that he or she is not going to be fair. So we asked the former police offier one simple question, "Given your background in law enforcement, can you be fair in this case?"

He replied honestly, "No, I can't."

At that point we were satisfied, and didn't want to ask any more questions lest we prompt the officer to go on a diatribe about how police officers should not be sued because they have a very tough job where they have to make split-second decisions with their life on the line. A rant like that from an established officer could poison the whole jury.

The attorney on the other side, however, was very seasoned, and he saw a golden opportunity to rehabilitate the police officer or at the very least let him do a little jury education. After we completed our questioning, he immediately started in with the officer.

"Does the fact that you were a police officer mean that you are automatically going to favor the police officers in this case?"

"No, sir."

"Is the fact that you were a former police officer going to cause you to ignore the evidence in this case and just vote for the officers?"

"No, sir."

"So you can be fair to both sides in this case?"

"No, sir."

"Well, can't you put aside your background as a cop and just judge this case on the evidence?"

"No, sir."

At this point the other attorney realized he was not going to be able to save this juror from being rejected for cause, so he asked him a question designed to get him defending cops in front of the other jurors: "What about your background as a police officer prevents you from being fair?"

The former police officer took a deep breath and then started the rant, but it was not what any of us were expecting. He started off by saying that as an ex-cop he knew how undertrained the young cops were these days. He then went on to describe current cops as shoot-first-and-ask-questions-later types. He talked about never shooting anyone in his forty years in law enforcement, even though he had been in harrowing situations. He then wrapped it up by saying he could not be fair in this trial knowing what he knew about cops.

It was hard to tell who was more stunned—the attorney, the judge, or us. If we had written a script for the juror, it would not have been that good. Suddenly the tables had turned and our opponent was trying to get the ex-cop kicked off for cause and we were trying to get him through. But when we made an impassioned albeit flawed argument to the judge that he should stay on the jury, she just shook her head and started laughing.

"Gentlemen, I admire your ability to turn on a dime, but five minutes ago you would have been screaming bloody murder if I had left him on this jury. Nice try—now move on."

The problem with trying to fit jurors into stereotypes (and the problem with stereotypes in general) is that jurors are partly a product of their environment and partly a product of their experiences. A juror who may seem to be a perfect prosecution juror in a case may have been pulled over by a cop and had a very unpleasant experience that has led him to not trust police officers. Likewise, a juror who would appear to be strong for the defense in a DUI case, for example, may have a boyfriend whose father was killed by a drunk driver. Voir dire, when it works, is an attempt to get at these experiences and to try to determine which of them may be driving a person's thinking. But the rapid nature of the questioning and people's reluctance to expose their prejudices in front of others means that voir dire is one of the most difficult things for lawyers to get right. It is somewhat akin to speed-dating in front of eleven other people.

PICKING A JURY

The changes in the past decade have also resulted in us adjusting the way we select jurors. Old defense strategies like picking jurors who were not too bright or who were highly emotional have gone by the wayside. And as we have adjusted our thinking, it has become obvious that the prosecution has done so as well. It is now prosecutors who look for highly emotional jurors who are on the lower end of the IQ scale.

Although every case is different, there are certain universal things we now look for in selecting a jury. The first thing we want in a juror is intelligence. People who can analyze the evidence and who can think for themselves are crucial. The smarter people are, the better they are at understanding concepts like the presumption of innocence or what "beyond a reasonable doubt" means. Intelligent people tend to be more willing to reserve judgment and follow instructions.

We also want people who are unemotional. With prosecutors more and more relying on jurors to base their verdict on their emotional feeling about a defendant, it's important to get people who will not be carried away by emotion. It's never a good sign for the defense when the alleged victim is on the stand and jurors are crying. It's hard to determine how emotional someone is during our limited voir dire examination, so sometimes we do rely on certain professional stereotypes. Accountants, engineers, and computer programmers are often logical thinkers not overly swayed by emotions.

Another trait we look for is a sense of confidence or resolve, people who can stand up for themselves. Most of the time, a jury that can't reach a verdict is a victory for the defense, so we want people who, if they are not in the majority, can withstand the onslaught of sitting in a small room being yelled at to change their minds. It takes a strong, almost contrarian personality to stick to your guns in that situation.

The last thing we look for is people who might clash with the victim. For example, if the alleged victim is a young female, we will try to get a number of young females on the jury. That may sound counterintuitive, but it has been our experience that no one is harder on a young female than other young females. Men often feel protective of young women, whereas young women will often eat their own.

A few years ago we were involved in a trial where our client was accused of groping his assistant's breasts while at the office. The alleged victim was twenty-one years old, very petite, with curly blond hair and a baby face. From the moment she hit the stand, she began crying and she did not stop for more than an hour. She ended up blurting out something she was not supposed to say near the end of her testimony, and it caused a mistrial. When we left the courtroom, several of the younger female jurors were outside and talking in a circle. They approached us and began to vent. They accused the victim of being a phony and said she was setting our client up to get some money from him. They were very harsh on her demeanor and appearance and even said some things that we never would have dared to say in front of the jury. It was reminiscent of the H. L. Mencken line: "On one issue at least, men and women agree; they both distrust women."

By the same token, we obviously want jurors who will *not* clash with our defendant. If we have a defendant who is wealthy, we try to avoid putting people from lower income groups on the jury, because there is a good chance we are going to get an attitude of "you think you're better than us because you have money, so I will show you."

This was one of the big undercurrents in the Peterson trial, as several of the jurors as well as Laci's family referred to Scott as if he were a spoiled rich kid who did nothing but hang out at country clubs playing golf. It wasn't the truth—the Peterson family was upper middle class, and Scott had worked very hard to earn a partial golf scholarship to college, often juggling two and three jobs—but several of the jurors, based on their post-trial comments, seemed to believe that Scott was a spoiled rich kid.

Of course the majority of jurors are not going to fall into any of these neat categories. In the end, like most trial attorneys, we end up picking a jury based on gut feelings. In most trials, jury selection is a rapid process. As the attorneys, we are constantly writing down what the jurors are saying, paying attention to their facial expressions and body movements, and thinking of follow-up questions to their answers. It is a lot to have going on at once, and it is easy to find yourself having forgotten if it was juror number four who said she loves cops or juror number five.

Having picked hundreds of juries and been to countless seminars on how to pick a good jury, we do believe that jury selection is an area where experience and knowledge can pay off. At the same time, it would be disingenuous to create the impression that it is a perfect science, because at the end of the day the single most important factor in picking a jury is simply gut instinct. Maybe a juror reminds you of a favorable juror from another trial. Or the juror smiles a lot, and you feel like this is not some person angry at the world. It's scary when the life of a defendant can hang in the balance, but attorneys are human beings and can be swayed in the voir dire process the same way we all make gut decisions every day.

Beyond the questions over individual jurors, we have to think about jury dynamics as well. A jury with twelve strong personalities is great for the defense because twelve strong personalities are going to argue about everything and eventually produce a hung jury. But no jury is going to have twelve strong personalities—every jury is going to have some sheep who will just go along with the majority. If you have a strong case and you have a couple of larger-than-life personalities on the jury, you want a lot of sheep. If you have a weaker case, you want fewer sheep and more big personalities who will hopefully clash.

Another consideration is the quota of whack-jobs you are willing to put on your jury. These are the jurors who are so unpredictable that in jury deliberations they may vote based on what the defendant's astrology sign is. They are usually easily identifiable because during voir dire they have no qualms telling you about the government conspiracy to steal their latest invention to eliminate the need for gasoline (that guy actually stayed on our jury), or that they have been stalked by Barbra Streisand for twenty years (that woman didn't make the cut). Most cities have two or three wackos in a jury pool, but in Los Angeles you can usually double or triple that number. If your case is strong, you immediately eliminate the wackos because you don't want them interfering. If your case is weak, you embrace the wackos and pray they make it through the trial without doing something too crazy.

JURY DELIBERATIONS

Most trial lawyers and judges can tell you some bizarre stories of jury deliberations gone awry. Physical confrontations in jury rooms are not infrequent, and shouting matches are normal. Stories of tyrannical jury foremen, jurors who refuse to deliberate, and jurors who bring in law books or Internet articles are all part of jury lore. Many of the jury deliberation stories that have been passed down through generations of lawyers are legendary, but perhaps none is more famous or more retold than the story of a jury that was sequestered in a hotel during a trial in the 1960s. During that time, one of the married male jurors started a relationship with an unmarried female juror. After several weeks of being out of contact with her husband, the wife of the married juror called the court to ask just how much longer this trial was going to take. The court clerk informed her that the jury had reached a verdict two weeks earlier.

Our favorite jury deliberation story, however, is one that nobody could dream up. A particular juror in a case was acting rather unpredictable during the trial. She was admonished for falling asleep and for talking to other jurors during testimony. Her fellow jurors asked the judge to remove her, but in an abundance of caution the judge chose to keep her on the jury. She somehow managed to make it to jury deliberations, but on the very first day she refused to deliberate. After a prolonged silence, she said she would deliberate but only if her one request was granted. The request was that the other jurors would agree to watch the movie *The Last Emperor* before deliberating.

Conveniently, she had brought a copy of the movie in her purse. She gave no reason why she was insisting on this particular movie or what possible value it would add to the deliberations. The best anyone could tell, she just wanted to watch the movie with her new friends. Apparently some of the jurors were giving serious consideration to acquiescing to this demand (it is, after all, a pretty good movie). But eventually another group of jurors, who were perhaps horrified at sitting through a two-and-a-half-hour movie about the last Chinese dynasty, wrote a note to the judge explaining what was going on. Judges are notoriously cautious about removing jurors, for fear of creating an appellate issue, but this judge had seen enough. He told this juror to go watch the movie in the privacy of her own home.

Pops loves to tell the jury story of a trial he did where a witness for the defense turned out to be a little crazy. After thirty minutes of testimony he let the jurors in on a secret. He testified that the government had put a receiver in his brain and that his thoughts could be picked up on a transistor radio. After the jury began deliberating, they sent a note out to the judge—they wanted to know if he could send in a transistor radio.

Nothing is as protected and as clouded in secrecy as jury deliberations; they are sacrosanct. Exhaustive steps are taken to prevent the deliberations from being heard or interrupted. In some high-profile cases, jurors are sequestered, which means they are put up in a hotel until the trial is completed.

Upon being excused at the conclusion of a trial, jurors are free to talk to the attorneys about the deliberations. Consequently, what little we know about jury deliberations comes from these conversations. Conventional wisdom among lawyers is that hanging out and talking to jurors is an invaluable tool to becoming a better trial lawyer. You learn what you did well and what you can improve on. Our experience is the opposite: whenever we talk to jurors, even after winning a case, we usually end up wanting to bang our heads against a wall. Because all it does is reaffirm how little we understand—or anyone understands—about what makes a jury tick.

Winning a trial is an incredible, indescribable feeling. It is sheer elation mixed with a large amount of self-congratulation for being the greatest lawyer the world has ever known. The quickest way to burst that bubble is to talk with jurors. When you ask them if your brilliant closing argument, the one you stayed up all weekend working on, swayed them, they will look at you blankly and tell you they can't remember anything you said. When you ask if your withering cross-examination of the alleged victim convinced them he was lying, they will tell you that actually no, they thought he was telling the truth.

Invariably what convinced them to vote in your favor was some piece of evidence that you considered inconsequential or some witness whom you felt was relatively unimportant. There is something remarkably humbling about being told that the vast majority of the three months of hard work you poured into the case and all the clever legal machinations you made during trial were largely ignored. Yet the siren call of the juror conversation is too great, and after every trial we end up in the hallway asking the remaining jurors question after question.

But not every lawyer's experience with jurors after trial has been rough. One criminal defense lawyer we know well had just finished a three-week trial in which the jury hung. After the judge declared a mistrial, the defense attorney was outside talking to several jurors when a female juror approached him and asked if she could speak privately with him. He assumed that she wanted to discuss hiring him for a case, so he excused himself and accompanied her back into the now deserted jury room. Within seconds she had unzipped his pants, pulled up her dress, and was bent over the jury table. When he told us his story, we both had the same reaction: "Did she vote for you or the prosecution?" To us, this was the critical part of the story. It would be very hard to have sex with a woman who had just voted against you.

HUNG JURIES

In a criminal case, the jury's verdict must be unanimous (in most states that means twelve to zero) for either guilty or not guilty to a particular count. When the jurors cannot reach a unanimous verdict, the jury is declared to be deadlocked or, in court lingo, "hung," and a mistrial is declared. It doesn't matter how the vote is split; six to six, eight to four, or eleven to one are all hung juries. If they can't reach a unanimous verdict, a mistrial is declared.

If it is a serious felony trial that has lasted several weeks, a judge will likely let the jury deliberate for several days or even a week or more before agreeing to declare a mistrial. Judges in serious cases tend to push juries more to come up with a verdict, especially if the trial has taken a while (and thus has cost the state a lot of money). But a judge has to be careful to not force a verdict, because a court of appeals might very well reverse the verdict if it appears the judge influenced the outcome by insisting on a decision.

With very few exceptions, a hung jury is considered a victory for the defense. Prosecutors win the vast majority of trials in this country, so denying them a conviction is the exception. Furthermore, prosecutors will often elect to not retry the case, so your client gets a dismissal. A recent study showed that only about one-third of cases with a hung jury ever get retried—the rest are either dismissed or end up being pleaded. That's why when the jury announces that they are deadlocked, you usually hear the defense attorney immediately push for a mistrial, while the prosecutor begs the judge to send the jury back for further deliberations. Unbelievably, several years ago we actually had to litigate a case and go to the court of appeals to get a judge to reverse a ruling that there was no difference between a guilty verdict and a hung jury.

In a trial we did in Orange County that lasted three months, the jury was out for more than a week. On day eight, at 4 P.M., they sent out a note saying that they were not able to reach a verdict and several of the jurors were going to quit deliberating. We were in the courthouse when the note came out, and the judge indicated to us that he was ready to declare a mistrial. We were ecstatic because this was a case we were very pessimistic about, and now we were going to get a hung jury. But the D.A. who had tried the case was nowhere to be found. After a half-hour search for the missing D.A., the judge sent the jury home and told us he would declare the mistrial the next morning. The next morning, with the D.A. present, the judge brought out the jury with the intention of declaring a mistrial. Incredibly, the time away from the deliberations had caused some of the jurors to cool off, and they told the judge they would continue to deliberate. Four hours later the jury came back with a guilty verdict on several of the counts.

SEQUESTERED JURIES

In a high-profile case, a judge may order the jury to be sequestered to shield them from the publicity surrounding the case. Sequestration usually means putting the jurors up in a hotel and bringing their meals to them. Access to relatives and friends is limited, as is most social interaction. Sequestration is usually ordered as a last resort, but it was used in the O. J. Simpson trial and the Casey Anthony trial. (Interestingly, and perhaps not coincidentally, the jurors in those two cases, who did not see any of the pro-prosecution media onslaught, came back with not guilty verdicts.)

In a long trial, sequestration can be a huge burden on the jurors. Being away from family and work with only limited contact to both means that very few jurors are willing to serve on a jury panel that will be sequestered. However, in the Scott Peterson trial, one potential juror seemed willing to be sequestered. She was an elderly woman seated in the front row during the early stages of jury selection. After the judge finished giving his standard speech about jury service, she timidly raised her hand and asked, "Judge Delucchi, my husband wanted me to ask if this jury was going to be sequestered."

The judge kindly reassured her, "No, ma'am. You can tell your husband he can rest easy. We are not sequestering this jury."

Without the slightest attempt at humor, the woman smiled at Judge Delucchi and replied, "Oh, he won't rest easy. He was hoping we would be sequestered."

Judges disfavor sequestered juries not just because of the burden it places on jurors but also because of the additional cost of housing and feeding the jurors, a cost borne by the state. But despite the increased cost, jury sequestration may become more popular in the future because it can help control the number one form of juror misconduct in today's world: Google. We live in an age where people Google other people before having dinner with them. The most frequent complaint of jurors is that they feel that information has been withheld from them; and it has been—all manner of evidence is not allowed at trial, for various reasons. Judges instruct jurors over and over during a trial that they are not to read anything about the trial or watch any show that discusses it or do any independent research. But jurors can't resist Googling the case they're on.

It has gotten so bad that it can now affect whether we go to trial on a case. For example, we had a case where the defendant had a rape conviction from twenty-five years prior to the new charge. A search for this man on the Internet produced only the information that he was convicted of the sexual assault, with no details about what happened. Any juror searching the Internet would have quickly found this conviction and possibly been prejudiced against him. But the details of this sexual assault were a lot less ominous than a person would expect: when the defendant was twenty-two years old, he got drunk one night, took off all his clothes, and climbed into the apartment window of a woman he knew. A neighbor saw him go into the window and called the police. When the police arrived, the defendant was sitting at the kitchen table, naked, while the woman was pouring him some coffee. She was a little mad at him for pulling the stunt but not afraid in the least. The police arrested the defendant and he was charged with sexual assault. An inexperienced lawyer pled him out to the sexual assault to avoid a prison term. He would have been better off pleading to a lesser charge and doing a little time. Twenty-five years later we realized that there was a very good chance that if we went to trial with him on the new charges, none of which involved sexual assault, one or more of the jurors was going to Google him and come up with the conviction. It turned out to be one very important factor in our decision to not go to trial.

Jurors are regularly exposed for giving in to the temptation of Google. They might accidentally say something during jury deliberations that they heard outside the courtroom, or they bring an article they have printed out into the jury room, and then they are ratted out by one or more of their fellow jury members. In the past three years, that has already happened to us five times, and we expect that number to increase in the next few years.

STEALTH JURORS

As long as there has been jury duty there have been jurors finding ways to get out of it. It is not that people don't consider jury service important, it is just that most people cannot easily put their lives on hold for two weeks or two months to serve on a jury. Work responsibilities, child care issues, travel plans, and physical ailments are just some of the reasons people use to beg off jury service. These are referred to as hardships, and, for the most part, judges will release potential jurors from jury duty upon hearing what their hardship is. Judges, along with the lawyers, feel that refusing hardships is going to make for a very unhappy and troublesome jury. One judge in downtown L.A. routinely denies all but the most drastic hardships—a potential juror who was sick and vomiting was told to go to a doctor over the noon recess and be back for the afternoon session. Attorneys on both sides cringe at this type of forced jury service.

After you get by the hardships, the pool of potential jurors mostly consists of retirees, unemployed workers, housewives, students on summer vacation, and people with employers willing to pay for jury service. That can make it very hard on the defense. As we discussed earlier, we are looking for intelligent jurors, which often translates into people with high-paying jobs, like doctors, engineers, computer programmers, CEOs, etc. These days it is very rare that any of these types are going to not be excused for hardship. The founding fathers intended that the leading citizens of the community would serve as the jury pool for trials. Today most of the leading citizens are going to get out of jury service.

The past decade has seen a new phenomenon, especially in high-profile cases, of jurors who are not just willing to serve, but jurors who are dead set on getting selected. We call them "stealth jurors," and they're willing to do or say whatever is necessary to get on a jury, perhaps to further an agenda or to act on misguided belief that there are book and TV deals awaiting anyone who has served on a high-profile case.

Our first experience with stealth jurors was in the Susan McDougal criminal contempt trial in Arkansas. Judge George Howard Jr. was aware of the highly political nature of the trial, so he designed a jury questionnaire to ensure that people with strong political opinions would be weeded out. Two of the questions the jury had to answer were:

"Do you have an opinion, positive or negative, about President Bill Clinton?"

"Do you have an opinion, positive or negative, about Kenneth Starr?"

The first clue that perhaps there were stealth jurors looking to get on the panel was that a full 48 percent of the respondents claimed they had no opinion one way or another about either Clinton or Starr. That was laughable. In the winter of 1999, the only person in the country who felt the same way about both men was Hillary Clinton, and that was only because she wanted to kill them both. Once we knew that about half of the jurors were lying on their questionnaire, both sides had to figure out which camp each juror likely fell into.

In the end, we felt reasonably sure that we were able to get at least five jurors on the panel who were stealth jurors in our favor. There is no way to know for sure, but after the jury had acquitted Susan on two of the three counts and hung seven to five in favor of acquittal on the other, one of the jurors complained that several jurors had made up their minds from the very start.

The Scott Peterson trial presented a very different problem. We knew there would be stealth jurors, but we knew they'd all be on one side: ready to convict him. We also knew that if a person chooses to lie, it is very difficult if not impossible to weed him or her out during the voir dire process. Because of the huge amount of publicity, there were two phases to jury selection for that trial. There was a first round where jurors filled out questionnaires and were then asked questions by the judge and the lawyers. If they were deemed acceptable, they would be told to return in a few weeks to go through the second round of selection.

In the end, we managed to catch and remove three stealth jurors. The first two were caught when they were bragging to people around them that they had gotten past the first phase and they were going to fry Scott. In both cases, the stealth jurors were overheard by people who reported it to the court.

Mark: The third stealth juror was the most insidious. She was a young woman in her midtwenties, with a charming personality and a constant smile. She was a psychology major and was working on a master's degree. When I questioned her, she talked about how she had initially assumed Scott was guilty but that she had had a talk with her father, who convinced her that it was unfair to jump to conclusions. When she recognized the case she was being called on, she gave it a lot of thought and came to the conclusion that if it was her brother on trial, she would want the jury to presume him innocent. She even went so far as to tell us that she had wrestled with the whole idea of being on a death penalty case, because she was not sure she could handle the responsibility. We loved her because we knew we were not going to get jurors on this case with no opinions—the best we could hope for was jurors who would at least try to be fair. Here was a girl who had admitted she had an opinion but had successfully convinced herself of the importance of being fair. That was as good as we were going to find in this case.

A few nights after her performance in the courtroom, we received an e-mail from a total stranger in Minnesota. He told us that he had been in a chat room discussing this case with a woman who claimed she had made it past the first round of jury selection. She also wrote that she had suckered those dumb defense attorneys (that part was true) and was going to make sure she got on the jury to convict Scott. He sent us a copy of the chat, which gave us enough clues to easily figure out who his chat buddy was. We turned it over to a very unhappy judge who was now looking at his third stealth juror.

When the young woman came back for her second round of questioning, she had no idea she had been outed. The judge let me cross-examine her first, and I began by being very nice to her, getting her to repeat much of what she had said the first time in court. After a few minutes of that, I pulled the chat conversation out and began to read through it, pausing every few seconds to let her squirm. The woman looked like she was getting sick. She stammered out nonsensical answers to the questions, but I was not about to let up on her.

Then the judge chimed in. He threatened her with contempt charges and told her that he was seriously thinking of letting her spend the night in jail. When he finally let her go, she fled from the courtroom as fast as humanly possible.

Those three were the stealth jurors we caught, but we can't say if any others got on the jury. There was one juror we had a lot of doubts about, and we debated back and forth whether to keep him on the jury. Finally, we agreed to not bounce him because he had been accused in a domestic violence incident and we felt he might have a mistrust of police officers and the system in general. Instead, once he was on the jury, he made it clear from day one that he was pro-prosecution. When the prosecutor would question a witness, this juror would be writing furiously, taking copious notes. Whenever we got up, he would stop writing and fold his arms and glare at us.

Midway through the trial, a local attorney who would later become a dear friend, Paula Canny, approached us and gave us some information that this juror had been hanging out in a local bar talking about the evidence and the other jurors. The judge called him into chambers, but he denied that he had been talking about the case. This particular judge had a quick trigger in releasing jurors, and on two separate occasions he came close to letting this guy go, but in the end he could not pull the trigger on him.

During jury deliberations the foreman sent a note to the judge, saying that he felt he was being threatened and then told the judge in chambers that it was this particular juror who had threatened him. It was obvious that the two men had very different opinions on the case, and the foreman felt the juror was going to do whatever it took to get a guilty verdict. The judge's solution was to let the jury foreman go rather than kick the bully off the jury. If the Peterson verdict gets overturned by the appeals court, the removal of the jury foreman will likely be the basis for the reversal.

To no one's surprise, when the trial was completed, this troublesome juror was the principal one calling networks to do interviews and trying to get a book published. Unfortunately for him, he was not telegenic, and he got bypassed for the interviews by a number of the other jurors. He did, however, collaborate with a number of the other jurors on a book about the case. We found it rather interesting that these jurors who claimed to be so upset by Laci's death were not upset enough to forgo trying to make a buck off her murder. Apparently empathy does not trump the desire for fifteen minutes of celebrity.

The trial of Michael Carona, the sheriff of Orange County, California, proved that stealth jurors not only exist but are being actively recruited. Carona, a polarizing figure during his reign, was on trial for several counts of financial crimes, including selling favors in return for gifts and cash. As jury selection was about to begin, a popular Southern California radio show, *The John and Ken Show*, began a campaign to convict Carona. John and Ken are classic "shock jocks" who play juvenile pranks on the air and see how far they can push the censors. In this case, John and Ken decided that Carona was guilty and decided to help the justice system reach that same conclusion. On the air they explained to the potential jury pool in Orange County how to lie to get on the jury in order to convict Carona and how to not get caught. Their show is extremely popular in Southern California, airing during the "drive time" afternoon rush hour slot, so they were reaching millions of listeners, including thousands of potential jurors. The defense attorney for Carona went to the judge and begged him to do something, but the judge essentially threw up his hands and said there was nothing he could do.

Carona was indeed convicted by a jury. There is no way to know how many of the jurors were affected by *The John and Ken Show* or how many lied to get on the jury. Before they begin voir dire, jurors take an oath to tell the truth, and we have seen several get caught lying about various matters. However, we have never seen one juror who was caught lying get punished.

COMMON JUROR ERRORS

If you talk to lawyers and judges about the performance of juries, most of them will tell you that they believe juries usually get it right. We agree with that; they do usually get it right. The problem is that *usually* getting it right when it comes to a person's freedom, reputation, or life itself is not very comforting to most defendants headed to trial. How good would you feel boarding an airplane if the flight attendant let you know that the pilot *usually* lands the plane correctly? Or if you were being wheeled into surgery and the nurse reassured you that the doctor *usually* does the operation correctly? No one believes that the criminal justice system is ever going to achieve perfection, but that is no excuse for not trying to improve the system.

We have to begin by understanding the most common juror mistakes. The most common juror error is reliance on eyewitness identification being inherently accurate. That reliance is misplaced. The majority of cases where the defendant was convicted only to later be proven innocent are cases where there was faulty eyewitness identification. For the most part these were not cases where the misidentification was done deliberately—it was simply a mistake, because human beings actually are not very good at eyewitness recall.

One of the most remarkable cases in American jurisprudence involved a woman named Jennifer Thompson, who was brutally raped when she was twenty-two years old. While the rape was in progress, Thompson made a vow to herself. She would memorize every single feature of her attacker, and if she survived, she would make sure he was brought to justice. She even convinced her attacker to turn on the light, so she could get a better look at him. After the incident, Thompson positively identified Ronald Cotton as the man who had attacked her. With a clarity that is rare in a victim, she got on the witness stand and swore to the jury that she was 100 percent absolutely sure that Cotton was the man. She had concentrated so hard that night there was no way she could be wrong. Cotton was convicted solely on her testimony.

Another man, Bobby Poole, was in prison for a series of rapes in that area around that time, and he bragged that he was the one who'd raped Thompson and that Cotton was doing his time for him. Based on some legal technicalities, Cotton was granted a second trial, and his defense attorneys pointed the finger at Bobby Poole. When Thompson was shown the picture of Poole at trial, she said that there was no way this was the man and that it was definitely Cotton. Again, she was absolutely sure. Cotton was convicted again.

Eleven years later, DNA evidence was run and it showed that Poole, not Cotton, was the rapist. Cotton was released from prison. Thompson, to her everlasting credit, has become one of the staunchest critics of eyewitness identification, going on television and radio shows telling people just how unreliable it can be. She talks about how unconditionally positive she was of her identification and yet how wrong she turned out to be and warns that there are a multitude of other cases out there with innocent defendants. Amazingly, Cotton never became angry with her, forgave her for the testimony, and they are now friends.

At times, the witness's inability to properly identify the defendant can even be comical. During an assault preliminary hearing we did, the prosecutor asked the alleged victim to identify the person in court who had assaulted him. The witness looked around the court for a while and then promptly identified the court reporter. The prosecutor asked him if he was sure that was the right person, and he repeated that it was definitely the man sitting behind the machine typing away.

All of us want to believe that we are reliable eyewitnesses of what goes on around us, but the truth is that we are terrible at it. Stress, obstructions, short time frames, distance, eyesight quality, and other factors we tend to discount all mean we often get it wrong no matter how hard we try.

Recently we did a wrongful death case in which two police officers shot and killed a young man they claimed was about to attack them. Six different witnesses observed the shooting. All six told different stories about what they saw, and several of them contradicted one another on major points. None of the six was lying. The reason that their stories differed so dramatically was that none of the six was walking along expecting to see a police shooting. If someone had told them ahead of time that in one minute there was going to be a police shooting at the street corner and to concentrate on what happened, it is likely their accounts would have been much more in sync. But life doesn't work like that.

We have already discussed another juror error—total reliance on a defendant's confession. Confessions are the holy grail to prosecutors. It doesn't matter if every single piece of evidence can point toward another person and all the witnesses they put on can be torn apart on cross-examination. If they have a confession, they just introduce it and the case is over. Nothing else matters—that is how solid confessions are in the minds of jurors. There is an almost universal belief that nobody confesses to a crime they did not commit. But in reality they do, and with a great deal more frequency than prosecutors and cops would have you believe.

The third major error juries make is convicting on emotion rather than evidence. It is very easy to develop a personal dislike, even hatred, for the defendant and decide to convict him or her for being a bad person. Prosecutors understand this and they try to exploit it as much as possible. They attempt to introduce evidence that has no real relevance to the case but casts the defendant in a bad light. Getting witnesses to say superfluous things on the stand, for example that the defendant cursed at a police officer or that the defendant treated someone poorly or that the defendant was unfaithful to his wife (or her husband), is common practice. We once faced a D.A. who was desperate to get into evidence that our client had called his wife fat to her face. It had absolutely nothing to do with the case, but he knew that the jury was going to hate the defendant if he could get it in. Wisely, the judge refused to let it be introduced.

Not all judges are so wise; many let prosecutors turn trials into a perverted version of *This Is Your Life*. People the defendant has not seen in years or may not even remember are paraded into court and allowed to testify that the defendant wronged them in some way. You may recall the final episode of *Seinfeld*, where everybody in the characters' lives comes back to testify against them. We would have found that a whole lot funnier if we weren't living it daily.

A couple of years ago, the prosecutor stood up in a murder case we were in and told the judge that the defendant had a propensity for violence and he could show it. He then brought in a witness who recalled that twenty years ago the defendant got really mad at him and *threatened* him. The defendant didn't actually do anything to him, but he threatened to do something to him. That evidence was allowed. He was then allowed to bring in an ex-girlfriend from twenty-five years ago to testify that when the defendant was twenty-three years old, he got into an argument with her and *may* have damaged her car to the tune of $600. For good measure, the prosecution was allowed to bring in another ex-girlfriend, from fifteen years before, to testify that the defendant had argued with her and called her a nasty name. As a final indignity, they brought in a witness who more than a decade before once saw the defendant get angry at his dad because he was late for a breakfast meeting. The guy had led a nonviolent life, but the prosecutor dragged up a bunch of arbitrary incidents from when he was a very young man. The prosecutor knew that if he could just make the jurors dislike the defendant, they might be more willing to convict on the flimsy evidence in the case.

But the most frustrating juror error is when you talk to a juror afterward and are told that he or she voted to find the person guilty because the juror is really good at "reading people." These are the people who believe they have some magical power to look into a person's eyes and determine if the person is lying. Despite the common misconception, the only thing you can tell by looking into a person's eyes is if they are bloodshot or not. Our experience is that the same people who are so good at "reading people" are invariably the ones who gave $10,000 to some guy to invest in the platinum mines of Peru and have not heard from him since.

Along those same lines are the jurors who tell you that they felt the defendant was guilty because he or she was acting nervous in the courtroom. No kidding—wonder why? Maybe because the defendant's life was on the line and he or she was depending on twelve strangers to get it right, and one of them thought the defendant was guilty because the defendant was nervous. Most people get nervous taking a driver's license test. Judge Patrick Haggirty, one of the brightest judges in L.A. County, recently noted that it is the guilty parties who are actually less likely to be nervous because they know they are likely to be found guilty. It is the innocent ones who are truly scared.

CHAPTER EIGHT

Media—Shame on You for Believing What We Say

In December 2001, famed novelist Dominick Dunne did a media blitz in which he revealed to a stunned audience that he had the inside scoop on the disappearance of Washington, D.C., intern Chandra ·Levy. According to Dunne's sources, Congressman Gary Condit liked to hang out at the Saudi Arabian embassy (Washington's answer to the Playboy mansion), where he never ran short of booze and hookers. While at the embassy, he complained to some of his Saudi hosts that Ms. Levy, with whom he was carrying on an affair, was driving him crazy and he sure wished she was gone (wink, wink). The Saudis, always an accommodating lot, made sure Congressman Condit was no longer bothered by Ms. Levy by having her dropped from a plane into the Atlantic Ocean.

It made for a great story and was duly reported up the chain of news shows, but it lacked one important element—it had not one grain of truth to it. Dunne, a best-selling author and occasional contributor to the magazine *Vanity Fair*, had suffered the unthinkable tragedy of having his daughter murdered by her boyfriend. Since that time, he had begun a second career as a victims' advocate, covering trials and writing about them from the prosecutor's side. Given his personal tragedy, his advocacy was certainly understandable, but like many others, he'd let himself be blinded by his drive to find someone—anyone—responsible for a crime. He was sure that Gary Condit had murdered Chandra Levy—any rumor or innuendo that could help hasten Condit's arrest and/or conviction was fair game. And thus Dunne went on a national radio show and told this ridiculous story.

Congressman Condit was not going to stand by and just take it. We had just begun representing him on the criminal investigation, and we referred him to a friend and one of the top defamation attorneys in the country, Lin Wood. Lin had successfully represented Richard Jewell and later the family of JonBenét Ramsey. Wood filed suit against Dunne for the libelous statements. Many attorneys wouldn't have bothered with the suit; TV and radio had been spewing innuendo for so long that the bar for libel had gotten ridiculously high. Suggesting a congressman helped in a murder was actually a fairly tame accusation in comparison to some of the other stuff out there.

But Wood and Congressman Condit held strong and refused to abandon the lawsuit. Once the federal judge declined to dismiss the lawsuit, Dunne and his lawyers recognized this was not a case they wanted to put in front of a jury. Dunne quietly settled the case with Congressman Condit and also apologized, although he refused to take "personal responsibility," the same thing he so often accused criminal defendants of not doing. Instead, he resorted to excuses, blaming everyone but himself for giving out the bad information.

The truly interesting part of the Dunne/Condit defamation case was not the rumor that Dunne repeated, but rather his unique defense. As reported by the excellent legal writer Jonathan Turley in his commentary on the case, Dunne made an argument in his legal papers that cuts to the very essence of the problem with today's legal coverage. Dunne said that the show on which he repeated the story (the long-running *Laura Ingraham Show*) was not taken seriously by anyone and no one really believed him. Dunne was admitting that lies were standard on shows like this and was hoping to convince the court that lies told on shows known for broadcasting lies were therefore harmless. His attorneys were wise to settle before this defense was put in front of a jury.

The gist of this argument is that no one really believes the crap they are putting out there—it doesn't matter what they say, because it is simply entertainment. But it does matter, because that is not how they advertise their shows. It's not acceptable to say that shows like *Nancy Grace* and the *Laura Ingraham Show* are "only entertainment." Nancy Grace is on a network called HLN, for Headline *News*, and the promos for her show trumpet how she is the only one with the guts to tell the real truth. Ingraham is well-known for claiming the media is biased and she is the only one willing to tell it like it is. Guests like Wendy Murphy are interviewed on shows with real journalists, like Greta Van Susteren. How is the public supposed to differentiate between journalism and entertainment when the networks don't do it themselves?

There is a large segment of the population that believes that a television network would not let someone on TV tell lies. We have had numerous arguments with people over something they heard on television, and when we explain that the person was lying or repeating a false rumor, they invariably say that if that were true they would be sued. What they fail to realize is that libel laws are very protective of free speech, and it is very difficult to succeed in most libel cases, which is why so few people pursue them.

People do believe rumors and ridiculous accusations, and not just people who believe the *National Enquirer* or the *Globe*. Not only do many of the potential jurors we speak to absolutely believe what they hear from these shows, they repeat it as fact, and it very much affects their outlook on the system. When reporting on Hollywood, rumors and gossip can be fun, and they are actually a part of the publicity machine that keeps the entertainment industry rolling. But the criminal justice system is not some division of the entertainment industry. When that tabloid mentality is applied to the criminal justice system, it can cause serious problems. These are real people's lives. There has to be some level of decency and some level of responsibility, even with the tabloid media.

MAINSTREAM MEDIA V. THE TABLOID MEDIA

The media in this country is an easy target because any mistake it makes is going to be in print or on video for all to see. It is the favorite whipping boy of both sides of the political spectrum. It also is heavily criticized by most of the participants in a high-profile trial, because the media is inevitably going to report things differently from the way the conflicting parties see them. In short, the media comes in for a lot of undeserved abuse. Much of the time the media is criticized as if it is some type of monolithic, one-cell organism that includes everyone with a microphone or a pen. That is an easy trap to fall into. A lot of shows and news telecasts still focus on information and trying to educate the public. But increasingly, with the advent of the twenty-four-hour cable channels, there are many shows that are nothing more than verbal *Jerry Springer*s in which rumors and lies are used to spark ratings, and two people yelling at each other is the method for "informing." We see what criminal defendants call the new "axis of evil": cable shows report unsubstantiated rumors, which jump to the morning shows, and from there to the cover of *People* magazine. By the time that process has taken place, many urban legends have morphed into accepted facts.

Within the mainstream media are reporters and interviewers who are trying to find the facts and report them to the public. They don't always get it right, but then again we have yet to do a perfect trial either. When they make a mistake, it may be out of carelessness or even laziness, but it is rarely out of malice. In high-profile criminal trials reporters often drive the lawyers crazy by focusing on things that are largely irrelevant and not hitting on the things that are important. But in fairness the media does not have access to everything the lawyers know, nor can they necessarily know what direction the lawyers are headed, because they don't see all the discovery in a trial. They only see what is laid out in evidence that day and have to speculate how that piece fits into the bigger picture. A lot of them do a very good job of doing just that.

One of the first lessons we teach new lawyers is that the media is not their friend. Admittedly some reporters have become loyal and trusted friends, but we always remember that, like us, they have a job to do. That job may include sucking up to you, buying you dinner, or maybe even flying you on a private jet to an interview location, but they are not doing it because of how much they love you. It is a business and the minute they have what they need from you, they are on to the next story. After the Scott Peterson trial, a lawyer who was a constant commentator and in high demand tried to get in touch with a reporter who, during the trial, called him five to ten times a day. After the trial was done, she wouldn't even return his call.

That is the nature of the business and new lawyers must quickly develop a thick skin. Reporters often trash us and our clients, but we will grant those same reporters an interview if we think it can help our client. The client and the client's family always want to know why we would grant an interview to someone who has just attacked us. The reason is simple: we realize that most articles about our clients are going to be negative because it is usually pretty hard to write a puff piece about someone accused of murder or a sexual assault. But still we'll give interviews in the hope that the next article won't be as negative and may include a couple of the defendant's talking points. Holding a grudge in this business only hurts your client.

For the most part, I don't believe the mainstream media court reporting is much different than it was twenty years ago. The biggest difference in the mainstream media is the sheer volume of reporting. With the rise of the twenty-four-hour cable networks, reporting on sexy court cases has become one way of filling the time. This is where the problem begins. You can only report so much on what evidence was presented and what it means. But most important, where the facts end, the tabloid media begins, and that is the big difference in the past twenty years. Tabloids will report every rumor and even add some rumors of their own creation. Of course, the overwhelming percentage of rumors is not about what a good person the defendant is and how likely it is that the defendant is innocent. And you have to feed your readers' appetites.

The lifeblood of the tabloid media is based on repeating rumors from dubious sources and to be generous in embellishing those rumors. The tabloid blood supply has been increased exponentially by the rise of blogs and various other news-interested Web sites. Anyone with a computer can now go online and insist that he or she is friends with the defendant's girlfriend and that she blurted out that the defendant had confessed to her that he murdered the victim. Other blogs don't want to miss out on providing what visitors want, so they repeat it and soon it is making the rounds of the Internet chat rooms as established fact. The tabloids get wind of these rumors and a story appears on page 8 of the *National Enquirer* that the defendant confessed to the murder. Within a day of the tabloid printing the story, one of the angry blond white women is reporting that she has a scoop. Her sources tell her (they love to start sentences with "my sources tell me") that the defendant has confessed to the crime, which just proves he is a guilty scumbag. She starts the self-righteous rant on how the defense will try to keep this important evidence out and how it is not fair to the victims that his confession may not come into evidence. In truth, the prosecution will never even try to introduce this evidence, because it is made up. But a future juror will be watching the show or will see the confession in the grocery store checkout line or read it on some blog and will end up sitting on that jury feeling that the defense has pulled some trick to get that confession excluded.

And sometimes tabloid reporting goes beyond irresponsibly re-publishing other people's lies. Cloaked in self-righteousness, they appear to believe they can say whatever they wish, true or not, because they are the good guys.

Look at our favorite, Nancy Grace. She built her career on a tragic backstory of the murder of her boyfriend and how that led her to become a prosecutor and to stand up for victims of crime. Fair enough—a good story and an understandable reaction. But the actual story was not enough for Grace because it didn't allow her to fit in all her pet peeves, like ignorant juries, sleazy defense lawyers, lengthy drawn-out appeals, and career criminals who are let back out on the street. So she made up a story that fit her agenda much better. In her retelling, her fiancé was murdered by a complete stranger who robbed him of $35 and left him to die. The twenty-four-year-old murderer was arrested and turned out to have a lengthy criminal record, but he had been put back on the streets. He denied any involvement in the killing and never confessed. The prosecutor asked Grace if she wanted them to go for the death penalty, and in a moment of weakness she said no. When the trial ended, she was forced to agonize for three days while the jury determined the defendant's fate. The convicted murderer then began a string of appeals that kept her wounds open. In short, her outrage at how the system treated her when she was a victim led her to become the superhero prosecutor that she is.

The unvarnished truth came out in an article researched and written by Rebecca Dana in the *New York Observer*. Grace's fiancé was not murdered by a complete stranger—the murderer was actually a co-worker of his. The defendant was not someone with a lengthy criminal history who had been let out by a liberal judge. He was a nineteen-year-old man with no criminal record. He did not deny his involvement but instead confessed on the night of his arrest. The prosecutor did in fact ask for the death penalty at trial, but the jury refused to give it because the defendant was mildly retarded. Grace did not have to agonize for three days of deliberations because the jury came back within a matter of hours. The defendant did not file any appeals, although later he filed an application for one that was denied. There was no lengthy appeals process. In reality, the system treated Nancy Grace quite well, and justice was served promptly and swiftly.

Grace is willing to take a case, even one that is already sympathetic, and create an entire fantasy world around it designed to ratchet up people's emotions and convince them that the system is unfairly weighted toward defendants. The irony is that journalists working for everything from the *Washington Post* to the *New York Times* to CNN to Fox News have been routinely fired from their jobs for making up stories, including background stories about their own lives that were not true. The tabloid media is held to a different standard, though. After all, as Dominick Dunne put in his legal papers, they're not expected to tell the truth.

Perhaps the best example of using lies to inflame a story comes from Wendy Murphy, whose crazy antics were covered in Chapter 1. Murphy became obsessed about the Duke lacrosse team scandal, the one where numerous white Duke lacrosse players were accused of gang-raping a black woman at a party. The case stirred up a lot of national interest not only because of the graphic sexual nature of the alleged crime but also because of the racial implications of privileged white boys devaluing the life of a black woman. Wendy Murphy jumped into the case with both feet, appearing on every show she could as an advocate for sexual assault victims and bizarrely suggesting that there is no such thing as a false sexual assault claim. As it turned out, this case became a classic example of a false sexual assault claim when it was shown that the entire story had been fabricated.

Professor K. C. Johnson of Brooklyn College has since coauthored a book on the Duke case. His research led him to write a blog piece on

Wendy Murphy and eighteen distinct, verifiable lies she told on television during the entire mess. Again, this was not spin she was promulgating but actual, easily verifiable lies. Among those lies was the assertion that the men had refused to cooperate with police. In fact, they had immediately cooperated, provided DNA samples, and taken lie detector tests. Murphy became obsessed with a broom handle she said was used in the rape and which she claimed would have the Duke players' DNA on it. No such broom handle existed, and there was never any accusation of the alleged victim being raped with a broom handle. She also insisted that the woman had been given a date rape drug that caused her to not struggle. Toxicology reports showed that no such drug was in her system.

The same thing happened with another regular commentator, Michael Jackson's personal prosecuting journalist Diane Dimond. Her "investigative reporting" always seemed to lead in one direction—Michael Jackson's guilt. There was a reason that when Santa Barbara district attorney Thomas Sneddon raided Neverland Ranch he only allowed one journalist to accompany him—Diane Dimond. She spent the entire time leading up to trial claiming to be an independent reporter while essentially acting as Sneddon's press secretary. Years later, when she covered the Casey Anthony trial, she wrote an article telling us how she just could not lie. She was raised so well that she was a beacon of honesty, incapable of not telling the truth.

Yet Dimond spent more than a decade telling lies about Michael Jackson, primarily on the tabloid show *Hard Copy*. She is a lot better than most of the angry blond white women at couching her stories in language that lets her off the hook when she is challenged. She invariably would do an interview about Jackson in which she would tell the audience about the multiple unnamed young men whom he victimized and whom she has interviewed, but who are unwilling to come forward. Of course, they were willing to tell her, a perfect stranger, all about how Jackson abused them. She would pair this with mentions of the settlement for $30 million that Jackson paid an early accuser (a figure that is also not accurate). After trashing Jackson, she would then make sure she stated that of course she was not saying he was guilty. Technically, she never uttered those words, but she has made it clear that she believed he was.

By her own argument, her claims were ludicrous. She asserted that Michael paid a young boy $30 million after the boy made allegations, yet that there were also many more children who wouldn't come forward. Really? There was not one struggling family of one of these kids who thought that if they even quietly made the allegations to Jackson's attorneys, it wouldn't be worth a couple million? That is ridiculous. In this litigious day and age, they'd have been racing one another to the courtroom.

And if her assertion was true, why wouldn't she have given these names to her best buddy, the Santa Barbara D.A. Tom Sneddon, who made a career of trying to bring charges against Jackson? He could have filed charges on the boys' behalf, or at least subpoenaed them to testify at Jackson's trial.

One of the first things we did when the charges were made by the one boy against Jackson was to send our investigator around to talk with kids who had been at sleepovers at the Jackson house, or with children of the employees who were around a lot, or anybody we thought might have pointed a finger at Jackson. Not one kid ever said anything happened—just the opposite. Yet amazingly Dimond found a number of boys, none of whom were willing to be named or willing to collect $30 million, who had been victimized by Jackson. And we know she must be telling the truth because she assures us that she wouldn't lie.

BLEEDING INTO THE MAINSTREAM MEDIA

As discussed, the tabloid media is one thing. But the fact that the tabloids are constantly out there spreading innuendo and outright lies puts the mainstream media in a quandary. A story about a trial is being broadcast repeatedly on numerous shows and all over the Internet. Everyone has heard it, so it becomes nearly impossible for mainstream reporters to just ignore it in their coverage. Their solution: instead of confirming or denying the story or even talking about where it came from, they simply say the story is out there and they can neither confirm nor deny it. This has the practical effect of validating the rumor, which goes from crazy person's blog to being an established, public fact. It is amazingly simple. For example, a blogger could start a rumor that President Obama was not born in this country, and within a week the story would be on all the major networks. Oh, wait a second . . .

For those who don't believe the mainstream media could ever be that gullible, let us revisit the experience of our client Congressman Gary Condit. When Chandra Levy went missing, it didn't take long for the police to learn that she had worked in Condit's office and that there was some type of relationship with her. That information soon leaked to the press and the frenzy was on. It started with the tabloids, and the angle they took was not surprising. They went crazy with stories of Condit murdering Levy—how he murdered her, how she was pregnant with his child, how he held orgies at his apartment, and even one story that he was a serial killer of Washington interns.

The story had all the necessary elements—missing photogenic girl; sex; an easy-to-hate, philandering politician villain; and a dozen wild rumors to keep things stirred up for a long time. Before long, the tabloid media was publicly labeling Condit as a murderer even though there was not a shred of evidence to show that he had anything to do with Chandra Levy's disappearance. In fact, most of the evidence pointed away from Condit, including a timeline that would have made it virtually impossible for him to have killed her.

With the tabloid media plugged in, it was inevitable that the mainstream media would become heavily involved. At first it was just straightforward reporting, but soon the rumor mill made its way to network TV. During a disastrous interview that Condit agreed to do with ABC's Connie Chung, he was asked questions about a number of things that were straight out of the *National Enquirer*. For example, Chung asked Condit if it was true he had planned to marry Levy and that he had promised her he would leave his wife. She also asked him if it was true that the day she disappeared, there were a number of frantic calls from her. These were stories that had been circulated in the tabloids but had no basis in fact whatsoever.

Condit couldn't answer a lot of the questions because of the ongoing investigation, and he came off seeming evasive. It was a no-win scenario and further contributed to the growing sense that he was hiding something. With blood in the water, the media then ratcheted the rumor mill even higher, and before long virtually every silly thing imaginable about the case was being at least mentioned in the mainstream media. Stories of Condit's association with the Hell's Angels motorcycle gang spurred an entire week of speculation as to how they could have been involved in Levy's murder.

Shortly after the Connie Chung interview, Condit hired us to represent him. Over the course of representing Gary, it became apparent just how absurd the idea of him harming Chandra was and how much the media was influencing the investigation. We started to push back hard. When Ms. Levy's body was found in Rock Creek Park in Washington, D.C., a place she frequently went to jog (and not in the Atlantic Ocean), it still did not stop the speculation about Gary. Eventually, with the help of a private investigator we hired, it became apparent that there was a different, much more logical suspect. This man had been prosecuted for assaulting two other women in the same area where Chandra was found and was serving a prison sentence. Yet instead of focusing their attention on this man, the authorities continued to plague Gary and his family. In the end, it took 9/11 to stop the Condit frenzy. It was almost eight years later, after an exposé by the *Washington Post*, that Ingmar Guandique, the man we had identified, was arrested for Ms. Levy's murder. He went to trial, was found guilty, and was sentenced to sixty years in jail.

At the apex of the Condit media frenzy a Fox News poll showed that 44 percent of Americans felt that Condit had murdered Chandra Levy. Although not one single piece of evidence linked Condit to Levy's disappearance, the media coverage of the incident was so full of rumors and lies that almost half of the American public was convinced of his guilt. If Congressman Condit had been arrested and charged with her murder, there is a very good chance he would be in jail today serving a life sentence.

WORKING WITH THE TABLOID MEDIA

Mark: After the Susan McDougal trials, I became a regular guest on shows like Good Morning America, Burden of Proof, *and* Larry King Live. *At the time, these appearances were just about being interviewed regarding a case in the news and answering questions that were routine, about legal procedures or potential strategies of the lawyers. After a couple of years, that gave way to shows where I would be a panel member with one or two other lawyers, and we would offer our opinions about a legal issue. Soon that evolved into the format where I was pitted against a pro-prosecution type who would disagree if I said the sun was going to set in the west. These were set up to be legal duels, a criminal law version of the old show* Crossfire, *and the idea was to try to produce fireworks that would increase ratings. On shows like this it's virtually impossible to make a logical, cogent argument in the fifteen-second sound bite before your opponent starts trying to talk louder than you.*

I soon cut back on my television appearances, staying only on Larry King Live *because the day after every appearance on that show, the phones at the office would ring off the hook. The best part of that was not the volume of calls but rather the types of cases we were receiving. We suddenly found that we could pick and choose our cases, and we were getting some great ones. Our motivation for taking cases was not how large the retainer was but rather how interesting the case was.*

A lot of people assume the reason I do television is because I like the celebrity that goes along with it. In reality, at least three out of every four people who recognize me on the street come up to me and say they know me but they are not sure from where. Finally it hits them and they spit out, "You're that lawyer." I smile and say yes, which is then followed by, "I knew it. You're O.J.'s lawyer!" In the beginning, I would correct them, but now it has gotten so frequent and so difficult to explain that when they say, "You're O.J.'s lawyer," I just smile and nod. Occasionally, I will shake their hand and say, "Yes. I am Johnnie Cochran." That always leaves them a bit confused.

Around the time I slowed down my TV appearances was about the same time that the angry blond white women were starting to come into their own and flex their muscles. Television legal commentary was giving up on discussing strategies or legal procedures and was now going full steam with the Nancy Grace model—pick a case with a great deal of emotional value, find a likely suspect, and then demonize the hell out of that suspect. A good-size segment of the population will always tune in to hear an angry diatribe directed at some person who they are being told is evil. Hate sells—always has. There was a reason public hangings were among the best attended events of their day.

As I watched some of these shows, I found myself getting increasingly upset, but not at the angry blond white women. I expected nothing better from them. What really bothered me was some of the defense attorneys who were appearing on television to supposedly represent the defense's point of view or, more accurately, how the system is supposed to work. Many of these self-identified defense lawyers were at best lukewarm in their defense of the suspect; at worst they seemed to be apologizing for being defense attorneys. In some instances you could flat-out tell that they didn't want to upset anyone or take a position that might get them some hate mail.

You don't become a defense attorney to win Miss Congeniality. This country has a tremendous history of defense attorneys fighting for unpopular causes, whether it is the teaching of evolution, the advancement of civil rights, or the presumed innocence of a suspected killer. We believe that we have nothing to apologize for—on the contrary, it is one of the most noble callings in the system.

I have started going back on television whenever I am asked and can fit it into my schedule. I want people to understand that there is another side to the story or at the very least that the defense should be heard. I have commented on

Barry Bonds, Casey Anthony, Dr. Conrad Murray, the Duke lacrosse team, George Zimmerman, and Jerry Sandusky. In every single appearance I have tried to present a view from the defense's standpoint. In some cases I don't agree with the defense viewpoint or the defense strategy, but it still needs to be put forth.

It is important to note that this is not a political issue, i.e., some wild liberal notion that is anathema to conservatives. It is the basis of our criminal justice system and is supported by people from all sides of the political spectrum. For example, when I have appeared on Sean Hannity's show, both television and radio, he has been among the most fervent supporters of the right to a fair trial. He was one of the few who tried to slow people down in the rush to convict Scott Peterson, not because he didn't think he was guilty, but because he felt that the defense should be heard.

The bottom line for me is that you can't have media coverage of a case that considers "balance" to be a rabid prosecution view versus a milder prosecution view. I don't ask people to believe what the defense is saying; I just want to make sure that they hear what the defense is saying. I don't like the yelling and the silliness and the absurdist comments that go along with tabloid media, but it is important to at least try to stop it from being a complete railroading of every person even suspected of a crime. Especially since much of the televised vitriol is now leaking into the courtroom and the cases themselves.

USING THE MEDIA—KNOWING WHEN TO TALK AND WHEN TO SHUT UP

When you're a lawyer to celebrities, you're going to have to deal with many accusations made in the media. We frequently find it necessary to respond to the rumors and negative stories about our clients, so we almost always oppose gag orders. A gag order is an order by the court for both sides to not say anything to the press. Since it applies to both sides, that's fair, right?

Not so fast. In reality what happens is the prosecution holds a huge press conference to announce the charges, talks at length about the details of the case, and then provides the press a copy of a criminal complaint that lists all of the offenses and how they were allegedly committed. In essence, they lay out their entire case to the media. Then, when the defendant hires an attorney, the prosecution will file a motion with the court to issue a gag order for both sides as if they are trying to be fair. This way they can be the final word anyone hears on the case.

Mark: Not every case warrants a media blitz, at least from the defense. A perfect example was the Chris Brown case. On a Sunday morning around 6 A.M. I received a call from super lawyer extraordinaire Kenny Meiseles, who said that Chris Brown was being arrested for hitting Rihanna. I told the friend I would get there immediately to take Chris into the police station to be booked.

After hanging up I wandered down the hall to my seventeen-year-old daughter Teny's room, turned on the light, and asked her, "Who is Chris Brown and what is a Rihanna?"

She buried her head in her pillow and began muttering. The only words I could make out were "old" and "lamest dad ever."

Despite the huge media crush wanting something from the Chris Brown camp, we felt that the D.A. was going to be a lot more willing to work with us if we kept everything out of the media and sorted this out behind the scenes. That was easier said than done. At the time, Chris was probably the most popular figure in the pop world, often being compared with a young Michael Jackson. He also had a deservedly squeaky-clean image.

But there was no good reason to feed the media; it would likely anger the judge and D.A. I was about to negotiate with. There were a lot of false rumors out there about the incident, but I knew the case was not likely to go to trial, so there really was no jury pool to taint. In the end, I was able to work out a very reasonable plea bargain. It is my belief that any media appearances by Chris or myself would have scuttled those plea negotiations.

Despite my well-earned reputation as a media whore, most people would be astonished to learn that I reject numerous opportunities every month to hold press conferences. Semi-celebrities or ex-employees of a celebrity frequently want to hire our firm to hold a press conference and announce some shocking detail they have about a real celebrity in order to shake some money out and get their fifteen minutes of fame. I am just not interested. When I hold a press conference or grant an interview to the media about a case, it is because I feel it will help the client's case. Our firm is not exactly underpublicized, and if I feel the prosecution is using the media to taint the jury pool, we are more than likely going to respond or maybe even issue a preemptive attack. But otherwise it's better to keep quiet.

Sometimes using the media can help a client's case a great deal, and we are certainly not above manipulating the media in our favor. In fact, one of our firm's greatest achievements was a direct result of using the media to send a message. It was especially important because it provided us with an opportunity to help correct an incredible injustice arising out of the genocide of the Armenian people by the Turkish government.

Mark: One day I received a call from my mother asking that I speak to one of her closest friends, Seta Marootian. Seta and her husband, Marty, were family friends and had the distinction of being the only other Armenian family that I knew of in my neighborhood back in the 1960s. That conversation started what was to become a more than ten-year legal odyssey in pursuing the Armenian Genocide cases.

Marty had a policy from an insurance company that had been issued to his uncle during the time leading up to the genocide (i.e., around 1915). I would later learn that some American insurance companies had found that selling life insurance policies to the Christian communities in Ottoman Turkey was a very lucrative business. At least it was until the genocide. Marty had for years been pursuing payment on the policy but wasn't getting any traction. He had sued the company in a class action lawsuit but was not happy about the results, so he and Seta asked if I could get involved. Up until that point, I had focused almost solely on criminal law—my experience in civil cases, especially class actions, was very limited. Nevertheless, I was fascinated by the subject matter and anxious to work on any case that would further the cause of genocide awareness.

One of the lawyers who was already on the case was Brian Kabateck, a highly successful civil litigator in Los Angeles with a sharp legal mind and an even sharper wit. We quickly set up a meeting with Brian to see if we could work together, and we hit it off immediately. It turned out that he was half-Armenian on his mother's side and had a personal interest in the litigation. In retrospect, there must have been some divine guidance involved in Brian and us joining forces on what we would soon come to call the "Genocide" litigation.

The first case with Marty and Seta went through what civil lawyers call the "discovery" phase. That is where requests for documents are made from one side to the other. As it turned out, the insurance company had kept very good records of the policy holders in a warehouse on the East Coast. Looking through the insurance policy paperwork from ninety years ago was fascinating. The policy cards contained the name of the policyholder, the village the policyholder resided in, the policyholder's occupation, spouse's name, children's names, and the dates of the payment of premiums. The entries for the premium payments were marked in large part by month and year and had been paid in gold coins.

As we were looking through the policy cards, it became apparent that in each village the premiums had stopped being paid in the same month of the same year. This happened time and time again in each village. Pretty soon a pattern emerged that literally showed the map of the Genocide by dates as each village or territory was wiped out. You could chart the course of the Genocide through Ottoman Turkey with these policy cards that had been locked away in a warehouse in New Jersey for decades gathering dust.

There were thousands of names on the policy list that we had assembled. As you might imagine, after we did the publicity on the settlement there were thousands of claims, including many for the same policyholders. We expected that, since over the course of several generations there might be all kinds of lineal descendants. What was surprising, however, was that for almost one-third of the policies there wasn't a single claim whatsoever. Entire families had been wiped out—not a single survivor lived to carry on the family's name.

Mark: Initially we did not have much success. The companies had little interest in settling, and it looked like another prolonged battle. This was roughly the time that Larry King was gearing up for one of his anniversary shows. I was a frequent guest and a huge fan of Larry (who is still one of the best interviewers in the business). A friend and the producer of the Larry King Live *show, Wendy Walker, called and asked if I would do an hour as a guest during the anniversary week. I was conflicted about this. I was in an extended trial in Orange County and just coming off the Peterson case, still racked with emotions over that verdict. After talking with Wendy, whose intelligence and humor is only exceeded by her tenacity, I agreed to do the hour on the condition that in the last segment I would get to talk about something other than Scott Peterson or Michael Jackson.*

She agreed, so Larry made the trip down to the hotel I was living in by the courthouse and we did the show live from there. True to their word they did let me talk about something other than Scott and Michael in the last segment—we started talking about this insurance company and the Armenian claims and whatever I could get in about the Armenian Genocide. The next afternoon I got a very excited phone call from Brian. He told me that the insurance company's lawyer had called him earlier that day. They had offered to immediately go to mediation, a process where both sides meet with a judge to try to informally resolve their claims. They even agreed to use Judge Dickran Tevrizian, one of the most respected federal jurists on the bench at the time, who also happened to be Armenian. I was floored.

"Brian, I can't believe this. What the hell happened?

Brain started laughing and said, "I think you can probably figure out what happened when you hear the one condition they put on the mediation."

"Okay. Give it to me. What is the condition?"

"Well, the condition is that you shut up and stop talking to the press."

The case did proceed to mediation before Judge Tevrizian, and the lawyers and the general counsel for the insurance company were a class act. They genuinely wanted to pay the policyholders and wanted to resolve the case. Many times when we are fighting large corporations in lawsuits, they will fight us tooth and nail over every little detail. This insurance company and its lawyers took the opposite approach; they wanted to do the right thing.

Ultimately the case settled for $17 million and became the first case of its kind to settle in this type of litigation. But even the settlement administration became an education. Once the amount was agreed on, we were required to publish or give notice to the class of affected claimants. We did this by newspaper publication, Web site, radio, and television. We advertised in virtually every Armenian newspaper and magazine in the world by listing the names of the victims of the Genocide who had purchased policies. The amazing thing was that we would hear from people who were so excited to see their grandfather's or grandmother's name in the paper—not because they were getting the money, but simply because seeing the name in the newspaper actually verified their existence. Unlike most families, where jewelry or paintings or books might be passed down through the generations, these families had nothing left of their ancestors to cling to because their families had been driven into the desert and left to starve to death. Seeing their ancestors' names on the list gave the families a sense of pride that at one point these men and women had been successful enough to have afforded insurance and that they were real people with real dreams. It may have not been much to hang on to, but it was something.

|||||

But sometimes it is not just a question of going to the media—it is a matter of who gets their first. We learned that the hard way in a case that involved the San Francisco Zoo and a tiger attack that left one young man dead and two other young men injured. We were hired to represent the two young men who were injured, but before we could even see the police reports on the case, the zoo started a media campaign to publicly attack the two boys and make them the villains.

On Christmas Day 2008, two brothers, Paul and Kulbir Dhaliwal, along with their close friend Carlos Sousa Jr., decided to visit the San Francisco Zoo. Near closing time, they were lingering outside the tiger exhibit eating nachos. The zoo was almost deserted. Suddenly one of the tigers, Tatiana, leapt over the wall and began mauling Paul. Sousa bravely managed to get the tiger's attention, but the tiger then attacked and killed him. The Dhaliwal brothers ran to a nearby concession stand and begged the young man inside to let them in. He refused. A few minutes later, the tiger, tracking the Dhaliwals' blood, reappeared and began attacking Kulbir. Miraculously, he survived. The police, who had originally been prevented from getting into the zoo, were finally let in and they shot and killed the tiger.

The zoo was not exactly remorseful. Almost immediately articles began appearing that the boys were to blame for the tiger's escape. First was a story of how the boys had been taunting the tiger. That was followed by a story about how the boys had actually been throwing things at the tiger, including pinecones and rocks, which were found in the tiger's enclosure. Other stories that followed included that the boys had slingshots and were actually dangling over the fence when the tiger attacked. Every day was a new revelation that blamed the boys and deflected attention from the zoo.

The campaign was as effective as it was inaccurate. The zoo got out in front of the story and succeeded in shifting the blame and the spotlight from them to the boys. The Dhaliwal brothers were so outraged by the smear campaign that they hired us to sue the zoo. When we got on the case, we found out just how effective the press had been. Other than Scott Peterson, no other case we have done has generated the kind of hate mail we received for representing these boys. Most of the e-mails talked about how the boys should be dead but the tiger should have been spared. There were even calls for the district attorney to file charges against the boys for killing the tiger.

As the onslaught was occurring, we were at a decided disadvantage. No discovery had been produced and we had no access to the police reports. We had no idea if what the zoo was saying was true and we had no way to find out. The zoo claimed to be quoting police and witness reports, which they had access to and we didn't. All we could do was tell the papers that we did not believe that what was being put out was true and that we would eventually have the evidence to prove it.

When we did finally get a copy of everything, it turned out that the zoo's entire story had been a hoax. Worse than that, they had covered up the real reason for the tiger attack. There was no evidence the boys were taunting the tiger. The only even remote evidence they had to suggest this was a young girl who thought she saw some boys earlier yelling at the tiger. As the zoo later admitted, visitors yell at the animals all day long, usually in an effort to get their attention. The story that the boys had been throwing rocks and pinecones and that they were found in the cage was directly refuted by the lead investigating officer. The officer told us that it appeared that the zoo even went so far as to try to plant rocks and pinecones inside the enclosure after the fact. Next, we learned that the zoo had been underfeeding Tatiana, and she had dropped a considerable amount of weight since coming over from the Denver Zoo. We also learned that Tatiana had attacked one of her trainers the year before and tore up that trainer's arm. The zoo was fined for their carelessness in that incident. Finally, and perhaps most important, the zoo fence was almost four feet under regulation, a fact they initially denied, and this was what had allowed the tiger to escape. And they had had absolutely no contingency plan for what to do in the event a tiger escaped its unsecure pen.

When we had all the facts, we immediately went on the offensive with the truth of what happened at the zoo that day. The police reports detailed the zoo's lack of planning and their lack of cooperation when the police got there. The *San Francisco Chronicle* and other local papers started running stories about the zoo's negligence. The problem for us was that by the time we went on the offensive, the story had solidified in people's minds. The boys had taunted a tiger and they got what they deserved.

During our investigation we received a number of e-mails and calls from ex-employees and former volunteers at the zoo, alleging a number of complaints about the mistreatment of animals, including underfeeding and improper safety measures. The zoo knew they could not afford a scandal that would not only prompt an investigation but would likely dramatically harm fund-raising. Not many people want to give to a zoo that is alleged to have mistreated animals.

In the end, after all the big talk about going after the boys at trial and defending the zoo's practices, the zoo quietly settled, paying the boys $900,000. If they really thought the boys were to blame, they would have taken the case to trial and let the jury hear all the things the boys did to taunt the tiger. They knew they couldn't, because the story wasn't true, and rather than be exposed, they simply wrote a check.

|||||

Every year we are asked to speak to lawyer groups about the media and how to deal with reporters. Our advice is that you can no longer ignore them and hope they go away. They are not going away. Ignoring them or complaining about them is not going to eliminate the problem. The only way to deal with the media is to go right back at it. Don't let rumors get out there, and if they do, don't think they won't be heard. Don't let lies go unchallenged. Try to get to them first with preemptive strikes when possible. More and more, the media, both mainstream and tabloid, plays a role in the outcome of trials. If you're a trial lawyer, dealing with the media is now part of your job, and that is not going away anytime soon.

CHAPTER NINE

The Best System in the World???

From the first day a young lawyer enters a courtroom until the day that lawyer's retirement party is held, the one phrase the lawyer will hear at least one thousand times is "We may not have a perfect system, but it is still the best system in the world." This concept is so ingrained in American lawyers that it is not even debated. The law is in many ways like a religion to attorneys, and the belief that we have the best system in the world is our chief article of faith. But like ministers who have had a crisis of faith, both of us have had seminal moments in which we have questioned whether our legal system is truly the best or even one of the best in the world.

Mark: I began to have serious doubts about the system on a snowy, wintry day in Cleveland, Ohio, in 2001. We were representing a prominent member of the local community at his sentencing hearing in federal court. He had pled guilty to keeping a storage unit that contained decades-old explosives near his suburban home in Cleveland, where he had been vice president of Cuyahoga Community College. The FBI believed that some of the explosives had been used in an attack by Armenian freedom fighters on the Turkish Mission in New York in the eighties, and that the remaining explosives were being stored for future use. The former college vice president was never implicated in any attacks, but the storage unit had his name on it, and it was asserted by the FBI that he had at least agreed to store the remaining explosives.

My client was a much admired figure in the Armenian community, a charismatic speaker and a forceful lobbyist who had spent time as the head of one of the prominent Armenian activist organizations. For his sentencing hearing, Armenian supporters from all over the country flew in to pack the courtroom, with an overflow group having to wait out in the hall. Virtually every person in that room had either been an eyewitness to the Armenian Genocide or had had a close relative who had perished at the hands of the Turks.

There was a palpable tension hanging in the air because the judge in the case was allowing a representative from the Turkish government to speak during the sentencing hearing, and the government had flown in its top lobbyist and spokesman, Bruce Fein. Fein is one of the most repulsive human beings I have ever had the displeasure of meeting. Whenever the Turkish government wants to deny the Genocide, it sticks Fein out front and lets him spew a bunch of denialist trash about how the Genocide was nothing more than a civil war provoked by the Armenians. I knew what was about to happen and pleaded with the judge to not let him speak. I tried to explain that this would be no different from having a Jewish person being sentenced and letting some nut job get up and deny the Holocaust ever happened. There is no way that would ever occur in today's society. But therein lies the problem for Armenians—the Armenian Genocide has been largely ignored in this country because Turkey is supposedly an important ally. In recent years, even though forty-three states have recognized the Genocide and Congress twice passed an Armenian Genocide Resolution decades ago, the last several administrations have become tongue-tied every time the resolution is brought up. Despite almost every presidential candidate since Reagan saying he or she will recognize the Genocide, nothing happens once the president takes office.

Sure enough, Fein got up, and in front of a courtroom that included several Genocide survivors, he denied its existence. It was a hateful and mean-spirited speech, made even worse by the fact that the audience was filled with people who had never met their grandparents or aunts and uncles because of the Genocide Fein was now denying. There have been few instances in which I have been filled with such rage, and I came very close that day to doing something that would have lost me my bar card for life. I looked over at Pat, who hadn't even met an Armenian until he was in his thirties, and he was shaking with anger. You could hear sobbing from all across the room, but in a testament to the dignity of the Armenian people, Fein was allowed to spread this trash without interruption.

When it was over, I gathered with the Genocide survivors at the back of the courtroom and swore to them that I would do everything I could as a lawyer to make sure they were not forgotten. But as I walked out of that courthouse, I felt unsure that I even wanted to participate in a system that would allow something like this to happen. On the trip back to Los Angeles I seriously thought about whether I wanted to continue as a lawyer.

Pat: I began to have my own doubts after we tried a civil case in San Jose involving the large drug company Pfizer. Our clients were Dr. Dennis Mangano, a local cardiovascular surgeon whose dedication to medical research is unmatched, and the nonprofit company he had formed, IREF. He hired us to be co-counsel at the trial where he was suing Pfizer for stealing trade secrets.

Dr. Mangano's career has been marked by some of the most important medical contributions of our time. Mangano is truly brilliant, but instead of focusing his intelligence on making money, he has used his gifts for the public good. He has been featured on 60 Minutes and other programs for his groundbreaking research and for the thousands of lives he has helped to save through his research. There may be people walking the earth who have saved more lives than Mangano, but they are very few. He is a true hero, a man who has dedicated his life to bettering mankind.

Mangano had put together some of the most extensive databases for heart disease in the world. The drug company Pfizer wanted to purchase the databases to test a new drug, but they could not agree on a price, so the deal was *called off. That's when the problems began. Somewhat surprisingly, Pfizer appointed one of Dr. Mangano's top researchers, Ping Hsu, to its board. The fireworks started a year later when Mangano accused Dr. Hsu of giving database information to Pfizer. In essence, he believed Pfizer had used Dr. Hsu to get around paying IREF. Mangano was furious and filed suit against Pfizer and Dr. Hsu. The case went to trial in November 2008 in San Jose, near where Mangano lived.*

The trial lasted for two months. After three days of deliberations, the jury announced their verdict. They found that Pfizer had stolen the database information and used it without paying for it. They awarded IREF $38 million plus punitive damages, which would be set by a judge. (Punitive damages are essentially damages to punish the defendant and to ensure that the defendant will not repeat the behavior.) There was also interest added, which ran the total to more than $59 million. It was a tremendous victory for Mangano, who had risked everything in this lawsuit, spending every penny he had to finance it. The judgment would give him the opportunity to continue to grow IREF and build even more databases in order to save lives.

If the jury awards punitive damages as part of their verdict, the judge is almost always going to give the victorious plaintiff some amount of money. Not in this case. The judge awarded a big fat zero. And he was just getting warmed up. Shortly thereafter, based on a motion for a new trial by Pfizer, he vacated the entire $59 million award because he did not feel it was justified.

The vast majority of jurors in civil cases have no idea that at the end of a civil case, the judge has the absolute right to just throw out their verdict. The reason this is not widely known is because it is a power that is rarely used. Judges generally have a great deal of respect for the jurors being willing to put their lives on hold and serve, and they understand that it is a true slap in the face to ignore that service and simply implement their own decision.

But the judge in this case was willing to do so, and the jurors were understandably furious. They wanted to know why they had sat there for two months and listened very carefully to what was very detailed and difficult testimony, only to find out that the judge could summarily override the twelve of

them. Dr. Mangano was devastated. He had to lay off employees at IREF
and eventually shut it down. The case is currently on appeal, with the hope
that the appellate court will reinstate the verdict. The first judge in this case,
Gregory Ward, has since retired from the bench and gone back into private
practice.

The decision not only overturned the verdict of a very hardworking, consci-
entious jury, it also destroyed a nonprofit organization that had saved countless
lives in this country with its work. After the jury verdict, we celebrated not only
for having won but because we sincerely believed that the system had worked—
we had held one of the largest corporations in the world responsible for trying to
take advantage of a good and decent man doing important work. It was the
kind of case that makes you proud to be part of the profession.

With one swipe of a pen, though, that was all taken away. It seemed im-
possible that the very same system that had produced the incredible verdict could
allow that to happen. From that point on, my level of cynicism about the sys-
tem rose dramatically.

So do we really have the best system in the world? Before 1980,
that question would have drawn an unqualified yes. The judiciary
was the least politicized of the three branches of government. Judges
were not afraid of the next election, prosecutors were not grandstand-
ing for conviction, jurors were not serving just so they could be on
television, and defense attorneys were not too scared to do their jobs.

We have already mentioned multiple times that things have
changed dramatically in the past thirty years. We've mostly dealt in
anecdotes, but we should also take a look at a few of the statistics that
back up the anecdotes. In 1980, the prison population in America was
approximately 500,000. Today that figure stands at a little more than
2 million. In just thirty years, the prison population in this country
has quadrupled, yet no one believes that the streets are safer than they
were in the 1960s or '70s. In fact, despite the growing prison population, the tough-on-crime crowd continues to tell us how much more
dangerous our streets and neighborhoods are. The United States has a

little less than 5 percent of the world's population, but we currently have 25 percent of the world's reported prisoners. Since 1980, just the number of drug offenders in jail has risen 1,200 percent.

These statistics seem to suggest that our solution to crime is just to lock everybody up—is it possible that we are much less advanced than we like to think in our approach to justice? With other countries focusing on alternative sentencing procedures, including electronic monitoring and drug treatment centers, are we falling behind in the way we look at punishment and rehabilitation? After debating the question back and forth for the past few years with a number of the participants in the judicial system, we are prepared to say that we still believe the American judicial system is the best in the world—with one major qualification. The system is cracking at the edges with some serious issues that are not being addressed.

There are two things about our criminal justice system that are truly amazing. One is that a system created more than 230 years ago—when horses were the mode of transportation and the telegraph was the mode of communication—is still a working framework two centuries later. The second amazing thing is that there is so much resistance to tweaking a system that is more than two hundred years old. Jefferson, Adams, and Hamilton could not have foreseen the Internet, text messaging, blogs, and twenty-four-hour cable networks. They had no way of knowing about DNA testing or fiber matching. Technology in the past hundred years has changed everything dramatically, and virtually all areas of government have understood that and acted accordingly. Not so much the judiciary. The justice system prides itself on following precedent, which in turn lends itself to living in the past and refusing to even discuss what is currently happening in the world.

If the discussion does not involve getting even tougher on crime and putting more people in jail, then no elected official wants to address it. There is one exception: Senator Jim Webb, a Democrat from Virginia, is in his first and last term (he is retiring after one term). A true war hero, the navy secretary under Ronald Reagan, and a pro-lific writer, Webb has never been the typical Washington politician. He is as tough a guy as you would want to meet and no one would ever accuse him of being soft on anything. He is a problem-solver, and it did not take him long to realize that the criminal justice system is a problem.

In 2009, in the U.S. Senate Webb proposed the National Crimi-nal Justice Commission Act. The bill would have established a bipar-tisan commission of prosecutors, defense attorneys, judges, professors, and law enforcement officials to take a look at a broad range of issues in the criminal justice system, from prison overcrowding to the war on drugs. The commission would have then released its findings and recommendations, the first comprehensive report since 1965, on the issue of crime in America. The bill was widely supported across the political spectrum, gaining support from groups as diverse as the ACLU, the National Sheriffs' Association, and the Fraternal Order of Police, along with numerous other law enforcement agencies. The findings in the report would be nonbinding, but they would serve as a road map to future changes for Congress and the courts.

In 2009 and again in 2010, Senator Webb was unable to garner the sixty votes necessary to overcome a Republican filibuster and pass the bill. The vote was fifty-seven to forty-three. Congress does a lot of boneheaded things, but this one was a no-brainer. Even Reihan Salam, a writer for the conservative magazine the *National Review,* referred to the vote as "the insane refusal of 43 Republicans." What Webb was proposing was that a commission be formed to study the issues and to let the experts take a look at a system that was cracking and make recommendations that were in no way binding. Despite widespread support from conservative, liberal, and even lib-ertarian groups, forty-three supposedly educated senators chose to vote to stick their heads in the sand and ignore the problem. The ex-cuses they gave were ridiculous: the commission might recommend legalizing marijuana, the commission might recommend changing sentences on drug convictions, etc. Mind you, even if they did propose these changes, they would be completely nonbinding recommendations.

Since the U.S. Senate refuses to form a commission to even suggest tweaks to the system, we decided to offer some suggestions to fill the void. These suggestions are far from all-inclusive, but they are at least a starting point for discussion.

1. **Appoint judges rather than elect them**. As we discussed in Chapter 5, removing politics from a judge's decision gives the judge the freedom to do the right thing rather than the politically convenient thing. Judicial review boards, like medical review boards, can deal with misconduct and remove judges when necessary.

2. **Judges need to play a bigger role in plea bargaining**. As it stands right now, there is very little a defendant can do if the prosecutor makes an offer that is ridiculous or just way out of line. Some judges will try to pressure one side or the other, while other judges simply stay out of the mix. Judges need to be given the power to do more than just cajole or suggest; they need to have the power to drop charges brought by the prosecutor and facilitate a plea bargain. If the prosecutor's offer is reasonable, then they can validate it. If it is not, then they can change the offer to something that the defendant can agree to.

    Orange County, California, has begun a unique version of this idea. The prosecutor in a felony case will make an offer for what the prosecution believes a case is worth. The defendant's attorney can then choose to meet with a retired judge, Robert Fitzgerald, who has been doing criminal cases for more than thirty years, and the attorney can then present the case to Judge Fitzgerald for his opinion of what it is worth. If the defense attorney likes Judge Fitzgerald's offer better than the prosecutor's, the defendant can then agree to take that deal and plead in Fitzgerald's court. If the deal is the same or not as good as the prosecutor's offer, then the defendant simply thanks Judge Fitzgerald and takes the prosecutor's offer or goes to trial. It is not a perfect system, but it at least allows for another set of eyes to look at a case and does not leave the defendant at the sole mercy of a prosecutor's whims.

3. **Jurors should be allowed to be told about jury nullification**. When the founding fathers set up the jury system in the United States, one of the principal reasons they chose to implement the system was so that members of the community could be a check on overzealous prosecutors. If a prosecutor was unfairly or unevenly distributing justice in a case, the jury could simply choose to not follow the letter of the law and "nullify" the case. Jury nullification has a long and storied history in this country, including helping to create the freedom of the press, encourage civil disobedience for civil rights, free Vietnam conscientious objectors, and gain women the vote. It was jury nullification in the Susan McDougal case we did in Arkansas that helped put a stop to the out-of-control Whitewater investigation.

Despite this history, jurors are actually never told that they have the power to nullify in a case. In fact, the law specifically prohibits attorneys from arguing jury nullification to the jury and a judge from instructing the jurors that they can use it. The concept is that the jurors must be told that they are to follow the law, and if they ask about jury nullification, they are to be told it is a violation of their jury oath and that it is unlawful behavior. Fortunately, some jurors in our past history have chosen to ignore this instruction and exercise the power to slow down overzealous prosecutions. But they should not have to be scared that they are violating a court order or doing something wrong—they should be told that they have the power to nullify if they choose.

This issue has gotten so silly that a man in New York was actually arrested outside a courthouse for carrying a sign telling the jury they could nullify in a particular case. If prosecutors are so scared that a jury will reject their case by exercising jury nullification, then perhaps it should be a signal to them to take a much harder look at the case.

4. **More jury sequestration**. In cases where the media interest is high, judges need to be more willing to sequester jurors. In the age of omnipresent communication, it is virtually impossible to be shielded from news reports on a high-profile case. Simple tasks like getting groceries become problematic because the tabloids at the checkout stands have headlines that are misleading or unfounded. Even at some gas stations, there are television screens on the pumps blaring out news while you fill your tank. During the trial of John Gotti Jr., there was a confrontation where Gotti was alleged to have threatened a witness in court. The New York tabloids ran with the story on their entire front pages even though the threat was disputed. There was no way a juror could have missed the headlines blaring out at them from every newspaper box in the city. No matter how conscientious a juror is, the media onslaught is inescapable. The only solution is to control the environment so that jurors are only in two places—court and their hotel rooms.

5. **Revise prosecutorial immunity**. As it stands today, it is virtually impossible to file a civil suit against a prosecutor for anything the prosecutor does under the cloak of prosecutorial

duties. Intentionally hiding discovery, lying in a closing statement to a jury, knowingly putting on a witness that is giving
false testimony—all intentional acts, all of which are covered
by prosecutorial immunity. A prosecutor can deliberately
break the rules and convict an innocent man and walk away
with no repercussions.

And it keeps getting worse. The Supreme Court recently
took up the case of *Connick v. Thompson* (the Connick is for
District Attorney Harry Connick Sr., and yes, it is his father).
Thompson was on death row for fourteen years and was weeks
away from his execution when an investigator for his defense
team discovered an exculpatory blood evidence report that
had never been turned over to the defense. Thompson was
eventually released, and he sued the D.A.'s office. During the
civil suit, one of the assistant district attorneys admitted that
he had intentionally withheld the evidence. It was also learned
that four other prosecutors were aware of the withholding
from the defense. In the civil case, Thompson was awarded
$14 million in damages by a jury. However, the Supreme
Court, in a five-to-four decision, overturned the jury verdict
and left Thompson with nothing. In an opinion written by
the always sympathetic Clarence Thomas, he stated that
prosecutors needed to be protected from these types of
lawsuits and that there are other avenues to discipline wayward
prosecutors, specifically reporting them to their state bar
association, which can them discipline them.

Of course, state bar associations never do anything. In the
report *Preventable Error*, a detailed study done by Pulitzer
Prize–winning writer Maurice Possley and one of the gen-
uine heroes of our legal system, Kathleen "Cookie" Ridolfi,
the authors researched cases between 1997 and 2009 in
California and found 707 cases where a prosecutor was found
by a court to have committed misconduct. When misconduct

is found to have occurred, the court is required to report it to the State Bar of California. Of those 707 cases, a total of 6 prosecutors were then disciplined by the State Bar of California. That amounts to less than 1 percent. And these were cases where the court had already made the determination that misconduct had occurred—the state bar did not even have to investigate. This is very disheartening to defense attorneys because there is a general feeling that if we sneeze in the wrong direction, the state bar is going to investigate us. In fact, we are relatively sure that last sentence will probably get us investigated by the state bar. Yet a prosecutor can be found to have intentionally hidden evidence that sent an innocent man to jail and walk away without so much as a slap on the wrist.

A partial solution is to give prosecutors the same qualified immunity that police officers have rather than the absolute immunity they now enjoy. They argue that this will provide a chilling effect on their office and their duties. Our answer is we hope so. It is about time that prosecutors were held accountable for intentional misconduct. Right now, they have no one to answer to. A couple of good lawsuits and perhaps they would think twice before deciding to deep-six evidence that could prove a defendant's innocence.

6. **Post-conviction DNA analysis**. Both prosecutors and defense attorneys agree that DNA testing, when conducted correctly, is very accurate. In fact, both sides regularly request it before and even during trial. But there are thousands of men and women who are sitting in prisons across the country who never got the opportunity to prove their innocence, because the DNA evidence in their case was never tested. The vast majority of states do provide for post-conviction testing, but the laws are usually so restrictive that very few prisoners are

eligible for the testing. Most prosecutors are opposed to post-conviction testing for one very simple reason: they are scared to death the results will show how many innocent people they have put in jail. Already, the Innocence Project has freed more than 295 previously convicted defendants, and it has done it on a very limited budget and only being able to look at a small percentage of cases.

States need to take restrictions off of DNA testing for convicted prisoners and fund expanded testing. States and counties somehow manage to find extra funding for additional cops, adding new D.A.s and building new jail facilities. A little of that money needs to go toward making sure that the people they are so intent on putting in those facilities actually belong there.

7. **Implement the double-blind procedure for eyewitness I.D.s.** Faulty eyewitness identification was the factor in 75 percent of the 295 cases where the Innocence Project was able to show that a convicted defendant was innocent. In many of those cases, the eyewitness was either brought in to view a lineup that included the alleged defendant or was shown what is known as a six-pack—six pictures, each one numbered, with the alleged defendant's picture as one of the six. In both situations, an administrator (usually a police officer) was present and essentially ran the viewing. The problem is that in many of these cases, the administrator gives either verbal or nonverbal cues indicating which person they want the witness to pick. The cue can be as subtle as a finger on top of one of the pictures or as non-subtle as a suggestion that the eyewitness take a closer look at number three.

In the double-blind method, the administrator of the six-pack or the lineup is unaware of which picture or person is the alleged defendant (i.e., the administrator is going into the viewing blind as well). Obviously, that prevents the administrator from giving any kind of cues to the eyewitness.

In addition, all identification procedures should be videotaped and audiotaped to ensure that there are no cues given. Videotaping is no longer an expensive proposition—most cell phones can record video today. There is no excuse for not videotaping and audiotaping, other than that the administrator does not want the jury knowing how the identification was made.

Furthermore, there are still many courts in the country that do not allow the defense to call experts on the problems with eyewitness identification. If the prosecution is going to be allowed to rest their case on or just support their case through eyewitness identification, then the defense should be allowed to show how fallible it is.

8. **Changes in sentencing for drug offenders**. An entire volume of books could be written about the absurdity of drug laws in this country. It is a topic that goes well beyond this book. Suffice it to say that our prisons are packed with non-violent drug offenders serving sentences that often surpass those convicted of second-degree murder or sexual assault. Sticking drug addicts (as well as the mentally ill) into jail cells rather than focusing on alternative sentencing has finally caught up with us. As discussed earlier, prison overcrowding is a serious issue that presents a real threat to public safety as well as major budget issues. But Congress can't be bothered to address that issue. They are too busy declaring March to be National Rodeo Clown Month.

9. **Remove dogs from the courtroom**. We need to preface this section with the comment that we are not dog-haters— quite the contrary. Between the two of us, we have four dogs

and one of the most dog-friendly offices in the country. Like most dog owners we are convinced our dogs have rare gifts that few other dogs possess. For example, Pat is convinced that his dog Lucy is smart enough to not only fetch the newspaper but to do the *New York Times* crossword puzzle.

Unfortunately, this blind allegiance and love of our dogs has filtered into the courtroom. One of the fastest growing areas of police investigation is K-9 searches. Police officers stop a vehicle and have the dog sniff for drugs, or in arson cases have the dog sniff a defendant's clothes for starter fluids. In some cases, police will give a dog a piece of clothing from the defendant to sniff and then take the dog to a location to see if the defendant was present at some point or what direction the defendant headed off in.

It is not that dogs don't have some use in police investigations. They can be a valuable aid in searches for missing persons or in sniffing out drugs at airports. But as Andy Rebmann, one of the leading experts on dog handling in the United States, told us, police dog trainers have gone from getting the dogs to do basic things they are capable of doing, to believing that their dogs possess all types of magical powers. This translates into the trainers giving their dogs cues to "alert" on vehicles or clothing, and that in turn is used as evidence to convict defendants. Russ Jones, a former police officer and dog handler, said that one reason he now opposes the war on drugs is because "ninety percent of these dog-handler teams are utter failures. They're just ways to get around the Fourth Amendment."

10. **Professional jurors**. The idea of having people who go to school to become professional jurors has been batted around for years by legal experts. It is a concept that is decades away from being implemented (if ever), but it deserves to be

studied. People wanting to become professional jurors would get a college degree and then attend jury school for a year. During that year they would be taught a basic understanding of the criminal and civil codes of the state, learn the most common jury instructions, practice jury deliberations, and sit in on actual trials. Upon graduation, they would take a test, and if they passed, they would spend the first few years doing misdemeanor trials while they worked their way up to felonies. Supervisors would occasionally sit in on jury deliberations to make sure everyone was doing their job fairly and according to the law.

Jurors who sit through a number of trials have a much better sense of what is a good case and what is not. They have a frame of reference that onetime jurors simply do not have. They also understand the instructions better, so there is less chance of jury error. Professional jurors, at least theoretically, would also be better on multi-count, complex cases, especially those involving financial crimes, because they would have had past experience in dealing with difficult concepts.

The huge downside of professional jurors, aside from possible constitutional issues, is the cost. Pay for jurors in most states is ridiculously low, and professional jurors would be a huge added cost to the system. It would also be very difficult to transition from our current system to one with professional jurors. It may never be workable, but it is an intriguing idea that deserves to be given an in-depth study.

All of these changes represent steps toward fixing a system that is in need of repair. But the first step has to be the recognition that there is a problem and it has to be fixed. In that respect, the country is very much like an alcoholic who is refusing treatment.

Alcoholics refuse to admit they have a problem—they often

manage to function on a day-to-day basis, so they insist that they don't have a problem. Whenever they succeed, they use it as an example of how they can handle their alcohol consumption; whenever they fail, they simply blame it on something else.

That is essentially where we as a country are with our justice system. We refuse to admit we have a problem, because we don't want to face the consequences. We hold up the day-to-day functioning of the system as proof that it must be working and working well. When it fails, we simply blame the judge or the defense attorney or whatever is convenient and hide our heads in the sand. Alcoholics Anonymous preaches that a true alcoholic will not get help until he or she has hit rock bottom and has nowhere else to go. Hopefully, this country is not going to wait until the system hits rock bottom before taking a hard look at making changes.

The biggest challenge, however, may be not in providing structural changes to the system, but rather in changing public perception of the system. The factors noted in this book—the politicization of the judicial system, the O. J. Simpson trial, and the rise of the angry blond white women—are all issues of public perception.

So how do we fight these factors and restore balance to the system? Some balance can be restored when people's perceptions of individual issues like confession and eyewitness identification change. As more and more wrongly convicted defendants are freed, the defense bar needs to keep the pressure on, constantly reminding the public about the inherent problems with these types of evidence. Defense attorneys need to focus on these issues, talk about the studies done, and hammer it home on every possible occasion. The media has been used to create the current public perception—there is no reason it can't be used to change it.

Defense attorneys need to do what we do best—fight back. For too long we have let politicians and the tabloid media put us on the defensive about what we do for a living. We represent what is best about America, a country founded on the principles of fairness and making sure the rights of the minority don't get trampled by the whims of the majority. We need to stop being defensive about it and stand up to the arrogant bullies who would prefer to gut the Constitution while telling us what great Americans they are.

We need to take pride that what we do for a living is the very essence of what this country was founded on—a group of outnumbered men and women who stood up to the enormous power of an overreaching state and demanded justice. Amazingly, even in those heated times, we did not lose sight of the very principles that would be the foundation of this country. A British soldier, Captain Thomas Preston, was charged with being one of the men who ordered the firing that killed numerous colonists at the event known as the Boston Massacre. Unsure if he would be able to get a fair trial in this new colony, he turned to a young lawyer from outside of Boston to represent him. The young lawyer's name was John Adams, and even though he was among the most fervent of the patriots clamoring for independence, he agreed to represent Captain Preston. He felt that, were the captain to be denied a fair trial, the very basis for the colonists' fight for independence would be nothing more than empty slogans. Adams did this even though he knew it might very well ruin his practice and even put his family in jeopardy.

Adams started a tradition that has been the centerpiece for the criminal justice system ever since. Defense attorneys have for years put aside their own personal feelings and even disregarded their own safety to ensure that the founding fathers' vision for this country is not destroyed by mob justice. Clarence Darrow went into a hornet's nest in east Tennessee to defend a teacher for teaching evolution. Thurgood Marshall and numerous other civil rights lawyers risked their lives to defend the rights of African-Americans in courtrooms across the country. Atticus Finch may be a fictional character, but he represents the hundreds of criminal defense attorneys across this country who stand up every day against overwhelming odds and a system geared against them, to fight for their clients not because it is the popular or most financially rewarding thing to do, but because it is the right thing to do. It is a tradition that we carry on proudly more than two hundred years after its founding, even when public opinion is dead set against our clients and the mobs are starting to form. It is why we can honestly say that there is nothing better than standing up in a courtroom and announcing that we are there for the defense.

Pat: I would simply like to thank my family, friends and two loyal dogs for their unwavering support while this project has been ongoing for what seems like a decade. A special shout-out to my niece Sarah Harris Wallman for her editing skills and suggestions while simultaneously going through her first pregnancy. It was not always easy to determine whether she was throwing up from morning sickness or from reading the early drafts. I would also like to thank our editor at Gotham Books, Patrick Mulligan, for his willingness to work around our trial schedules and for his numerous suggestions that made this a much better book. Also to Emily Wunderlich and Lisa Johnson at Gotham, who have been so encouraging and helpful in leading us through this process and continuing to offer encouragement. Finally, to our agent, Deborah Grosvenor, for her enthusiasm about the book and invaluable advice on how to convince someone to actually publish our rants.

Mark: It is always impossible to thank everyone who played a role in either providing source material for the book or who have been supportive of me in both my personal life and my career. I would like to acknowledge a special few, however, who have been with me through a lot of trials (literally) and tribulations. The best starting point would be my family—my mother, my wife, and my two children, Jake and Teny, and, of course, my father, Pops, who if you have read this book you realize is my hero. Some of the great lawyers in the country (many of whom are now judges) have been gracious enough to have worked with me over the years, giving me their time, advice, and friendship. It would require an entirely separate book to mention them all, but I would be remiss to not at least mention three who were particularly helpful to me throughout my career: the Honorable Warren Ettinger, the Honorable Dikran Tevrizian, and the Honorable Armand Arabian.

Finally, I want to send a special thanks to Sandi Mendelson, Judi Hilsinger, and David Kass and the entire team at Hilsinger-Mendelson for their work.

Together we would like to gratefully acknowledge the work of the best legal team in America, the lawyers and staff at Geragos & Geragos. Thanks to Shelley Kaufman, Tina Glandian, Hagop Kuyumjian, Ben Meiselas, Setara Qassim, Tony Benitez, Aja Matelyan, Alice Wenk, Edgar Martinez, Sandra Sanchez, Lala Asheghie, and Art Badalyan. This acknowledgment will serve in lieu of any future raises.